Spectacular Cities

Spectacular Cities

Religion, Landscape, and the
Dialectics of Globalization

IPSITA CHATTERJEE

OXFORD
UNIVERSITY PRESS

OXFORD
UNIVERSITY PRESS

Oxford University Press is a department of the University of Oxford.
It furthers the University's objective of excellence in research, scholarship,
and education by publishing worldwide. Oxford is a registered trademark of
Oxford University Press in the UK and in certain other countries.

Published in India by
Oxford University Press
YMCA Library Building, 1 Jai Singh Road, New Delhi 110 001, India

ISBN-13: 978-0-19-946513-2
ISBN-10: 0-19-946513-4

Typeset in ITC Giovanni Std 9.5/13
by The Graphics Solution, New Delhi 110 092
Printed in India by Replika Press Pvt. Ltd

To Ma and Baba

Contents

LIST OF FIGURES   ix

PREFACE   xi

ACKNOWLEDGEMENTS   xv

1. Introduction   1

2. Culture and the Dialectic Approach   17

3. In the Name of the Father, the Globalization,
   and the Holy City, Amen!   36

4. Transcendental Landscapes: Akshardham Temples
   in the US   68

5. Mapping the Fantastic: Akshardham Temples in India   110

6. Subjecting Globalization: The Class and Gender
   of Globalization   144

7. Conclusions: Spectacular City as Synthesis   175

BIBLIOGRAPHY   184

INDEX   192

ABOUT THE AUTHOR   195

Figures

4.1 Atlanta Temple: Cluster of curvilinear and spherical
domes adorned by golden *kalashas*, or pitchers   71
4.2 Intricately carved pillars at the Atlanta temple   72
4.3 *Chhatris*, or umbrellas, in the outer periphery of the
Atlanta temple   73
4.4 An intricately carved foundation base at the
Houston temple   75
4.5 The Houston temple complex consists of acres of
manicured lawns and gardens   76
4.6 Signs placed at the Atlanta temple's entrance to
advertise the temple food court   91
4.7 Museum display at the Houston temple listing spiritual
leaders from history and proto-history in the different
regions of India   96
4.8 Museum display at the Houston temple featuring India's
diverse flora, fauna, cultures, and languages   97
4.9 Museum display at the Houston temple celebrating
India's contribution of the concept of zero and proudly
proclaiming its historical lineage in astronomy,
geometry, and mathematics   98

4.10 Museum display at the Houston temple prominently
      emphasizing India's 'unparalleled contribution to
      science, philosophy, architecture, and education'   99

7.1   Coniferous forest in Dubai airport   176

Preface

Spectacular Cities: Religion, Landscape, and the Dialectics of Globalization
is inspired by a desire to understand the globalizing world as it
really exists. Too often, we understand this globalizing reality through
concepts, analyses, flow charts, and PowerPoint presentations that do
a good job of projecting a slice of that reality but leave one with the
desire for the whole cake. Is there a way to talk about reality as it actually unfolds, rather than in a piecemeal, sequential way that is convenient for communication, but is an unfortunately simplistic version of
the chaos? The chaos appears as chaos because we have been trained
to simplify through analysis and such simplification is a necessary and
important precursor to cogent communication. But what if simplification is an ideological exercise? What if, in the process of simplification,
we are producing reality? What are we missing then? It is very important to be clear here: I am not anti-intellectual, and I am particularly
in favour of academic conceptualizations, but my question is, what if
we can adopt an academic ideology that cogently communicates reality
in its complexity? Complexity is important, because it depicts reality
in its chaotic glory. The mess has something to say, and by sequencing
it, fragmenting it, and reducing it, we are reducing its ability to speak.

This book is therefore a quest for an approach towards understanding globalization as a glorious mess. Globalization does not singularly
unfold as an economic process here, a cultural process there, and a
political process yet somewhere else. Economic globalization does not

unfold as a neat stage that is then followed by cultural globalization, and then again by political globalization. We academics look at it that way because we are economists, or anthropologists, or geographers. Here, however, I hope to transcend an analytical approach by treating globalization as a totality. This, I hope, is a dialectical approach to globalization that can understand the components of chaos in a relational context where the relations are internal to the components, where any attempt at mechanical separation will dissolve the reality. In other words, I hope to study culture and economy in a relational assemblage through what I call the 'city-as-synthesis'. The city, to me, appropriately permeates all aspects of culture and economy, hence showcasing how they inflect while constituting globalization today. This does not mean that globalization cannot be found in rural contexts; it simply means that I have chosen the city as the appropriate receptacle for revealing the dialectics of globalization, because the urban condition is the reality that I know well.

Spectacles tell a lot about reality; they are gigantic chaos. Imagine, for instance, the spectacle of a roller coaster: the bumps, twirls, loops, and knots that make it up. They are complexly constructed and energetically ground the thrill of real life. I use spectacular landscapes: the temple complexes of BAPS Swaminarayan Hinduism in Atlanta, Dallas, and Houston in the United States (US), and in Gandhinagar and Delhi in India. The temple complexes, also known as Akshardham temples, have acquired a transnational global presence, with hundreds of temples all across the world, a transnational diaspora of followers, an ample cyber presence, and, most interestingly, a spectacular physical presence. The temple complexes loom large and appear out of sync with their urban environment. They crop-up like ancient monuments of intricate carvings, domes, and arches, but the reality is that the hoariness is only a pretense; the temples are actually quite new. These spectacles assume definite characteristics in Indian cities, where they are packaged with theme-park-style rides, sound and light shows, and dioramas using fibre-optic technology. These spectacular landscapes in the US and India are more than geographic sites; they form narratives of migration, transnationalism, spiritualism, national identity, multiculturalism, and racism. These spectacular narratives are simultaneously cultural and economic, because such is the inflected nature of their existence, in which it is impossible to separate one from the other. That is why

I use their relationality and their inflection to reveal the constituted materiality of globalization. The spectacular city, therefore, adequately synthesizes the chaos of globalization. I simply follow it and bring it to the pages of this book. In other words, the book is a chaos—it is a mess—and I do not attempt to restore any order to it, because I believe that the complexity of chaos can convey more about globalization than the simplified order of academic analysis.

Ipsita Chatterjee

Acknowledgements

I am extremely grateful to all the scholars who have done the brilliant work of conceptualizing globalization—sometimes I cite you in this book, and sometimes I critique you, but I critique you because your work made me think, and informed my intellectual consciousness in a profound way. I am particularly thankful to Dick Peet and Ed Soja for their geographic ideas on dialectics, which I have so often used in the past and which serve as the intellectual starting point for many of the discussions here. Dick is a great friend and mentor; very few people can say that their friends were mentors and their mentors were friends, but I have that! Dick continues to inspire my intellectual world. My infinite gratitude goes to the members, volunteers, and monks of the Swaminarayan sect who patiently answered my questions and showed me around.

Ma and Baba are my heroes. As I was writing this book, Baba went through such hard times health-wise, but even in his sickest and weakest moments he would wave my previously published book to whoever came to visit him, promising them that a new book was forthcoming. Ma's courage, fortitude, patience, and ability to silently bear the weight of the world are qualities I aspire for but cannot meet. This book is for the two of you. Baba and Ma are the thesis and antithesis of my life: Baba constantly disparaging intellectual elitism and emphasizing the importance of a hands-on education, and Ma constantly instilling a thirst for learning and all things book-wise even when she did not have the time to pick up a book after the gruesome chore of taking care of everyone.

Butola Sir is probably the first person who taught me to think dialectically. He is a whirlwind of ideas and he can sweep over you and leave you completely swayed. He had that effect on me during my Jawaharlal Nehru University (JNU) days. Looking back, I realize now that what is unique about him is his ability to understand the world in its complex relationality, rather than seeing it in fragments. Dialectics is the spirit of this book—I am immensely grateful for Butola Sir's influence.

My friends inspire me intellectually in so many ways, and they are the light of my life: Jayson, Ginu, Jagdish, Chandip, Suvarna, Reji, Deb, and Amalia are always a part of me, as well as a part of this book. Paul Hudak is an excellent chair, leading the geography department at the University of North Texas with a sensitivity that creates a support system for this kind of work. Many thanks to him for being supportive and flexible in all those moments when motherhood called. Waquar is my whole world, academically and otherwise. We grew up together and grew to understand the world together; we are a contradiction that exists together. His intellectual curiosity, kindness, generosity, and love humble me every day. I do not say this enough, but I am so grateful that Waquar lives in my world, and I am so grateful that I met him. Nadia is the most dialectical person I know; children are a mass of contradiction, petulant at one time and endearing the very next moment, demanding and at once giving, annoying, and at once sweet. Thank you, little Nadia, for putting up with a mother who has to divide time between you and so many other things!

1 Introduction

Globalization has become a major preoccupation, both academically and otherwise. The term itself is simple enough to resonate, and yet so abstract that it can mean anything. It resonates as an increased familiarity with the globe, and this increased familiarity is brought about by the information technology revolution, the use of plastic money, and the faster movement of commodities over great geographical distances. In real, everyday lives, it means that the labels on our shirts show that they have travelled the globe before coming to us. It means that it is possible to watch Bollywood movies made in India at the moment of their release in faraway Austin, Texas. It means that certain layers of people—the urban middle class, the corporate CEO, or the media baron—travel further and more frequently for work and pleasure. It also means that McBurger travels to Beijing, and that Thanksgiving is celebrated in Delhi. At the same time, it means that trade barriers collapse and Third World economies find their markets flooded as corporate giants like Pepsi, Walmart, Nike, and Lays swiftly buy up indigenous companies. It also means that sweatshops and export-processing zones replace government-subsidized factories in the industrial belts of the Third World. These are major changes in the lives, livelihoods, and landscapes of everyday life, and therefore, it is natural that tomes have been written to understand, define, conceptualize, and explain it.[1] It is therefore not my objective, amidst this rich and diverse conversation on globalization, to add yet another volume that will align with either one or two of these schools and reinforce something that has already been said.

My objective is a little different and, in order to elaborate on what it is, I need to communicate the frustration I have experienced for some time in my conversations on globalization. The frustration stems from the fact that globalizing reality is not a sequential reality or a fragmented reality; it is neither as if economic globalization unfolds first, followed by cultural, political, and urban globalization, nor as if economy changes in one part of the city, and culture globalizes in another part. As a complex assemblage, globalization unfolds as a reality where culture, economy, politics, and the city alter in tandem as a social totality. In other words, globalization does not unfold sequentially as an economic act and then a cultural-political act on a spatial stage called the city. Yet, many economic analyses of globalization tend to follow that sequential ordering, if, that is, they make their way into cultural explications at all. Many cultural analyses make no attempt to unpack how cultural changes mutate alongside economic and political changes. If a globalizing urban condition has no explicit sequential ordering or spatial fragmentation, then why have we been sequencing and compartmentalizing it in the conceptual worlds of our textbooks? Why have we been talking about neoliberalism as an *economic* mode of production to the exclusion of the *cultural*? Why have we been talking about McDonaldization and Disneyization as if they are a *cultural* rather than an *economic* onslaught? If reality is always a complex assemblage, how can we develop a language and mode of conceptualization that is not a theoretical closure on the dynamic and complex assemblage called social totality? This is where the frustration becomes more intense. When we see with our eyes, live our lives, touch and feel around us, and breath and exhale, we experience reality as social totality; however, when we communicate it, the experts have, somehow, always found it wise to sequentially order reality, separating space from society and segmenting the economic realm from that of culture and politics, layering the economy as the base upon which they slapped the frostings of culture and politics. Is there no conceivable way to conceptualize globalizing society as a social totality, so that we can completely understand reality in each historical-geographical moment? Is there an approach to conceptualizing and then communicating reality so that it does not become fragmented or sequenced, but instead remains an organic whole in its complex cultural and economic entirety? In the interest of being as clear as possible—because I do think that clearly communicating my frustration will make my objectives clear—I will provide an example here. Consider an egg. An egg can be analysed as an economic entity, in which case an economic conceptualization will see it as a commodity and understand the context of its production, whether it was produced in the factory or a farm. What was the context of labour in its moment of production? Was the factory mechanized? What kind of wage was paid to the labourers involved in its production? What was the nature of the farm? Was it a family enterprise? Was it organic? All these questions are important for pricing the egg, labelling it, and understanding why it is found in its ultimate location. The egg is also a cultural concept, leading to questions of why it is produced, how it is produced, and why it becomes a commodity for the market instead of travelling straight from the chicken coop to the breakfast table that depend on the culture of food preferences, nutrition, and dietary behaviours, and norms about vegetarianism and non-vegetarianism. Concepts like cage-free, free-range, happy chickens, and no-animal testing are economic and cultural concepts, and they have specific meanings and specific pricing in the historical-geographical moment of food production. Finding a way to talk about the omelette in its cultural and economic entirety without fragmenting it or sequencing it so that the yolk does not separate from the white is necessary, because once it does, it is hardly an omelette. The omelette is a good thing, even a great thing, because it provides the essence of the egg in its entirety in each bite. Conceptualizing the globalizing reality as a social totality can be a great thing, because it comes closest to conveying the essence of reality in its entirety. That, I think, should be the purpose of every academic endeavour. Therefore, in an effort to address my frustrations head on, I decided to use the omelette to understand the egg. The city is the omelette; it is the perfect synthesis of globalizing urban condition in its entirety, an organic whole imbricating the culture and the economy in such a way that the white and yolk cannot be separated if we do not want them to be. Therefore, I use the city to understand the dialectics of globalization. I am attempting a dialectical approach to globalization, which means that I want to understand globalizing reality in its entirety without fragmenting or sequencing it.

In other words, I do not analyse globalizing reality with the aim of conceptualizing neoliberal economics, postmodern capitalism, corporate culture, or the leaky state. I attempt to approach urban reality as a synthesis of globalization and—in approaching the city in its cultural, economic, and spatial entirety—I hope to explicate the dialectics of globalization. The dialectical approach to social reality is different from the analytical approach. An analytical approach slices, fragments, and sequences reality into boxes and categories, and then understands them as externally related in a mechanistic way. The boxes—such as economy, culture, landscape, and society—are fragments that each have their own properties and idiosyncrasies, and can be understood as individual systems that then fit together like mosaic to form a whole. In contrast, the dialectical approach is a relational approach to reality, in which the economy, culture, landscape, and society never exist as separate boxes, and cannot be isolated in a petri dish, because any attempt at mechanical separation means that the organic whole will cease to exist. In a dialectical approach to reality, concrete things are always in a context of interrelations with each other within a larger totality. The context of these interrelations is an integral character of reality that is not external, accidental, or mechanical. In that context, therefore, the city serves as the organic whole, the social totality, the cell-pigment that permeates all aspects of reality—the economic, the cultural, the social, the political, and the spatial. Therefore, we must understand the concrete components of this social totality in the context of their interrelation with each other, so that the cultural cannot be understood if separated from the economy, or the spatial, and so on and so forth. Any attempt to isolate any of these concrete components decomposes the cell, leaving the city unexplored, un-understood, and un-theorized. The city provides the synthesis, the context for all the relations and interconnections that make up the social totality.

In studying the city-as-synthesis, I focus on the temple complexes of BAPS.[2] These complexes are also called Swaminarayan temples or Akshardham temples. BAPS is a reform movement in Hinduism that originated in Gujarat, in western India, in the eighteenth century. It was revealed by an ascetic Swaminarayan, who later became the primary figure of worship when the religion was institutionalized. From its beginning as a small religious congregation, the Swaminarayan sect has assumed global proportions, with a strong international presence in many countries of the world that is largely financed by the Gujarati-Indian diaspora. The national and transnational presence of these temples, their awe-inspiring material form, and their even more vociferous cyber presence have earned them a migrant fan following that transcends the narrow bounds of their sect. In many ways, the Akshardham temples in India and abroad materialize the inter-relationality of globalization in their urban form. A major characteristic of these temple complexes is the overbearing presence of gigantic, intricately carved marble temples, replete with arches and domes and vast courtyards and gardens looming large in the major cities of the world. They represent an urban form that is in a dialectical tension between religious traditionality and globalizing modernity, crystalizing a social totality that is an interesting amalgam of social, economic, cultural, and political contexts. Therefore, to reveal the dialectics of globalization, I explore the Akshardham temple complexes of Delhi and Ghandhinagar, near Ahmedabad in India, and those in Atlanta, Houston, and Irving-Dallas in the US. A close look at the temple complexes, and at the people's narratives that form in and around them, reveals, concretely and close-up, the organic interconnections between space, culture, and economy. They provide excellent contexts for dialectically understanding globalization, because they reveal, in their urban form and presence, a synthesis in which the economy is indissolubly imbricated with culture and with space. In the following chapters, I have struggled to find a language that maintains the dialectical approach's integrity in revealing these imbrications in their full complexity, so that I do not inadvertently segregate reality into synthetic components, therefore reducing reality to a caricature. I have relied on semi-structured interviews of priests, monks, volunteers, and visitors at the temple complexes, collected over a two-year period. Some interviewees requested that their names not be mentioned, and, therefore, the names used here have been made anonymous or intentionally left out. I have also maintained detailed field-diaries, which often substantiate the concreteness of the various imbrications. There were stringent restrictions on photography in the temples, so, wherever allowed, I have used photographs to convey the image of the city-as-synthesis. The excerpts of interviews and field observations were used as qualitative data to inform and empirically substantiate my efforts to reveal the dialectical nature of globalization.

In Chapter 2, I search for an appropriate method for understanding and explaining culture, because I anticipate that, in the city-as-synthesis, culture will appear in a strong interrelation with other aspects of reality.

I begin with a discussion of the idealistic, as opposed to the materialistic, approach to culture. Idealism assumes that culture is always already *there*, while materialism, on the other hand, contends that culture is *produced*. My dissatisfaction with the idealistic approach is that it does not go far enough in explicating why culture is *there*, and how it came *about*. On the other hand, my critique of the materialist approach is that it often becomes a crude variety of economic determinism that assumes culture is a superficial manifestation of deep economic activity. Economic determinism is often echoed in the base-superstructure model of Marxist materialism, in which the realm of production or the economic sphere is assumed to be either the basis of society or the deep structure on which the superstructure of society is superimposed. The superstructure is the realm of politics, culture, religion, and other forms of mental and conceptual faculties that are institutionalized for the distribution, allocation, and transportation of that which is produced in the realm of the base, or deep structure. Weber's (1992) idealistic analysis of culture served as a critique of this Marxist version, because Weber insisted that cultural rationalities, like religion, informed and produced certain kinds of economic rationalities. Therefore, protestant ethic (culture) was the cause behind the emergence of the spirit of capitalism (economic), which was the result. A dialectical approach, however, steers clear of causal analysis, and hence the challenge directly facing me in this chapter is, as Peet (2000: 1230) said: 'How to conceptualize relations between parts of life that meld into one another?' Peet answered by claiming that the culture-economy spatial dialectic of regional formations can offer a conceptual starting point for a radical geographic analysis of culture. Culture-economic spatial dialectics co-position economy, culture, and space without giving causal significance to any of them, as the idea is to give equal presence to economy, culture, and space in order to understand regional modes of production as an assemblage of all three. Williams (2009) also criticized the base-superstructure approach, arguing that the base-superstructure approach artificially separates social signification from production, thinking from acting, and economy from culture when, in reality, they are the same historical-geographical moment. He proposes 'mediation' as the link for understanding the real world as constituted by more than one thing at once (Williams 2009: 97). However, Williams was quick to point out that, although better than crude reductionism, 'mediation' still suffers from the fact that it implicitly necessitates the existence of two separate categories, between which mediation must happen. Therefore, the objective of this chapter is to find a way to reveal the 'constituted materiality' (Williams 2009: 108) of globalization, so that the relationality between economy and culture is highlighted. The point is to avoid a tendency towards categorization, sequencing, and causality that will seal off all possibility of a dialectical representation of reality.

This chapter explores the tendency, in geography, to bring space in as a lens along with culture, economy, and society, so as to understand the geographical elements of the constituted materiality of social totality. In that context, I discuss the debates that transpired within radical geography regarding the need to understand space as an axis of social reality. Soja's (1980: 224) 'socio-spatial dialectic', in which he argued that space plays an important role in value transfer within capitalism, was an important moment in the dialectical turn, but it has received very little attention in Marxist analysis. I review mediation, the culture-economy spatial dialectic, and the socio-spatial dialectic as possible options for resolving the reductionism seen in the Marxist base-superstructure approach to culture. I conclude that the city, as a concept, serves as the synthesis for explicating how culture and economy meld into one another in organizing the social totality of globalization. My argument here is that, in the real world, society and space are not separate categories, so there seems to be little conceptual purpose in synthetically adding space to society (as in the socio-spatial dialectic); dialectics is not a hyphen that stitches separate categories together in an external relationship of hyphenated links. For the same reason, the culture-economy spatial dialectic of distinct regional formations will also not work, because the dialectical approach, unlike the analytical approach, is not amenable to scalar fragmentation, as there are no local dialectics or meso-level dialectics that can be added together in order to reach a national- or a global-level dialectic. The city serves as a totality that synthesizes the economy, culture, and space into an interrelated whole. Therefore, I must look at the city-as-synthesis in order to understand the constituted materiality of globalization. In this constituted materiality, culture, economy, and space are not discrete boxes, but rather internally related and imbricated in such a way that they cannot be disaggregated in the first instance as well as the last. This means, in essence, we have been looking at the wrong problem:

the question is not how can we study culture, but rather how can we understand the constituted materiality of globalization? In answering that question, culture will be revealed in its intricate imbrication with economy, space, and all of the other aspects of social totality. The city-as-synthesis is not some local scale that can be added to other cities in order to understand the national or global culture. The city-as-synthesis is a concept, rather than a geographical site, that crystalizes the culture of globalization.

In Chapter 3, I delve into globalization. I explore the existing literature concerning globalization, and hence the existing approaches to globalization. Some see globalization primarily as an economic process: the unfolding of a neoliberal economic regime that ushers in privatization, deregulation, and free trade while phasing out the redistributive roles of the government, cutting back on social welfare programmes, removing subsidies, and spurring capital across nations. In the Third World context, the exploitative aspects of these economic impacts include the dismantling of the import-substitution industrialization regime, and hence de-industrialization, unemployment, the informalization of labour, the rise of export-processing and sweatshop jobs that are brought in by foreign corporations, a decline in social redistribution, and an increase in income inequality. Others primarily focus on the cultural aspects of globalization, seeing it as a massive global regime of corporatization and commodification, and hence one that irons out local cultural diversities, such as the formation of the hodge-podge and fusion culture of saree-wearing Barbies and chipotle-flavoured sushi. Some argue that corporatization will be victorious over all forms of local, authentic culture, which will lead to the homogenization of the cultural landscape. Others argue that it is not all that simple, because local, national, and regional cultures will interact with global, corporate cultures, indigenizing them in creative ways. A spatio-material lens for understanding globalization also exists, which is envisioned as 'time-space compression' (Harvey 1989a: 147), the 'space of flows' (Castells 2000a: 14; 2000b), the 'space of places' (Castells 2000a: 14; 2000b), and de- and re-territorialization (Appadurai 1990, 1996). This spatio-material approach claims that the neoliberalization of the global economy combines with the technological revolution to alter global space, and our imagination of it, in a profound way. Flows of information, images, money, ideas, and commodities de-root known geographies and produce new ones. This increased connectivity seems to annihilate geographical distance, creating a compressed world that involves a dense network of flows and places.

My attempt, in this chapter, is to synthesize these fascinating ideas into a complex whole, in order to understand globalization in its totality. In many ways, this chapter is the window into the entire book; it is the first opening to some method of doing away with my frustrations vis-à-vis approaches to globalization. I use the city as a receptacle for understanding the constituted materiality of globalization. Therefore, this chapter takes a conceptual look at the post-Fordist city (First World) and the post-liberalization city (Third World). Post-Fordism makes up the internal organic logic of globalization in the sense that it represents the dismantling of Fordist factories, and hence the unravelling of those old industrial cities that crystallized around the industrial economy. The result is often inner-city decay and suburbanization. Post-Fordism also represents the emergence of post-industrial cities that are focused on research and development, computer programming, software, digital technology, theme-park entertainment, and tourism. The First World city therefore synthesizes the contradictory impulses of post-Fordist globalization, while also simultaneously decaying, hollowing, suburbanizing, and morphing into cities with gated enclaves, privatopias, and mixed-ethnic neighbourhoods prized for their diversity. Globalization is a cultural-economic dialectic of disintegration, gentrification, redlining, de-industrialization, joblessness, the picturesque growth of enclaves, hybrid architecture, digital suburbs, and silicon valleys. In the Third World, where Fordism was not as profound, the dialectics of globalization can mainly be understood as post-liberalization realities in which liberalization indicates the structural adjustment of the economy and the adoption of neoliberal policies. The post-liberalization city in the Third World is also a contradictory synthesis of de-industrialization, informalization, and intensification of poverty and slums, as well as the simultaneous urban revitalization that produces 'world class' landscapes overnight in the form of gigantic malls, riverfront boulevards, gated communities, and theme parks. How is it possible to conceptualize these contradictory dialectics of globalization that unfolds as cultural, economic, and spatial realities in a tight nutshell? To answer that question, I look at Baudrillard's (1993, 1994), Harvey's (1989a), and Jameson's (1984) conceptualization of the postmodern condition—which is a condition, a reality, and a phase that coincides with globalization—because these are brilliant attempts at conceptualizing globalizing realities. The chapter draws on Baudrillard's notion of the prevalence of sign value in the era of globalization and postmodernity—an era in which identity, signification, and image have acquired precedence over substance, material, and use value. I examine Harvey's and Jameson's contention that neoliberal globalization forms the foundation for the postmodern, superstructural manifestation of culture in the form of ephemeral identity politics, commodification, and signification. My critique of Baudrillard is that he peels off culture, isolates it, and allows it to transcend its moorings in the economic and spatial dimensions of reality. My problem with Harvey and Jameson is that, in their effort to substantiate culture, they wander into a domain that assigns the economy the primary causal agency for the production of culture. The dialectics fall short in both counts. I use examples from cyberspace, more specifically the presence of the sacred/religious in cyberspace. By looking at churches, mosques, and other religious institutions that go global by using Facebook, YouTube, and the internet, I indicate how these institutions resolve the cultural (religion) and economic (call for subscriptions, memberships, selling CDs, confessions, and sacred rites) through a cyber-material city, a transcendent space where culture always unfolds with the economy. Therefore, globalization is not a *post* to modern, a hyper-cultural phase *after* the era of the economic, and it is not *late* capitalism emerging out of a *cultural logic*. Instead, culture has always been integral to the modern and the time after, and it has always been intricately imbricated in all phases of capitalism, always existing as the veneer and the underside, the base and the superstructure. Culture permeates the economy, and the examples I draw from the internet substantiate how the cyber-material city is a culture-economy synthesis.

In Chapter 4, I use my fieldwork at the Akshardham temple complexes in Atlanta, Houston, and Irving-Dallas, as examples of a dialectical approach to globalization. I first claim that the temple complexes should not be understood as geographic sites, because they internalize the metabolic processes (culture and economy) of the social totality of globalization. Hence, they are more than just fantastic landscapes; they are transcendental materialisms of built form, narratives, texts, perceptions, and oral histories. Transcendental materialism borrows from Hegel's transcendental idealism, in which Hegel argued that history progresses through contradictions between ideas. An initial idea or thesis is contradicted by another idea, the antithesis, and evolves into a new synthesis that influences human action and transforms the world. Ideas therefore produce action, as each synthesis soon becomes a thesis and once again is challenged as civilization proceeds towards the perfect, or absolute, idea. Each synthesis transcends its more imperfect predecessor, moving history towards perfection, hence 'transcendental idealism' (Stewart 2000: 465). On the other hand, I argue that, following a Marxist materialism, material conditions drive globalization, and ideas are materially produced as an integral and inseparable aspect of material existence. Therefore, the city-as-synthesis and the Akshardham temples are transcendental materialisms—new materialisms secreted over older ones—and as these new materialisms transcend the older ones, the city, and globalization, evolve. These new materialisms are sometimes woven together with other materialisms many thousand miles away, thus defining the dialectics of globalization. Examining these materialisms closely, the chapter reveals the dialectics of globalization through immigrant narratives, oral histories, and perceptions. 'Localism-globalism' is a label I use to indicate how the same temple complexes are intensely local, familiar, safe havens, and homes for Indian immigrants of a particular generation, while they are also, at the same time, large, fantastic, magnificent, and global landscapes for second-generation American-Indian youth. 'Dollar divinity' is another example of transcendental materialism, where the transnational production of the sacred is an expensive political–economic process of negotiating visa issues for godmen, priests, and cooks, of keeping the books, collecting donations, and dealing with city regulations and the law. It also indicates how the sacred produces itself through food courts, gift shops, and rental spaces, all of which are important income producers. Therefore, as an exemplar of globalization, the Akshardham temple complex brings out the inflection of culture and economy in materializing globalization. 'The nation in global circulation' is an example of how Akshardham temple complexes transcend their geographic location in American cities by grounding the immigrant Indians' patriotic fervour for the nation they left behind. The temple complex becomes an impromptu India, a nation left behind, and globalization makes this possible. At the same time, this patriotic fervour is mediated with respect and love for America and American multiculturalism, which produces an interesting symbiosis of Indian-Americanism. 'Racial disjunctures' are contradictory materialisms of globalization in which the immigrant landscape must embrace the 'racial others' who find their way into the temple complexes from the host city in which it is placed. The 'other' is desirable and welcomed because she is a testimony to the temple's popularity. However, at the same time, she is often alienated and mistrusted, as she is considered too profane and too culturally bankrupt, needing salvation. Globalization, therefore, is constituted by the many contradictory materialisms that exist in a relational context to each other. These materialisms have transcended other materialisms that existed before them to produce a sedimented geography of globalization. The archaeology of globalization must, therefore, understand the myriad transcendental materialisms that relationally constitute its dialectics.

In Chapter 5, I produce a cognitive map of the Akshardham temples in Ghandinagar and New Delhi, India, particularly a cognitive map of the spectacular, themed landscapes for which tickets are sold to an audience. A cognitive map is, as Jameson (1984) indicated, a postmodern subject's ideological representation of her place in the world, in other words, her ability to map her city. It is ideological because there is a link between what the postmodern subject imagines herself to be and how she represents herself on the map. Jameson called this ideological link the representational dialectic. Alienation happens when the postmodern subject is no longer able to map her position in the city and the social totality. Disalienation involves regaining the ability to find one's position, and thus it is empowering. In the cognitive map of the Akshardham temple complexes, I juxtapose the spectacles of Vedic boat rides, mystique India dioramas, Sat-Chit-Anand water-laser shows with the themed spaces of Disneyland. I use disalienation, alienation, cognitive maps, and representational dialectics to understand how the production of fantasy in the religious sphere, particularly in the context of globalization, can be theorized. Using the cognitive map of the spectacular, themed spaces of Akshardham complex, I argue that globalization provides a new representational dialectic that prevents disalienation. In other words, globalization keeps us alienated and disempowered. In order to substantiate this disalienation and disempowerment, I compare religion with capitalism, purposefully blurring their boundaries to indicate how organized religion can function as a factory in which accumulation must take precedence. Just like capitalism, accumulation in the religious sphere is also fraught with contradictions: it needs donations, contributions, and worldly wealth to survive and expand its reach, but it must preach the need for alienation from those very base material attachments—in other words, alienation from accumulation—to its disciples. I argue that an organized production of fantasy, or what I call 'mapping fantasy', provides the temporary resolution to these contradictions. An increasing amount of capital is extracted and invested in the production of spectacular fantasies—like Vedic boat rides, mystique India dioramas, and laser shows—which allows accumulation to proceed unhindered. At the same time, these fantastic spaces are programmed and themed to teach the values of alienation from accumulation. Globalization—with its ability to circulate technology, engineers, ideas, funds, and themed spaces—creates a dialectic between what a postmodern subject is and what her religion has mapped for her. It is possible that, in 'acting out' this ideology of cultural production–consumption, we may develop a critical distance from this sphere of stupefaction. Disalienation will result, and we can then produce alternative maps of who we are and of our position in the city, and in doing so produce an alternative globalization.

In Chapter 6, I take a good look at who shapes globalization. However, in the spirit of the dialectical approach, I want to emphasize that this is not a Cartesian analysis of a subject fashioning an object called globalization. Instead, I am interested in understanding how the materiality of globalization is shaped. In doing so, I am particularly interested in querying the subject that shapes globalization and in the process gets shaped. Following phenomenologists, I argue that subject or subjectivity is not some nebulous mental faculty separated from the body. Doing away with Cartesian dualism, phenomenologists have claimed that the tangible and intangible, the mind and the body, our position in the world, and our perspective of the world are not separate entities, but simultaneously exist in the 'body-subject' as embodied positions that can never be synthetically severed. It is that version of the subject, or subjectivity, that I wish to use. However, I argue that phenomenological understanding does not go quite beyond the individual, and we therefore need to take recourse in Marx in order to understand embodied subjectivity in the group context. For Marx, consciousness is inescapably bound to the material act of labouring and existing, but this consciousness is never insular; it is always a social act, a collective act of labouring in a group or class. Therefore, class-consciousness is defined by the body-subject's situation in the context of labour and accumulation. The constituted materiality of all reality, including the globalizing realities, must therefore be a class act. The city that synthesizes this materiality of globalization must therefore also be a classed reality. I also argue that class is always imbued with gender. There can be no genderless class, or classless gender, and hence the constituted materiality of globalization is informed by a gendered-classed subject co-constituting a gendered-classed city. I query the spectacular landscapes of the Akshardham temple complexes in Houston, Atlanta, and Dallas in order to understand how they shape a gendered and class-based globalization. I look at religious patriarchy in the Akshardham complexes in order to understand how it has become soft and more porous in the contemporary context of globalization, leading to the inclusion of the 'worldly' American Gujarati women. It is my argument that, through an increased porosity or softening of religious patriarchy, capitalist patriarchy is enabled, or left un-critiqued. The women subjects who shape the new global religion, the new migrant-consciousness, and the new globalizing city emphasize that their economic emancipation is attained through carefully balancing their reproductive roles (household work) with their productive roles (jobs). In other words, these women subjects never disrupt the sexual division of labour at home, and thus carefully nourish familial patriarchy while they take on productive roles outside the home. The softened religious patriarchy consents to a woman's participation in production only after she has performed her gender roles at home. Being able to do both is the new subjectivity of the globalizing women. In doing both, the woman subject engages in a class act: the act of accumulation. She aids accumulation, directly and indirectly: directly by becoming the modern entrepreneur at work, and indirectly by legitimizing the sexual division of labor at home so that her man can participate in production free of any caregiving responsibilities. A globalizing religious patriarchy celebrates her economic emancipation on the condition that patriarchal capitalist accumulation is not disrupted in any way. Therefore, not only do capitalism and patriarchy depend on each other, but capitalist patriarchy also depends on religious patriarchy. The gendered subject is always engaged in a class act, and a class position is a gendered act. My women interviewees belonging to the middle-class and their male counterparts shape accumulation through the religious and capitalist patriarchy, and that is the constituted materiality of globalization. Such is the dialectics of this materiality that separating cultural questions from economic questions will leave a disembodied subject, a partial consciousness, and a fragmented city that does not exist in reality.

Understanding globalization is the goal of this book, but the path to understanding is not a simplification of reality into containers, boxes, and arrows that appear neat and nice in textbooks while failing to encapsulate the real world. The path to understanding is complex, because the real world is complex; globalization is complex. I am confident that the dialectical approach I attempt in this book is the best way to communicate this complexity. Dialectics reveals the constituted materiality of globalization, a materiality that is constantly shaped and reshaped by culture, economy, politics, society, space, class, and gender all in unison. The city synthesizes this unified process, and the city-as-synthesis is complex enough, manageable enough, and specific enough to reveal the imbricated, relational nature of social totality. The task at hand is to be sufficiently cognizant to avoid slicing this synthesis into oppositional categories like base versus superstructure, culture versus economy, production versus signification, space versus society, and class versus gender. Because analysis has been the predominant mode of enquiry (at least in the social sciences), we have been trained to internalize a 'common sense' second nature that approves fragments, sequences, and boxes. It is hard to indiscipline one's mind to escape from the prison of the mechanistic analytical tradition and train it to think in a complex manner. Indisciplining would require moving away from cause-and-effect-, flow-chart-, and Venn-diagram-based analyses. I hope to achieve a very indisciplined approach to the social totality of globalization in this book. I take spectacular landscapes, particularly the temple landscapes and narratives surrounding them, as examples for approaching complex-constituted materiality. I choose these fantastic landscapes because, in analytical thinking, they are immediately categorized as cultural landscapes, just as the World Bank and the stock exchange are immediately boxed as economic landscapes. It is my hope to use the temple landscapes to demonstrate how culture is not a synthetic veneer overlaying the discrete foundation of the economy, but rather how they are imbricated in constituting the materiality of reality. I hope that *Spectacular City* can appropriately communicate the complexity of globalization in its cultural and economic entirety without simplifying it and reducing it into a caricature of reality. I also hope that the same can be done for the economy, and that it would be possible to see the World Bank, the IMF, the stock exchange, and the treasury as culturally imbricated, all in the interest of completely understanding the totality of globalization. That, however, is another book.

Notes

1. Some have understood it as the spread of the democracy of free market (Friedman 1999), others as the rise of the empire (Hardt and Negri 2000), and yet others have said that globalization is just a de-politicized and superficial way of talking about capitalism and its spread across the globe (Giminez 2004). Harvey (2005), Peet et al. (2003), and Stiglitz (2002) devoted much energy towards understanding the neoliberal nature of contemporary globalization. Peet has understood it through the inner workings of global governing institutions, like the World Bank, the International Monetary Fund (IMF), and the World Trade Organization (WTO). Harvey has devoted years of work towards a historical-material analysis of the capitalist mode of production and its unravelling as neoliberalism and globalization. Stiglitz has understood globalization as the rounds of structural adjustment imposed on various post-socialist and Third World countries. Others, like Appadurai (1990, 1996), Barber (2000), and Ritzer and Malone (2000), have looked at globalization through a cultural lens, often understanding it as the co-existence of the contradictory forces of corporate-homogenization and local diversity. Still others have looked at the nation and its mutation in the era of globalization, asking questions such as: does the nation hollow out; does it leak; is it dissolved into a regional entity like the European Union (Brown 2001; Ohmae 2000; Hetne 2001; Strange 2001)? Some scholars, like Davis (2004) and Sassen (1991), have taken an urban perspective to understanding how the city transforms under globalization. Davis concentrated more on the deep, structural violence that the city must absorb in the wake of neoliberalism and structural adjustment, and hence the deeper entrenchment of exploitation, increase in poverty and joblessness, proliferation of slums, and the ubiquitous proletarization of the poor. Sassen, on the other hand, understood how the city is implicated in large and small global flows in such a way that it often transcends the nation in its scale and outreach to become a 'global city' (Sassen 1991: 12).

2. Bochasanwasi Shri Akshar Purushottam Swaminarayan Sanstha.

2 Culture and the Dialectic Approach

Why Is Culture Material/Immaterial?

Culture is a word that resonates with everyone; it may mean something specific to every person, but almost everyone can find some reference point to it. The reference point may be food, art, theatre, fashion, and range from the mundane—such as agriculture and horticulture—to the more intellectual, such as the development or improvement of the human mind as it is understood in terms like 'cultured people', 'cultured minds', and so on. It proves difficult, however, to abstract from the personal reference points to an academic definition. In *The Sociology of Culture*, Raymond Williams (1981) observed that there are usually two approaches to culture: an idealistic approach and a materialistic approach. The idealist approach understands culture as something that influences the human spirit, and thus influences our whole way of life. It is therefore infused in a whole range of social activities, particularly in cultural activities like language, art, and music. The materialist version understands culture as a direct or indirect product of a set of social activities. The social activities, and the culture that results from them, make up the whole social order. The idealist position assumes that culture is *there*, while the materialist position assumes that culture is *produced*. Production, in the materialist interpretation, refers to the production of culture through economic activities. In this chapter, I will take a closer look at the materialist position, and discuss its various reformulations, since these form the theoretical position of this book. It is not that I consider the idealist position to be conceptually poor—ideas are important catalysts in the production of history, and culture is indeed a set of ideas, traditions, and customs that are instrumental to informing a whole way of life—but I note that what is silent in the idealist interpretation is an analysis of why culture is there. Where did it come from? Who put it there? Are humans genetically predisposed to culture, or does it come from somewhere else? These silences inspire and drive this book towards a deep and critical look at materialism, a crude version of which claims that culture emerges from economic activity, a position that has been criticized as economic determinism. Therefore, the larger conceptual purpose is to understand the materiality of culture, and its inflection with ideas, without sinking into an abyss of economic determinism or floating into a cloud of idealism. This is an endeavour that is difficult, because the world is usually understood and interpreted in conceptual categories that are then defined by phrases that reduces the chaos of reality into an order of certainty; for example, we have conceptual phrases like culture, economy, territory, landscape, society, politics, time, and space, to name a few. These phrases reduce all the processes of the social order into separate compartments when, in reality, they are always tied to each other and happen together. In that context, tracing a causal relation of which activity produced which process is often only an intellectual and academic exercise that simplifies the complexity of reality so that it can be effectively communicated to an audience in order that they can, in turn, interpret reality in the same way as the person who initiated the exercise.

My attempt here is to understand how some of these conceptual categories are tied together to produce the tapestry of reality. In particular, how are culture, economy, and territory inflected in defining a landscape of socio-spatial and temporal reality? What is the best way to analyse culture so that it is not relegated to a residue, an aftereffect of the economy, while simultaneously avoiding the superimposition of culture as the 'super-organic' influence that, from out of nowhere, determines all of society? Since I am a geographer, I will attempt to do that through the lens of geography, which means that space, territory, and landscape will each be important ingredients in this conceptual journey, although I will not limit myself only to the geographic literature. Peet (1997: 37) makes an important remark regarding the lack of astute and deep inflection in these conceptual realities in geography:

Culture is brought into economic analysis, as though culture is a separate and subordinate realm, mainly at moments of theoretical crisis, when purely economic analysis obviously cannot suffice: a motive here, a type of behaviour there, a consumer preference every so often, after which the analysis returns as quickly as possible to 'objective certainty'. This continuing lack of integration, for example, the new cultural with the new industrial geography, is partly because a synthetic project is complicated. But it is also because the movement for theoretical reform got stuck on 'the complexity of agency' or 'the multiplicity of identity' rather than engaging in a complete rethinking of the social and cultural origins of economic institutions, behaviours and actions.

The 'theoretical reform' that Peet alluded to refers to the radical turn in geography, which he spearheaded in many ways. This radical turn provided sharp and nuanced critiques of the quantitative revolution, which held that reality was often reduced to simplistic mathematical and statistical models or consumer-behaviour research that happened in an imaginary, isotropic space. The radical turn successfully called for research that attempted to understand the human condition in more complex ways, where issues like poverty, inequality, and exploitation were not simplistically reduced to imaginary individuals on a geometric space who behaved according to the laws of physics. However, Peet also argued that this theoretical reform 'got stuck' because cultural analysis became too pre-occupied by the subject or agent and her/his identity. In a theoretical effort to bequeath power to social groups as part of a conceptual effort to make the 'agent' visible in the structure–agency debate, cultural analysis became lost in the multiple subjectivities of the agent. This is not a bad outcome, except for the problem that cultural analysis stopped at that point, instead of taking it further and putting a similar conceptual effort into understanding the complexity of 'structures' and how they work to exploit.

A more complete theoretical reform would therefore require a conceptual tool that uses culture and economy in a creative tension, as well as using it to analyse some aspects of the social totality (structures of exploitation) without losing sight of the agent, who is part of this totality but not entirely imprisoned by it. In Marxism, structure as a concept arises in the preface to the *Contribution to the Critique of Political Economy* (Marx 1970: 20–1), where Marx contended:

> In the social production of their existence, men inevitably enter into definite relations, which are independent of their will, namely relations

of production appropriate to a given stage in the development of their material forces of production. The totality of these relations of production constitutes the economic structure of society, the real foundation, on which arises a legal and political superstructure and to which correspond definite forms of social consciousness. The mode of production of material life conditions the general process of social, political and intellectual life. It is not the consciousness of men that determines their existence, but their social existence that determines their consciousness.

A crude interpretation of this Marxian materialist analysis understands the economy as the foundation, or the deep structure, of society, and as the realm where classes enter into relations of production and transform nature through their labour. The value generated from this 'real foundation' is then managed, circulated, accumulated, invested, and inherited through a 'legal and political superstructure' that provides the interpretive devices that enable social groups to understand, explain, and rationalize their material realities, and hence informs their consciousness. The layer of the superstructure that informs social consciousness is the realm of religion, culture, the market, the state, and the military. Thus, culture is the ideological realm that is connected to the material, because the latter produces the former; in this kind of analysis, culture is always the by-product of the economy. I will return to the use of base and superstructure in Marxist analysis later in this chapter, because it is germane to the understanding of culture that I want to propose in this book. For now, however, it suffices to say that Peet called for a different kind of analysis that does not relegate culture as the 'subordinate', or as a 'behaviour' here and a 'preference' there.

Cultural, Economy, and Space

A dialectical view of society is one where we move away from causal interpretations to an interpretation in which different constituting factors (sometimes co-aligned and sometimes contradictory) are co-present, in their supportive or opposing ways, to produce reality. For Peet (1997: 37), a link between culture and economy that arrives at a cultural-economic geography is achieved through the 'mediation of subjectivity', which can be specified by the concept of 'economic rationality'; that is, the logic people give for their economic action, and how they rationalize their overall successes or failures. Peet contended that these economic rationalities are discursively formed and displayed (as a set of ideas represented as value systems, codes of behaviour, customs within families, communities, and religious orders). Thus, economic rationalities are culturally created and, therefore, the spaces where they are found (that is, the geography) are also intricately interwoven with cultural, ethical, and traditional discourses to produce 'regional discursive formations' (Peet 1997:38). In the context of North American capitalism between the eighteenth and the twentieth centuries, Peet discussed the discursive system found in New England, with Boston as its capital and the Puritan religious ethic as its mode of cultural regulation, as well as a Virginia system and a Philadelphia-Quaker system. Using the New England discursive system as his case study, he indicated how an entire new industrial-economic rationality was produced in the region; an economic imagery that draws from Puritan religious ethics of hard work and repetitive, organized labour to attain the grace of God—by answering one's calling in life and, in the process, making a profit and investing in the local community—while relying on scientific innovation, because God is not involved in the mundane realities of everyday existence. Such a religious-cultural imaginary allowed for the thriving of a regional economic system grounded in modern industrial capitalism, profit making, and the continuous re-investment in profit. The cultural-economic imagery also transformed the regional landscape into mill towns with congregational churches, representing the sites of cultural-economic production, as well as other landforms, such as the schools, universities, libraries, and concert halls that emerged due to the generous charity of the industrial elite. Profit was not spent in pomp and merrymaking; rather, the stoic and Spartan puritan ethic propelled its re-investment into socially conscious charity imperatives that allowed for its re-investment in education and culture. Thus, culture produced a distinct economic system, which in turn produced new sites of cultural and economic production.

In an effort towards a more culture-historical materialism, Peet (2000: 1230) reflected:

> Economy is not a sphere separate from, yet somehow dominant over, other dimensions of social existence. Economy is merely that set of material and cultural practices most directly involved in the reproduction of existence. How to conceptualize relations between parts of life that meld into one another?

Using Weber's analysis of the Protestant ethic as the catalyst in the foundation of the modern industrial revolution, Peet complicated Weber's interpretation by arguing that a uni-causal explanation in which culture (the protestant ethic) is the sole determinant of the economy (capitalism) is an interesting starting point, but not an entirely accurate representation of the chaos of reality. Instead, he argued for a radical geography that attempts 'cultural-economic' analysis in which culture and the economy are dialectically intertwined. In other words, culture and the economy are so complexly inflected that it is impossible to separate one from the other in order to arrive at a distinct cause–effect equation. Instead of a causal analysis, he made a dialectical attempt that also tied space into the analysis. Different regions (space) contribute a distinct and different economic culture to the global capitalist system; therefore, a cultural-economic spatial dialectic would be the best conceptual tool.

Base-Superstructure and Culture

As already mentioned earlier, in certain versions of Marxism, base is the 'economic conditions of production, which can be determined with the precision of natural science' while the superstructure is the ideological form for which the methods of investigations cannot be objective (Williams 2009: 78). Culture, along with other political and legal institutions, is therefore part of the superstructure, informing the consciousness of the society under study. Williams critiques this form of analysis as 'reductionism' that assumes the base and superstructure, which are two pre-existing and separable entities with no mutual constitutive processes between them. This orthodox and reductionist version, according to Williams, ignores the fact that thinking, imagining, and interpreting are material acts that are always accessible in material ways, such as the voices in a song, the colour in a painting, and the writing on a page. It is not as if human societies act on the material world as non-thinking, unconscious beings in a discrete material universe called the 'base', and when their material actions are over, they switch into the world of the 'super-structure' and engage in imagination and interpretation. Thinking and acting, when artificially separated, produce a conceptual sterility that cannot comprehend the complexity of reality. The separation of the base and superstructure separates the process of 'social signification' as a secondary act of representing reality that happens after the moment of the primary act of production:

> In Marx, in Engels, and in much of Marxist tradition the central argument about 'practical consciousness' was limited and frequently distorted by the failures to see that the fundamental process of social signification are intrinsic to 'practical consciousness' ... For the practical links between 'ideas and theories' and the 'production of real life' are all in this material social processes of signification itself.
>
> Moreover, when this is realized, those 'products' which are not ideas or theories, but which are very different works we call 'art' and 'literature', and which are normal elements of the very general processes we call 'culture' and 'language', can be approached in ways other than reduction, abstraction, or assimilation. (Williams 2009: 70–1)

Therefore, for Williams, a satisfactory comprehension of reality must understand the base and superstructure, economy and culture, production and signification, and act and interpretation as inextricably tied together, with no one aspect taking ontological priority over the other. Only then can a true dialectical view of culture emerge within the historical materialist tradition. Williams offered the concept of 'mediation' (2009: 97) as that constitutive link. Mediation is seen as the reconciliation of two opposites within a totality that hence emphasizes how each feeds into the other as a constitutive element. However, the problem lies in the fact that it is almost impossible to understand mediation without assuming two separate categories of reality between which the mediation must occur. Although Williams (2009: 99) prefers mediation to simple reductionism—because mediation, at least, has the ability to emphasize the constitutive materiality of the real world—he cautions that 'mediation' still continues to assume the role of an 'intermediary', never fully eliminating the gap between 'reality' and 'speaking about the reality'. The point is that the real and the act of speaking of the real are always constitutive moments; when we look at the real world, they always happen together and at once, and are never frozen in the discrete containers of the base and superstructure. Yet, when it comes to conceptually communicating this constitutive reality, we somehow always use a hyphen to separate these constitutive moments. This, according to Williams, leads to a rather sterile, simplistic, and reductionist analysis of reality, and he suggested, with caution, that mediation may come close to un-freezing this conceptual separation so that 'constituted materiality' becomes conceptually dynamic (Williams 1980: 108). This search for concept is the key for culture, because without a dialectical philosophy that expresses this constituted materiality and eliminates unidirectional arrows from the base to the superstructure, culture will always remain ontologically secondary to the economy, ensconced in the realm of interpretation, reproduction, and signification *after* the material act of production. When puritan culture actually existed in the real world, as Peet so elegantly indicated in his interpretation of Weber and the New England discursive system, it was a constitutive element in the mill-town capitalism of the region. So, how best can I, for the purpose of this book, attempt such a dialectical philosophy, which presents the constituted materiality of culture and the economy without becoming conceptually sterile and reductionist? Will mediation work? Or, would Peet's (2000: 1231) 'cultural-economic spatial dialectic' work better? At this juncture, before such a decision can be made, there is an urgent need to delve into a discussion on dialectics.

Dialectics

Sayers (1990), in his important critique of *Karl Marx's Theory of History: A Defense* (Cohen 1978), makes a distinction between *analysis* and *dialectics*. Analysis, according to Cohen, involves the disaggregation of the whole into discrete component parts that are then defined and understood as fragmented aspects of a totality in isolation. Sayers (1990: 142) claims that 'the effect of this method is to produce a fragmented and atomized picture of reality' where 'things are what they are; they have their being purely in themselves and quite independently of the context of their relations'. Dialectical philosophy, on the other hand, is the exact opposite of this:

> Dialectic insists that in order to understand the concrete nature of things it is vital to see them in the context of their interconnections with other things within a wider whole. For dialectic, concrete and particular things are always and essentially related, connected to and interacting with other things within a larger totality. This context of relations is internal and essential to the nature of things, not external and accidental. By contrast, the analytical approach, with its logic of external relations, has the effect of removing things from their context and producing an abstract account of them. It has the effect of fragmenting the world into a disconnected

series of atomic particulars and, thereby, producing a mechanical account of reality. (Sayers 1990: 143)

Therefore, Sayers stressed the importance of contexts, interconnections, and unity within a larger whole, where the context of relations that make up the whole are not imposed from the outside but rather are internal and organic to it. Sayers further clarified that dialectical philosophy is not opposed to distinctions, because it understands that an important aspect of comprehending reality involves making distinctions. However, unlike an analytical method, it insists that in reality different, similar, and opposed parts are in unity. Sayers provided several examples of Marxist concepts that illustrate his point. His example of the forces of production and the relations of production substantiates some of the elements of the dialectical method he emphasized:

> A machine, for example, requires people to build, operate, and maintain it—only given these is it a productive force. A machine is a productive force only in the context of certain relations of production in which it is employable productively. No doubt it is possible to remove a machine entirely from its surrounding social relations and consider it purely abstractly and in isolation ... But then one is no longer considering it as a productive force, but merely in its abstract material aspect, as a physical object. A machine is regarded in this way by the physicist or the engineer. This is perfectly valid and legitimate, if your interest is confined to its material properties, since a machine is indeed a physical object—a certain configuration of metal and other materials—and remains so, whatever the social context in which it is placed. The historian, however, is interested in the machine not merely as a physical object, but as an instrument of social production, as a productive force. And a machine becomes a productive force only in certain social contexts, only in certain relations of production. These relations are essential—that is to say, internal and not merely external—to its being as a productive force. (Sayers 1990: 145)

In the above example, the machine, under the analytical tradition, remains the exact same object irrespective of the social context in which it is placed, because the purpose here is to understand the machine as severed from its social relation and, therefore, the context of its placement is not important. The axe is an axe, consisting of parts like the handle and blade that can be gripped in a certain way to cut certain things. In a dialectical tradition, however, the axe is a tool if it is being used in the context of chopping, it is disposable refuse if it is lying in the junk yard, or it is a symbol for working people if it is being used as a political mascot. Therefore, the dialectical eye stresses the relational context of distinct elements in social totality. Without the context and the relations, the axe has no meaning. Drawing upon Hegel, Sayers thus insisted that all properties that things have are because of the relations in which they exist, such as in the following example:

> Only by reflecting light in a certain way does a thing manifest colour; only in and through its mechanical interactions with other bodies does an object manifest mass; only through its relations to other things in space does a thing show its shape, and so on and so forth. In short, all properties are 'relational'. (Sayers 1990: 153)

At least, some of the relations in which these properties exist are intrinsic to these properties, and dialectical philosophy stresses the intrinsic relations of those properties, unlike the many analytical orthodoxies that containerize and isolate properties in such a way as to make them exist only in absolute, rigid worlds abstracted from their contexts and connected only by relations that are external to them. In reality, things and their relations are not separate from each other, nor are things separate and isolated from other things; they are constantly in relation with one another, and that is how they manifest their properties, which, together with their relations, infuse into things and become their properties (Sayers 1990: 154). For example, humans are not just biological beings, and their identity is not some external relation that washes over them, because the formation of human identity is a continuous dynamic process of contextual relations. Separating the human from its identity means that the human no longer exists, and separating the identity from the human as if it were some external force means that the identity loses its context, and hence its meaning. Humans are always in a context of social relations in which they enable the identity formation of other humans in society. This identity formation is itself intrinsic to humans, as it fills up the very cells that make up their biological being. Therefore, Sayers, in essence, summarizes how a dialectical view attempts to understand the world as an organic whole, whereas the analytical tradition often understands the world as a mechanism of self-sufficient parts. He contrasts the clock analogy with the human body analogy. The clock is a mechanism, and if we break it into its parts, nothing happens to them; we can take some of these parts and add them into a new clock that we are building, and in such a case we thus add nothing to the process but our own methodology of disaggregation. The society, on the other hand, is like a human body, where each organ is in relation to another and thrives and develops its properties in relation to another, and where disaggregation means the end of life. For purely mechanical objects, the analytical methodology may be sufficient, but for more complex organisms, such as society, a dialectical view may be the most suitable. Those who pursue the analytical tradition claim that the chaos of intertwined relations in a whole society needs to be abstracted and separated, at least in theory, because the power of abstraction is often illuminating. Sayers, however, cautions that in order for them to be truly illuminating, we must remember that concepts are *abstractions* of reality and not reality-incarnate. In other words, the textbook should not impose iron laws of abstraction on the real world, because such laws freeze the dynamic, evolving, and contingent nature of reality into discrete containers in the deep recesses of someone's thought process.

A dialectical approach to culture is desirable because it promises to conceptually articulate the integrity of a chaotic reality, which is incredibly complex and therefore deserving of a non-mechanistic, complex appraisal. The dialectical approach has been adopted by many geographers who attempted to develop a historical geographical materialism after Marx's historical materialism. However, most major debates have centred on how to make 'space' a central aspect in the dialectical analysis of social processes. I have already mentioned above that Peet (2000) asked for a 'cultural-economic spatial dialectic' for understanding how different regions (spaces) are also at the same time different regional (spatial) discursive systems of culture and economic rationalities. Cultural-economic realities are, at the same time, spatial realities as well. Soja (1980), in his very famous article in the *Annals of the Association of American Geographers*, made an impassioned plea for making explicit how space was dialectically intertwined with social processes by propounding the concept of the 'socio-spatial dialectic'. He categorized Marxist academic work into three categories. The first category consists of those who are strictly antagonistic of the spatial and who retreat into an orthodox version of Marxism and claims that analysis should focus on class relations because the 'addition' of space creates fetishism by assigning too much autonomy to space. The second category often places space in the centre stage of its understanding of reality, but, when pushed to make an explicit choice, the social gains primacy over the spatial. Soja placed himself in the third category, which follows a Lefebvreian stance that calls for a socio-spatial dialectical approach:

> A socio-spatial dialectic is a productive and appropriate focus for the concrete analysis of capitalist social formations and for concerted social action. As an analytical focus, the socio-spatial dialectic is not aimed at submerging class analysis or elevating space per se to the level of a 'scientific subject' in Marxist science or presenting the organization of space as an autonomous structure with regard to fundamental relations of production. Instead, it serves primarily to specify explicitly that the social relations of production and social formations in general, as Marx himself observed, contain within them a fundamental vertical vs. horizontal structure affecting the position of all agents of production (i.e. people) and shaping a simultaneously social and spatial division of labor. In the development of Marxism, the spatial structure has remained, for the most part, externalized and incidental, a mere reflection of a deliberately despatialized concept of the 'social'. The social-spatial dialectic thus represents a call for the reinclusion of socially produced space in Marxist analysis as something more than an epiphenomenon. The argument, however, is taken one step further by suggesting that the vertical and horizontal expressions of the relations of production under capitalism (i.e., relations of class) are, at the same time, homologous, in the sense of originating in the same set of generative structures (e.g., the relation between labor and capital); and dialectically linked, in that each shapes and is simultaneously shaped by the other in a complex interrelationship which may vary in different social formations and at different historical conjunctures. There is no permanent and rigid dominance of one over the other in all concrete historical and geographical circumstances. Indeed, the historical development of the dialectic between social and spatial structures—the interplay between the social and territorial division of labor—should be a central issue in concrete Marxist analysis. (Soja 1980: 224–5)

The essence of the above argument is that space is not simply a mere reflection, a stage, or geometry or pattern etched by the processes of capitalist accumulation, but instead an active moment in the process of accumulation; therefore, production relations—in other words, relations between capital and labour—should not just be viewed in socio-economic terms but also viewed simultaneously in spatial terms.

However, the problem arises in his attempt to take this argument a step further by disintegrating the vertical and horizontal expressions of the relations of production. The vertical is seen as the exploitative class relations that exist between the bourgeois and the proletariat—the social division of labour—and the horizontal is the centre-periphery, or spatial, division of labour between centres of accumulation (the global north) and centres of exploitation (the global south). Drawing on Amin's work on the geographical transfer of value, Soja emphasized the implications: exploitation of the periphery means the working class of the periphery may be subsidizing the labouring class of the core. In other words, the proletariat exploits the proletariat, and therefore, the simple notion of bourgeois versus proletariat class struggle is rendered problematic. The production of space mystifies class struggle or, in other words, the horizontal (space) impinges on the vertical (class). These are important observations on capitalist accumulation and have received much debate within the annals of dependency and world systems theory. This is not the place to engage in an elaborate discussion on class, accumulation, and exploitation. Instead, what I want to point out in the context of this book is that Soja's intention is a vibrant spatial lens for the analysis of capitalism, because he truly believes that space is a neglected element of Marxist analysis that must be explicitly engaged with for the intellectual and practical transformation of capitalism:

> Thus the trans-formation of capitalism can occur only through the combination and articulation of a horizontal (periphery vs. center) and vertical (working class vs. bourgeoisie) class struggle, by transformation on both the social and spatial planes. (Soja 1980: 224)

The socio-spatial dialectic is thus the analytical tool through which the spatial (horizontal) is explicitly brought into the picture in such a way that neither the social nor the spatial has ontological primacy. The purpose is not to move towards a spatial determinism in which spatial structures have inherent autonomy, but to call for a 're-inclusion of socially produced space'. Soja clearly understood that, in reality, the social is never really separate from the spatial, and his argument is that the spatial has been left out of the Marxist analysis of reality and therefore must be re-included in a dialectical way. The problem, here, is two-fold: he is suggesting a rather un-dialectical process of re-inclusion—'a socio-spatial dialectic'—where he is assuming that in the conceptual world of theory the 'social' and 'spatial' are discrete containers that can be rendered dialectical when a hyphen is added between them *and*, as a step further, he is calling for an inflection of the vertical and the horizontal relations of production as an example of the dialectical analysis of global capitalism. In reality, the social and spatial are not discrete containers, and there is therefore no reason why they should, in theory, be discrete and separate; so the solution to a theory that neglects space is not to 're-include' it as a hyphenated add-on, but attempt a dialectical analysis that does not separate them in the first place. Second, disintegrating reality through concepts like the vertical and horizontal, where the vertical is assigned to the social (in this case, class relations) and the horizontal to space, proves problematic for the truly dialectical approach that Soja wanted to emphasize. Once reality is abstractly separated into conceptual worlds of the vertical and the horizontal, it is so often imprisoned within them that it becomes difficult to adopt a dialectical approach. Why are class relations ontologically posed on the vertical axis while geographic relations on the horizontal axis? Why are these relations conceptually posed in terms of height and breadth? In reality, all forms of exploitative relations (class, colonial, race, gender, and so on) simultaneously occur and produce the historical geography of capitalism; they are not pigeonholed separately in vertical or horizontal boxes. The horizontal and vertical are what Sayers would call abstractions, and they are not very illuminating, because we have forgotten that they are abstractions. They have come to acquire a life of their own, and dominate our conception of reality because of the primacy of Cartesian rationality in academic analysis, where dichotomous, rigid categories appear convenient. Unfortunately, the reality of capitalist exploitation is not that of a clock for which the horizontal parts can be fixed into vertical parts so that reality can function like a well-oiled machine. This discussion is pertinent for our approach to culture, because 'socio-spatial dialectic' may do to culture what base-superstructure does: just as base and superstructure separate the economy (base) from culture (superstructure), the socio-spatial dialectic may disintegrate the social (cultural processes) from space (form/landscape). Further discussion of the 'spatial dialectic' will make this danger clear.

At the same time that Soja was propounding his 'socio-spatial' dialectic—which became a very powerful concept in geography, producing

spatially embedded analysis of capitalism. His is not so much an argument for putting space into Marxist analysis, but an argument for making the spatial analysis of capitalism more nuanced by understanding regional and local specificities. In his critique of Peet, Smith (1979: 376) argued that the social and the spatial should not and could not be separated:

> 'Spatial relations' do not simply reflect 'social relations'; without the *spatial* periphery there could be no *social* relations between it and the core. Far from being different relations, the social and the spatial are different aspects of a single relation. We can separate them on occasion for analytic convenience but we cannot define them as separate in practice if our entire project is to combine them. (Emphasis in the original.)

With regard to Soja's 'socio-spatial' dialectic, this is what Smith (1979: 376) had to say:

> Soja perceived the problem precisely but is unable to solve it practically since he is unable to submerge the social-spatial dichotomy. In proposing the 'socio-spatial dialectic' he solves it philosophically using a severe dose of terminological overkill.

It is my argument, that while extremely important and urgent, the concept: 'dialectic' has often been used as just a word, a hyphen, and an add-on, rather than an approach to social reality. Dialectic is not a thing that can be broken down into sub-components to produce a scalar version from the local, to regional, to global. I indicated earlier, with the clock analogy, that the dialectical approach is antithetical to fragmentation and disintegration in a mechanistic way. Capitalism is, of course, embedded in regional, local, placial ways—and pointing as much out in the 1970s is an immense theoretical contribution—but the use of the term 'dialectic' is problematic here. Dialectics cannot be 'spatial', 'social', or 'socio-spatial', because it is an approach to reality that does not understand it as fragmented into social, spatial, socio-spatial, regional, or local. Peet's and Soja's brilliant effort to spatially conceptualize society become problematic because of the use of the term 'dialectic' within analytical categories that are abstractions. However, both their work, and Neil Smith's critique of their work inform my ideas as I revisit dialectics, this time, as an approach towards reality and its materiality.

Of course, Peet moved away from the concept of 'spatial dialectic' many years ago. In my discussions with him, as I wrote this chapter, he made it very clear that he was aware of the limitations of that idea, they are, he said, 'not particularly useful for your project'. Soja, on the other hand, has continued to champion an explicitly spatial logic. In his most recent book, *Seeking Spatial Justice* (2010), Soja explicitly sought to re-imagine justice and injustice as processes that are not merely inscribed on space, but are rather produced *by* space. The objective of this 2010 book is to coequally conceptualize spatiality and sociality, in the interest of developing a more comprehensive understanding of justice.

Towards a Dialectical Approach

So, how can we adopt a dialectical approach that does not render culture secondary to the economy, that abhors a base–superstructure dichotomy, and that does not tear space from society? Williams proposed two concepts: 'mediation' (2009) and 'constituted materiality' (1980). Mediation refers to the reconciliation between two opposites within a totality, hence emphasizing how each feeds into the other as a constitutive element. However, as I indicated earlier, Williams was aware of the limitations of the concept of 'mediation', which seemed to signify the existence of two separate categories between which one must mediate. 'Constituted materiality' refers to this inherent inner connection between humans and nature, so inherent that it is impossible to separate them and use dualistic languages like 'applying', 'exercising', or 'causing', because they always end up misrepresenting the constituted nature of materiality. How can a dialectical approach be initiated towards understanding globalizing cities and their cultural landscapes? How can the constituted materiality between humans and a globalizing urban condition be best understood dialectically? If 'mediation' is not adequately dialectical in explicating culture, the economy and space as an assemblage, how can we talk about urban landscapes and their globalization? Where should we begin? Should we start by theorizing the cultural dimensions of globalization? Should we start by theorizing the cultural and economic content of landscapes? Should we start by theorizing the globalizing city?

Albritton (1999: 67) uses Marx's *Capital* as an example of dialectical thinking to suggest:

> Ideally we would like to start with a category that is abstract and empty and yet permeates the whole, as does the category 'cell' in biology. And

if the object of knowledge is relatively self-determining, as is capital, we want a category that we can rigorously and clearly move forward until we come to grasp fully the inner logic that enables capital to be self-determining ... We need to start with a category that can unfold the historical specificity of capitalism ... The most logical starting point, then, for the dialectic of capital would seem to be the category 'commodity'.

The start of a dialectic is always a kind of 'bootstrap operation'. We assume the existence of capitalism, and hence start not with just any conception of the commodity but with a commodity that is 'ripe', or as it eventually becomes in a fully developed capitalist society. In other words we start with a capitalistically produced commodity, because this is the form of the commodity that is most 'ripe', even though we cannot fully understand what this means until we reach the end of theory. In other words the commodity in which we are interested is one that can become capital.

In our case, I propose starting with the 'city'. The city, and its urban condition, is the cell that permeates and absorbs culture, the economy, and the globalization of culture and the economy. It can unfold the historical and geographical specificity of globalizing culture while being rigorous and complex enough to reveal its inner workings. The city is already in existence, and it is ripe with globalization, or will eventually become ripe. The theoretical objective would be to reveal, dialectically, the constituted materiality of the city; a materiality constituted by the globalizing society that is the organic whole of which society and space are inherent and indissoluble components. The city avoids the base-superstructure dichotomy because it is a concept that reveals, bit-by-bit, the 'constituted' nature of its materiality, in which production and signification, culture and economy, society and space, and act and interpretation are from the very beginning, always together and never analytically separate—this is a 'city-as-synthesis'. Such a city-as-synthesis is a concept, not a geographic site, just as the 'commodity' is a concept. Therefore, at this juncture, I ask the readers to keep in mind that, for the rest of this book, our dialectical approach demands that we understand the constituted materiality of the city-as-synthesis. In doing so, the dialectics of globalization will unfold.

3 In the Name of the Father, the Globalization, and the Holy City, Amen!

Globalization has the universal appeal and conceptual rigour once possessed by the term 'modernity'. Being modern meant possessing the conveniences of urban existence that allowed human societies to transcend the daily frustrations of negotiating life. Pleasure would be extracted from things like television, the central-air-conditioned homes, and clear ice cubes in every glass of water, so that the banalities of repetitive existence would become bearable. It also meant medical doctors and medicine, and scientific discoveries that could reduce suffering and prolong life. Everyone wanted to be modern, or at least wanted to possess what was modern. Of course, the struggles of the Third World would define a different trajectory of modernity than that present in the First World, where industrial revolution was already ripe. In the colonized nations, the so-called 'harbingers of modernity',—the colonial rulers—were only interested in finding resource and labour that would feed the industrial revolution at home; therefore, modernity's prosperity, as well as its convenience and affluence, were intentionally concentrated in the geographies of the metropolitan cores. The history of colonization, therefore, complicates the postcolonial vision of progress in many Third World nations: how to develop through an 'indigenous modernity'? Can there be an indigenous modernity in which the postcolonial reality does not become a simplistic rendering of the colonizer's view of the world? In India, this was never conclusively resolved, and there instead existed a sympathetic tussle between the Gandhian and the Nehruvian models; a tussle between the Gandhian self-sufficient village community, which was labour-intensive and local, and abhorred the large and the mechanized, and the Nehruvian 'temples of modern India' (Nehru 1954, cited in Ahmed 2008: 202), a paradigm that celebrated big dams, large industries, and new technology. In spite of its many variants and detractors, modernity was, as a social praxis and intellectual project, larger than life. I say intellectual project because most disciplines, including the very social ones, went through a major modernizing phase during which time they were not only theorizing modernity, but also going through an onto-logical overhaul as they strove to become scientific in their analysis and predictive in their stance. I am not proclaiming the death of modernity and modernization here, or proposing to revisit the very important postcolonial critique of modernity. In this chapter, I am claiming that 'globalization' has become important in its appeal, as all-encompass-ing in praxis, and as deep as the discourse of modernity. Indeed, in many academic and non-academic circles it has been understood as the more vociferous way of globally spreading 'modernity' through trade, opening up of markets, flight of multinational capital, and unrestricted financial speculations.

Globalization has been a difficult process to intellectualize because, in reality, it has always existed. Peoples, communities, and nations have, to some extent, always been global through their trade, travel, and explorations. However, the Internet, information technology, plastic money, electronic banking, and frequent flyer miles have all clearly plugged us into the global in unprecedented ways. Therefore, an increasing desire emerged among journalists, intellectuals, commenta-tors, and pundits of all sorts to define it, capture its essence, and give it some flesh and blood so that it can become more tangible in ways that allow people to possess it, become it, and aspire for it. I remember that, in the intellectual world that I inhabited, I was in graduate school focusing on furthering research on identity and the nation-state and thought it was impossible to find anything that was not contaminated by the confusing term 'globalization'. Many treatises were claiming the end of the nation-state, the dissolution of national boundaries, and an increase in border porosity because of the new free-trade regime that reduced national economic regulations and allowed for the unhindered flow of capital, commodities, aid, and innovation. This led to what some scholars believed to be the 'hollowing out' of the nation-state and the rise of a regional state or a world community (Ohmae 2000; Brown 2001; Strange 2001). With the developed world's embrace of neoliberal regime and the forceful imposition of its Third World variant—the structural adjustment policies—it seemed that the nation-state, that hallowed receptacle of the modern condition, was slowly weakening. Neoliberalism called for a decrease in government regulation and an increase in the power of the free market. In the developed nations, this often meant a decrease in government programmes that provided assistance to the needy and vulnerable groups, thus exposing them to the discipline of competition at the marketplace. However, this also simultaneously meant a significant shrinkage in the responsibility and accountability of the state. In the developing economies, the World Bank and the IMF pushed governments towards austerity, the removal of subsidies, and border porosity, thus once again weakening the entrenched system of what used to be called 'License Raj' in India. It seemed that this theory was an adequate mirror of society, because nations and their gatekeepers, the national governments, were indeed transitioning to a more global economic regime.

So, is globalization a reference to the world's transition from more nation-based protected economies to a more free-market based global economy run under a more hegemonic policy regime referred to as neoliberalism? Or is there more to it? The academic and non-academic literature more concretely answered the first part of the question, while the latter seemed to be more difficult to conceptualize. A canon of work has been devoted to understanding the economic transition, ranging in perspectives from the left to the right. The intellectual left, within which I am emplaced, contends that the neoliberal regime has not been beneficial for the poor people of the world, because it has led to an increase in intra-national and inter-national inequality and the concentration of wealth in the hands of corporations, professionals, CEOs, speculators, and investment bankers to the exclusion of the poor and the middleclass (Harvey 2005, Peet 2007); it has intensified and magnified local economic crises to global proportions through contagion effects (Stiglitz 2002); and it has transformed pro-poor and redistributive policies in cities into the anti-poor, entrepreneurial strategies of gentrification, beautification, and slum eviction (Harvey 1989b; Baviskar 2003; I. Chatterjee 2004, 2011; Mahadevia and Narayanan 2006). The academic left has pled for a nuanced understanding of how globalization, with a neoliberal face, is grounded in place-specific ways that both follow and transform the pre-exiting path-dependencies of those places. This 'actually existing neoliberalism' involves moments of creation and destruction that morph into variegated geographies of local neoliberalisms (Peck and Tickell 2002; Brenner and Theodore 2002: 349). According to these academics, the political–economic aspect of globalization has been predominantly neoliberal, albeit with significant local flavours, and it is transforming the world in a profound way to create uneven geographies of privilege and deprivation. More specifically, the transition to a market regime has ushered rounds of privatizing public goods and common property resources like water, education, health, and forests, which have made these goods more expensive and less accessible to the poor. Reducing tariff barriers, licenses, and quotas may reduce red tape, but it has also allowed multinational corporations to take over Third World markets. Relaxing national regulations allowed for the outsourcing of First World jobs, increasing unemployment there, and giving special concessions to corporations has allowed for the corporate colonization of cities and towns edging out small businesses in the First World. The new intellectual property regime ushered in by the WTO has allowed for the commodification and theft of biotic resources from Third World environments through patenting by corporations based in the First World. The jobs flooding into Third World economies as a result of neoliberal globalization are low-end and highly transient jobs that exploit women in sweatshops, export-processing zones, maquiladoras, free zones, and call centres as they fly from nation to nation while investing nothing in local economies and often harshly exploit environments, generating economic vulnerabilities as they fly elsewhere. Therefore, indeed for this set of literature, a large aspect of globalization is the transition towards a global neoliberal regime and its associated impact on inter-regional and intra-regional inequality, inter-class and group inequality, labour and environmental exploitation, commodification and privatization, and neo-colonization through corporate control.

However, is there more to globalization? If so, is it in any way connected to the political economy of privilege and deprivation wreaked by the neoliberal global regime? There is a broad range of literature—mainly emanating from the fields of international relations and political science—that emphasizes the nation-state, governance, and sovereignty. One strand of this literature postulates the hollowing out of the nation-state through a leakage in national sovereignty that creates an integrated world order (Brown 2001; Ohmae 2000; Hetne 2001; Strange 2001). Contrary to the earlier argument, another group of theorists argues that the forces of globalization have not hollowed out the nation-state; rather, the nation-state has creatively re-formulated and re-produced itself (Berry 1989; Mann 2001; Slaughter 2000; Taylor 1995). Cultural theorists on the other hand, focus on the cultural implication of globalization, arguing that the flows of commodities, people, ideas, and information all produce a new geography of duality: the landscapes of corporate standardization/homogenization and the landscapes of heterogeneity, difference, and diversity. While the majority of cultural theories on globalization acknowledge that strong global-corporate flows of capital, commodities, and advertisements lead to a standardization of taste, preferences, ideas, outlooks, and ways of life, the result is not always complete standardization and homogenization. In fact, the cultural geography of globalization is a complex trope of homogenization, difference, and disjuncture that exists in a symbiosis. For Barber (2000), the globalizing world is often a clash between the forces of standardization, which he referred to as 'McWorld', and the forces of uniqueness or difference, which he referred to as 'Jihad'. McWorld is centrifugal, outward looking, and expansionary, driven by cutting-edge technology, and a desire to capture new markets and find new sources of raw materials. Jihad, on the other hand, is inward looking, centripetal, rooted, and parochial, and is interested in preserving its identity. These contradictory forces may exist in an uncomfortable contradiction within the same country, or they may be separately placed in different nations that are in collision. The complex topography of cultural globalization would involve the indomitable ability of McWorld forces to iron out differences and diversities in favour of a more homogenous topography of corporate standardization, because McWorld forces have the financial strength to push their worldview, because people are generally easily lured by the glitter of consumption. In the end, the map of cultural globalization would therefore reflect a cartography of corporate hegemony.

In the same light, Ritzer and Malone (2000) argued that the New Means of Consumption (NMC)—which includes franchises, shopping malls, superstores, home shopping television, theme parks, and casino hotels—changing consumption patterns while simultaneously alter-ing their manner of eating, entertainment, living, and thinking, thus generating a new way of life, not only in the US but all over the world, because the NMCs vociferously push the frontiers of emerging markets. Although Barber, Ritzer, and Mallone never discussed neoliberal policy, if we were to extrapolate their cultural logic to the previous discussion on neoliberal policy we could infer that the cultural manifestation of free-market globalization pushed through by the neoliberal regime would also lead to a process of cultural standardization. Appadurai (1990, 1996) articulated the existential angst of globalization when he said that the nation-state's hyphen is in tension as the nation is called on to represent the unique identities it contains while, on the other hand, the state is increasingly required to stay open to new flows of people, technology, images, capital, and finance. Ethnoscape, tech-noscape, financescape, mediascape, and ideoscape represent the new landscapes of globalization. Ethnoscape represent the fluid terrains inhabited by tourists, immigrants, refugees, exiles, and guest work-ers. Technoscape represent the invisible tunnels, air spaces, and cyber spheres through which technology flows, thus rendering impervious boundaries porous. Financescapes represent the new topographies of financial speculation that have been rendered so footloose that they no longer need to be confined to a nation, but rather can treat the world as a global casino with the nations as slot machines to be harvested as and when required. Similarly, television stations, newspapers, and maga-zines have now become global, carrying with them pictures, images and sound bites across nation-states, thus shaping a transnational and global civil society of bloggers and cybercitizens who inhabit the global mediascape. Ideas and ideologies are also increasingly uprooted from the places of their origin and circulated so much that they become global common property; thus, national and regional discourses of 'freedom', 'democracy', and 'war on terror' assume global purchase and spread. Appadurai talks about global diasporas and their sense of deter-ritorialization, and how this is often exploited by groups and institu-tions in the places left behind and elsewhere to create new networks of expatriate finances and cultural identification. Harvey (1989a: 147) used the term 'time–space compression' to explain how the general acceleration of the world through the information-technology revolu-tion, fast travel, footloose capital, and multinational and transnational corporations has allowed space to be overcome so easily that it is as if space has been annihilated and rendered redundant. Therefore, globalization creates an intense compression of space, because of our increased ability to overcome it in a much smaller amount of time. Castells (2000a: 14, 2000b: 77) believed that the new political geography of the world does not represent nation-states as the fundamental unit of existence, but rather 'spaces of places' and 'spaces of flows' that create a 'network society'. Places are not eroded and assimilated into a homogenous global village, but instead remain important senders and receivers of global flows. Some cities become more plugged into the global network, by sending and/or receiving flows of foreign direct-investment, migrants, commodity supplies, experts, and intelligence, therefore transcending their national containers to scale-up into a more global status. These global cities are the nodes, or coordinates, for the network of relations and processes that they are imbricated within to create a grid of places and flows that defines the world's political ecology and political economy.

Therefore, while there is a general agreement that globalization created a new topography of assimilation, homogeneity, and transnational interaction, there is considerable diversity in terms of how this topography is imagined. One way of conceptualizing it is through the landscape of commodification and corporate standardization; another through the multiple scapes of technology, people, ideas, finances, and media; yet another envisions it as the general compression of time and space, and the last looks at it as a network. Cultural and technological processes are important determinates in these conceptualizations, along with the economy. Therefore, in essence, this broadens our understanding of globalization by extending it beyond the realm of the neoliberal economic-policy regime and the hollowing out of the nation-state to indicate that globalization is as much a political–economic phenomenon as it is a cultural one.

Within this cultural conceptualization, there is a significant amount of intellectual energy devoted to further deepening the conception of standardization/homogeneity in globalization in order to indicate how those phenomena that may appear as assimilation, homogenization, standardization, Coca-colonization, Mcdonaldization, Disneyization, or Barbieization, are actually riddled with layers of heterogeneity, differences, and uniqueness that speak to local, national, and regional spaces. Appadurai (1990) used the term 'indigenization' to indicate that assimilation and standardization are hardly ever complete, and that global forces interact with local forces to develop into various indigenous versions of the global process. Therefore, what appears at first glance as the complete ironing out of local diversities actually metamorphoses in interesting ways as a new global–local synergy. Barbie, for example, goes 'ethnic', sometimes adopting the local Indian saree, bindi, and dark hair and at other times sporting the kimono and chopsticks. Barbie also goes brown, black, or pale according to local ethno-racial skin tones; however, it still maintains its model-like proportions—the long limbs, high cheekbones, and thin lips—irrespective of the body proportions of the local population of women. Therefore, indigenization only works to a limited degree: Barbie cannot go completely 'native', because it would then lose its corporate sign value, the essential soul that made it global in the first place. Ritzer and Malone (2000) used McDonalds as an example to study the variegated forms of global-local interactions, citing numerous examples of how local culture bleeds into the global corporate symbolism to produce a new semiotics of fast food. In Thailand, the burger patty incorporates chili powder and sugar, while in Hong Kong the service staff does not smile or greet customers as their western counterparts do, because according to local culture it is competence, directness, and unflappability that are prized, rather than pleasantry. In Beijing, McDonalds encourages a 'hang out' atmosphere where the customers sit around and chat in a family setting even after eating is done, rather than eating quickly and collecting food from the drive-through as is intended in the US. In Delhi, where, because the dollar prices of its food are simply converted to their equivalent in rupees rather than according to local purchasing power, the McDonalds' fare is quite expensive compared to cheaper local food, and so eating at McDonalds is an identity-enhancing practice for the upper middleclass and the rich. However, Ritzer and Malone contend that, in spite of this global–local interaction, McDonalds cannot go too native, or it loses the very mantra that revolutionized eating and food preparation in the first place. The other side of this interaction often involves resistance from those places under corporate onslaught, where there are complaints that McDonaldization is altering eating habits and luring youth and children away from fresh food and into a new culture of less nutritious fast food, and therefore has important ramifications on the local quality of life, health, and consumption choices. Many contend that McDonaldization symbolizes a new form of economic and cultural imperialism, because it involves the near-complete takeover of local markets and rapidly out-competing local food producers and street vendors who come from the poorest strata of such societies. The result is a loss of livelihood, erasure of food diversity, and alteration of traditional and cultural norms of eating, socializing, community life, and the organization of public space. Urban landscapes undergo massive transformations as glossy golden arches replace food shacks, food trucks, and food trollies. The 'cultural imposition' through Disneyization and Barbieization are also criticized: 'western' notions of beauty, standards of thinness, tallness, hair straightening, and skin lightening are globally circulated and, in spite of Barbie going ethnic, a certain gendered process of aesthetics, cosmetics, and eating behaviour is imposed that calls into question local gender identities. The globalization of Disney cartoons and the adoption of exotic tales like 'Aladdin' do not, according to critiques, inculcate an appreciation for Arabian fairytales in the United States. Instead, Aladdin speaks with an American accent and Jasmine looks like an American supermodel while both undergo some degree of skin darkening and emplacement in exotic castles in an exotic desert land.

Therefore, globalization is, in essence, a profound social change that permeates economic, cultural, and social life. As the uneven political economy of privilege and deprivation wreaked by the neoliberal economic regime accumulates privilege for CEOs, investment bankers, and corporate and media barons, and at the same time, heaping deprivation on the working class, farmers, women, and sweatshop workers of the world. This uneven political economy is also an uneven cultural economy because economic imperialism and neo-colonialism are, through corporate takeover, also forms of cultural imperialism. The organization and re-organization of social life through globalization does not happen in compartments where the economy transforms in one city and the culture is altered in another city and politics are reoriented somewhere else, nor is there a preexisting sequence where the economy transforms first to determine the course of cultural change and is then followed by political re-organization. The transformation of social reality through globalization involves the co-transformation of various economic, cultural, and political moments and, in most, if not all, instances, these moments cannot be isolated. Only in the analytical elegance of academic books can globalization be 'analysed' as a cultural process, or a political change, or an economic transformation; in reality, they happen all at once, feeding and bleeding into one another, and aiding and sometimes opposing one another. These transformations are hardly ever complete, sealed-off, and closed, and they do not unfold in the same way everywhere. Therefore, I propose that if we were to understand the geography of globalization dialectically, it may be useful to study all these transformative moments as co-positioned in the process of social transformation. To do that, a discussion of globalization in the context of the city becomes imperative, because the city, as discussed in the previous chapter, is an appropriate solvent of both culture and economy that can be as historically–geographically specific as we want it to be, or more generally dispersed as 'the urban condition' if we want such a dispersion. I am proposing a dialectical approach to globalization, not because it would solidify an academic niche for this book, or because I think it is novel and different from some of the other existing research on globalization, but because I think a dialectical approach can be valuable. It is true that the brilliance of analysis rests on the simplification of the chaos of reality so that simplified threads can be distilled from the very particular circumstances of their happening to be applied elsewhere—and there is also definite value in such analytical exercises—but I contend here that the process of analytical simplification may result in the compartmentalization of reality in a way that is not real. Inductive and deductive analyses, which come out of the positivist tradition, are heavily invested in prediction, which often requires model building and identifying patterns, compartments, boxes, and flow diagrams. However, social reality is hardly a chemical equation and sometimes models therefore do not work, or fail in their predictions. Therefore, instead, in dialectically approaching the city, I would like to understand globalization by letting reality flow into the pages of this book.

The City, Post-Fordism, and Post-Liberalization

Globalization of the urban condition has been described, especially in the Global North, as a transition from Fordism to post-Fordism. The French regulationist school divided the history and geography of capitalism into periods based on the dominance of certain processes: manufacturing between 1780 and 1870; machinofacture between 1870 and 1940; Taylorism, or scientific management, and Fordism between 1940 and 1970; and flexible production and post-Fordism, which began in the 1970s, continue to the present day (Peet and Hartwick 2009). Henry Ford's semi-automatic assembly line, higher wages for workers, and sociological surveys all formed an assemblage of control of labour and capital that allowed for the flourishing of gigantic factories and defined the way of urban-industrial life in the US and elsewhere. The factories had to be large and the workers they employed needed to be disciplined enough to execute the same soul-crushing movements day in and day out. A higher wage allowed the worker to dream of a home, car, and all the other middle-class comforts that labour could never have afforded. Therefore, the Fordist way of life organized urban existence around the factory, with the city set up to collect goods and distribute them to consumers. The efficient circulation of capital and its transformation into commodities, as well as their continuous consumption, required protecting the national economy from foreign goods through heavy tariffs that protected the homegrown capitalists. Therefore, the Fordist era essentially entailed a lower degree of globalization of capital and more nationally grounded investment. The 1970s marked a period of oil crises with embargo on oil exports to western nations, resulting in economic stagnation. The rigidities of Fordism—associated with long-term capital investments, labour markets, and labour contracts—failed to provide a fresh lease of life to capitalist development, and as a result locked 'big labour, big capital, and big government into what increasingly appeared as a dysfunctional embrace of such narrowly defined vested interests as to undermine rather than secure capital accumulation' (Harvey 1989a: 142).

Post-Fordism emerged as a solution to the crisis because it involved the dismantling of the rigid, large-scale Fordist factories, the dismantling and de-rooting of capital investment from the national sphere, a flexible mode of hiring and firing labour, and, hence, a new way of organizing urban life. Production need not be carried out within the same factory via the assembly line, and hence there was no need for long-term, rigid entrapment of capital in gigantic factory sheds and warehouses; instead, through rounds of de-regulation, capital would be rendered free, footloose, and flexible enough to fly anywhere on earth

in search of lucrative investments. Thus began the era of the globalization of capital, and hence, the globalization of the production process.
Capital would find sources of skilled yet desperate labour in the Global
South, who were too poor to protest and too desperate to unionize,
and engage them in super-exploitive productive endeavors in the
form of sweatshops, maquiladoras, export-processing zones, and free
zones, as they are variously known. The nations in the Global South,
which were also impacted by the oil crisis, were pried open through
structural adjustment programmes pushed by the World Bank and
the IMF. As the economies of Third World nations were forced open,
and as they dressed their cities to lure in global capital in the form
of mergers and take-overs posing as the hotel, hospitality, and retail
industries, they had to allow their labour and environment to become
vulnerable as they relaxed labour and environmental regulation. If
capital encountered resistance from labour unions or environmental
activists, it was now footloose enough to fly elsewhere, taking with it
its sweatshop jobs. Therefore, post-Fordism allowed for the vociferous
globalization of capital, binding the First and Third World realities in
a parasitic embrace that only grew stronger as nations went through
increasing economic and financial de-regulation and structural adjust-
ments. Labour, however, was not vociferously globalized, as passports,
visas, and citizenship issues remained real and, in many cases, became
even more ethnophobic, thus sealing-off national containers from
immigrating labor and guest workers. So, while economic realities
became more porous and connected, creating what Harvey (1989a:
147) referred to as the 'time–space compression', political realities
kept labour more place-sticky or nation-sticky. Anti-immigrant hysteria
became an accepted ideology of Tea Party politics in the US as white
labour in the First World lost jobs to outsourcing, and anti-immigrant
riots erupted in France in 2005. However, the predatory nature of
global capital—which favoured certain Third World nations as emerging markets, certain labour pools as more docile, and certain cities as
more up and coming—only entrenched exploitation by etching an
uneven geography of privilege and deprivation between and within
nation spaces. Thus, hip and up-and-coming cities and spaces within
cities transformed, overnight, into export-processing zones, towering
malls, commercial corridors, and office blocks that attracted labour
from other, more deprived spaces of the city, as well as other deprived

spaces of the nation, to create a new army of informalized proletariat (Davis 2004). Thus, the era of post-Fordism is synonymous with what is usually described as globalization, because it reduced national regulation, encouraged border porosity for capital, allowed capital to fly anywhere, caused a dismantling of nation-based Fordist factories, and encouraged a global geography of segmented production and assembly in which a garment is cut in Bangladesh, stitched in Honduras, labelled in Haiti, and embroidered in Sri Lanka.

The post-Fordist city is an interesting globalized reality. In the US, Fordist cities had long been abandoned by the middle class and the rich; as Fordism gained ground, white flight to suburbia introduced a city–country dichotomy in which the city became a geographical concentration of the poor with the white working class looking for a way out, and fresh waves of immigrants looking for a way in (Burgess 1925). The city encapsulated the concentration of poverty, a crumbling infrastructure due to the flight of tax dollars, decaying public schools, gang turfs, blight-stricken homes, and the 'uncivilized' and the 'unknown'. The Federal Highway Act of 1956 provided the necessary arteries of escape for the American white middle class, allowing them to live in their leafy, grassy, picket-fenced suburban homes and still commute to the city for work. The GI bill allowed veterans to procure suburban homes via low-cost mortgages, and a general re-structuring of domestic banking that subsidized homeownership encouraged a suburban geography in the US (Florida and Jonas 1991). Trends changed after the 1980s, with post-Fordism and the 'rusting' of the northern industrial cities, as the capital in the US moved from the North's industrial belt to the South's Sunbelt. The post-Fordist cities of the Sunbelt were based around service industries: research and development, data processing, digital technology, clean energy, theme parks, and entertainment and tourism forming the mainstays. Another aspect of post-Fordist globalization in (but not exclusive to) the Global North has been the deep and entrenched form of gentrification, which gained magnitude in the decade of the 1980s (Florida and Jonas 1991). Neil Smith (1996) famously described this process as colonization and likened the urban developers to 'urban cowboys' who went to reclaim the 'savage' city from the poor, the immigrant, the outlaw, and the homeless in order to bring it within the pale of civilization. With the slow dismantling of the New Deal's urban policy (Florida and Jonas 1991), and the transition from a managerial to an entrepreneurial state (Harvey 1989b), city governments were more prone to open urban spaces up to private investment. Identifying blight and imposing eminent domain became a new form of public–private partnership through which the inner city would be reclaimed, renewed, and rejuvenated by private capital in order to attract the young, white middle class back to the city. Post-Fordism, flexible production, gentrification, and urban renewal became key features of globalization for the Global North. While globalization has, at least in the lay context, been understood as the influx of exotic foods, music, clothes, the internet, social media, and fast travel, it also represents the dismantling of manufacturing, outsourcing of jobs, emergence of Sunbelt urbanism, and the emergence of the post-industrial landscapes of urban renewal for First World cities.

Most nations in the Global South went through a period of industrialization, although the extent to which this phase can be described as Fordist is questionable. Many nations, after gaining independence from imperial powers adopted some mode of industrialization, often under an import-substitution regime (Davis 2004; Stiglitz 2002), the aim of which was to become self-sufficient and to spur economic growth and employment, but the urban context did not necessarily always follow industrialization in the same way as in the Fordist cities. Many cities were already laid out as the collection points and port cities for raw materials that were then exported to the colonial headquarters, while others were administrative centres, religious and pilgrimage centres, and textile or steel cities, which received a further boost under post-colonial governance. Therefore, the colonial history and geography of different continents make the pre-globalization and post-globalization social realities complex. Therefore, in the Third World context, it would be difficult to identify a slice of history and geography that can be neatly labelled as a Fordist and post-Fordist regime. Yet, the nature of industrialization, the forms of governance, and the manner of investment have clearly changed for most Third World countries as they underwent structural adjustment and economic liberalization. In India, for instance, globalization meant economic liberalization, and hence the dismantling of licensing and quotas enjoyed by the import-substitution industries (Ahmed 2009). De-industrialization has been coupled with the rise of export-processing zones (Guha-Banerjee 2011), industrial homework, and a general rise in urban informalization (Roy 2005).

Alongside this, there has been a push towards urban entrepreneurialism that calls cities to become entrepreneurial, profit-seeking, and growth machines, which has unleashed urban revitalization programmes that call for massive slum eviction and city beautification (Baviskar 2003; I. Chatterjee 2009; Mahadevia 2002). The Indian gentrification is similar to the gentrification being pursued in Kuala Lumpur, Singapore, Beijing, Beirut (Bunnel et al. 2002; Yeoh and Chang 2001; Marinelli 2009; Roy 2009) insofar as they all involve a desperate urge to do away with the sediments and cobwebs of an urban past and re-produce the urban condition in the image of the skyscrapers of Manhattan. The purpose is to demonstrate that the city has 'arrived', gone global, and can now provide all the frills and trimmings needed to attract fickle global investors. Giant glossy malls in Kolkata sport Michael Kors, Ralph Loren, Tommy Hilfiger, Pizza Hut, and Chillies. This, in a city where thousands of tailors are master craftsmen in hand-tailoring clothes on order for as little as four dollars, and where street vendors sell a mind-boggling array of delicious food at a pittance. Therefore, globalization in the Third World entails, in essence, a dismantling of the formal manufacturing sectors, a rise in sweatshops, export-processing zones, industrial homework and informal work, and rapid urban renewal that is often accompanied by massive evictions, displacement, and the destruction of old landscapes. If Fordism signifies a largely pre-globalization regime and post-Fordism symbolizes a largely globalizing regime for the Global North, then, for the Global South, 'pre-liberalization' would signify a largely pre-globalization regime that emphasizes formal-sector manufacturing and urban development with distributive principles, and post-liberalization would signify a globalizing regime with increased informalization and an urban agenda that is largely entrepreneurial. However, even within those two broad phases, there would be a large degree of heterogeneity both within and between countries.

Globalizing, the Sacred, and the City

Organized religion, religious codes, religious institutions, and religious landscapes define modern identity and social reality. Enlightenment and modernity produced secularism as an alternative way of life, allowing for the re-organization of western societies into the separate spheres of the church and the state, which was indeed a big distinction from the pre-modern condition in which the church was the state. Yet, secularism did not eradicate religion from modern societies, but instead allowed for its preservation in the private sphere, where it often leaked into the public sphere of state politics in different messy assemblages. For example, the crucial significance of a presidential candidate's religion in US electoral politics, where the popular contention is that anything other than some version of Protestantism would be unacceptable to the public, or the headscarf controversy in France, which led skeptics to argue that Judeo-Christian symbols like the Cross are quite acceptable in the French public sphere and are worn by many as a pendant, suggesting that much of the hullaballoo about French secularism and headscarf-wearing is actually a veiled form of anti-immigrant Islamophobia (Murray 2006). Religion is an important dimension of reality, because it is simultaneously economic and cultural. It grounds life through customs, traditions, and rituals, as well as demanding respect and obligations while allowing for the accumulation of cultural capital in temples and churches. It depends on a thriving body of devotees who must donate and calls for new membership in order to continue growing. It is therefore interesting to understand how organized religion negotiates globalization in the city, because, since culture and economy are conjoined in forging the religious worldview, such an understanding would present the culture–economy dialectic of globalization, rather than presenting it as *cultural* globalization and *economic* globalization. In many ways, religion is as important as the Fordist factory in forging the urban condition. The aforementioned homogenization school of research argued that the globalization of free market ideology and the rabid promotion of consumption as the true and only sacred religion of all humankind would trump other ethno-religious identifiers to create a common topography of desire. In the shared topography of aesthetics and desire for commodities, the customs of fast food and the mantra of the fall collection would iron out the Kosher, the Hallal, the headscarf, and the skullcap. Therefore, for Barber (2000), the 'Macworld' forces will trump over 'jihad forces' because the glitter of consumption is far more alluring than the pull of particular, parochial, and archaic ideologies. In other words, Macworld represents corporate forces that are forever expanding outward, because they must continuously find new markets, or create them where none exists. Advertisement becomes an important mode of aesthetic penetration into the life worlds and worldviews of the un-initiated, and corporate forces pump capital, technology, market research, and ideas into these life worlds in order to manufacture desire and awe. Commodities become the new gods, because the sleek Ferrari, the lithe Barbie, and the strawberry-flavoured lip gloss must first be desired and revered if they are to be consumed, and so they must render the indigenous dolls, cars, and cosmetics profane. Barber contended that global corporations have the financial might and the ravenous, profit-seeking appetite to manufacture desire and reverence for the new global pantheon of Nikes, Levi's, Calvin Kleins, and Apples, which will create a new religion of consumption that would iron out local identity markers of caste, creed, clan, and tribe, which he metaphorically referred to as 'Jihad'. Post-Fordism and post-liberalization of First and Third World cities provide appropriate globalizing contexts that are now institutionally and culturally ripe to embrace this new religion of corporate consumption more vociferously than ever before.

Baudrillard (1981, 1993, 1994) contended that the postmodern (globalizing) world would be obsessed with the production and consumption of images and signs, as sign value would take precedence over the use value of a commodity, resulting in people buying things not because they find them useful, but because they are identity-enhancing symbols. The image, according to Baudrillard, will take precedence over the real, so much so that the difference between the real and the image will disappear. Fredric Jameson (1984) and David Harvey (1989a) are co-aligned in arguing that the postmodern era promotes the fetishism of the commodity to the highest possible level: globalization and the circulation of images and spectacles becomes so real that we assume our identity around superficial and fleeting cultural markers, which then leads us to celebrate differences, particularity, and locality. Our worldviews are informed at the superficial level, our understanding and analysis of injustice remains cursory and centres around issues of aesthetics, body image, and identity differences; as such, 'postmodernism is dangerous for it avoids confronting realities of political economy and the circumstances of global power' (Harvey 1989a: 117). Jameson (1984: 53) contends that postmodernism is therefore the 'cultural logic of late capitalism', because capitalism must survive through expanding its reproduction and generation of profit, which it can only do if it can create fresh reservoirs of desire in new markets or by rejuvenating old markets. The aesthetic production becomes the cultural logic that gives the post-Fordist, post-liberalization capitalist city a fresh lease of life by manufacturing reservoirs of desire. However, Jameson warned that cultural production and consumption is not benign, but rather has important political and economic repercussions on the global scale: 'yet American, postmodern culture is the internal and super structural expression of a whole new wave of American military and economic domination throughout the world: in this sense, as throughout class history, the underside of culture is blood, torture, death and horror' (1984: 53). Jameson and Harvey of course take recourse to a base–superstructure analogy in which culture is the expression of economic necessity:[1] the deeper economic needs of capitalism fuel aesthetic production, and the social reality of the consumer is so stupefied by the religion of aesthetics that they ground their urban politics within a superficial realm of cultural representation. Rather than looking beneath the fetishized, glossy surface of the commodity to see the domination of labour, the usurpation of their sweat and blood, the colonization of the Third World commons, and the war and neo-imperialism in oil-rich countries that all form the inner scaffolding of aesthetic production, the consumer's gaze remains captured by the glossy surface of culture that the post-Fordist/ post-liberalization city comes to represent through their malls, enclaves, gated communities, and boutique coffee shops. The moot point is two-fold. First, some academics believed that with the secularization and marketization of society, and the globalization of the market logic, the religion of consumption would erode identity markers that are rooted in pre-modern ethno-religious and other logics. Globalizing urban life, whether post-Fordist or post-liberalization would therefore be a receptacle of postmodern images, commodification and signification steeped in a postmodern religion of consumption. Second, this turn towards culture, identity-enhancing symbols, and the celebration of difference has a deeper and darker economic motor.

Where does this leave organized religion? Do aesthetic production and the spread of McWorld's forces obliterate religious identity? Does religion become co-opted into commodity fetishism? Is there a religious logic to late capitalism? According to Vasquez and Marquardt (2003: 60):

> As globalization deterritorializes and reterritorializes culture, religion enters into recombination with multiple media, giving rise to hybrid

cultural products that blur spatial, temporal, and conceptual distinctions
at modernity's core, juxtaposing Aztec sacred buildings and liquid architecture, as in the movie Blade Runner, or Vedic rituals with pop music
and videos, as in Madonna's 'Ray of Hope'.

In essence, they argued that, as more and more people migrate, more
and more ideas travel in the cyber world, and more and more commodities flow, religion is carried with them away from its place of origin to
new destinations, thus leading to an uprooting, or deterritorialization,
and re-rooting, or reterritorialization. This uprooting and re-rooting
leads to a give and take, an integration, in which the globalizing cities
comes into contact with local culture and worldviews and produces
a new hybrid form that renders previously self-contained worldviews,
fixed in place and time, very porous. However, Vasquez and Marquardt
cautioned against the ubiquitous celebration of hybridity, arguing that
hybridity need not always be enriching and emancipatory, but that it
is always enmeshed in power. Kamat and Mathew (2003) elegantly
brought out the dangers of oppressive hybridization in their work on
the Hindutva[2] movement in the US. They indicate how the flow of US
dollars to India, which they refer to as 'saffron dollars',[3] funded the
Bharatiya Janata Party (BJP) and its affiliate organizations in India,
allowing for expatriate funding of deeply inward looking, exclusionary Hindu politics that regard Indian nationhood as synonymous with
a Hindu nationhood in which all minority religions and cultures are
excluded as un-patriotic or foreign (Shah 2002; Kamat and Matthew
2003). In the US, a brand of Hindutva flourishes under American multiculturalism that contends that all cultures must be treated equally;
this relativism, which is the central core of American multiculturalism,
treats culture as ahistorical although, according to Kamat and Matthew
(2003:13), culture without history leads to an uncritical celebration
of difference. American-Hindutva is nurtured as a unique immigrant
cultural identity, a 'neglected civilization' that enriches diversity in its
foreign host society. The American-Indian youth, deterritorialized from
the actually existing horrors and exclusion of Hindutva politics in India,
re-territorializes American-Hindutva as a series of aesthetic sign values
replete with vegetarianism, Vedic rituals, yoga and breathing exercises,
colourful *diyaas*,[4] and ethnic dances. De-spatialized from the electoral
politics of India and de-contextualized from its history of producing
riot, attacking Muslims, and burning churches, American-Hindutva

becomes an adorable mix of enchanting hymns, mantras, fire dances, and beautifully carved marble temples in big cities—like Chicago, Atlanta, and Los Angeles—that are hungry for a splash of the ethnic, the intriguing, and the interesting in their post-Fordist city landscape. Levitt (2006) confirmed how the intensely American couple that strives hard for the intensely American dream, pursues an intensely American middle-class existence of a home in the suburb, two cars, and a decent job, is also intensely Gujarati, re-defining the borders of belonging by spending their weekends at the International Swaminarayan Satsang Organization (ISSO), a Hindu denomination based in Ahmedabad, Gujarat, India. In my own fieldwork among immigrant communities in Atlanta, Houston, and Dallas, the Swaminarayan temples clearly emerged as the hub for socio-cultural networking and support for the Gujarati Hindu Indian, although non-Gujarati Hindus also visit the temples. The immigrant Hindu attends weekend religious prayers and eats the communal vegetarian meal prepared at the temple complex by a cook who is brought in from India, while their children attend the morning Gujarati language classes, in which genders are carefully kept separate by sending boys to separate classes from girls. It is as if a slice of the sacred is experienced in the land of the profane, which is polluted by commodification, individualism, and the pursuit of superficial aesthetic desires. Globalization provides salvation by allowing the immigrant, at least for a couple of hours, to shed the profanity of foreign existence, the mundane pursuit of profit, the economic rat race for a house with a picket fence, and the constant plugging into the computer to keep abreast with the stock market as 'vices' that can be washed away and cleansed by stepping into the alternate geography of the alabaster temple complex.

The Post-Fordist hybrid geographies of immigrant mosques, temples, and churches allow for globalization and a grounding of the gods in the 'profane' cities of the world. These cities were adopted by immigrants in pursuit of profit; the existential angst between resolving an economic existence while also staying true to one's 'cultural' urges is resolved by the globalizing city. The more global the city, the more hybrid it is, allowing for a mosaic of ethnoscapes (to borrow from Appadurai 1990: 297). The religious ethnoscapes of American-Islam, American-Hindutva, American-Latinos, and the African churches are more than just religious edifices; they are a dialectical geography of globalizing social reality in which economy and culture—use value and sign value—contradict and blend with each other to produce an urban spectacle. The spectacular city is a dialectical landscape, because it is not simply a superstructural representation of the deeper, more substantive political economic 'underside of culture' (Jameson 1984). It is also not just a simple veneer of the aestheticization and commodification of religion. In other words, post-Fordism/late capitalism is too complex to be adequately conceptualized within a base-superstructure framework where culture is an aesthetic varnish that can be scraped to reveal an underside—fuelled by blood, torture, and death—where the real machinations of economic exploitation and political power play out. Late capitalism is not *driven* by a cultural logic, and postmodernism is not a stage *after* modernism. The spectacular city is also not a site at which the cultural logic of aesthetic consumption and the production of sign values give a fresh lease on life to *late* capitalism. There is no doubt that culture circulated as images, identity-enhancing signs, semiotics, logos, and aesthetics have an ever-increasing presence in our lives, and one cannot quarrel here with Baudrillard's excellent conceptualization. There is also no doubt that cultural difference, the struggle over identity, and recognition are important aspects of contemporary urban reality. However, my contention here is different: it is not as if culture has suddenly gained pre-eminence over the political economic in this *late* stage of capitalism that manifests as *post*modernity: it *has* always been *as* important, if not in the form of signs and images, then in the form of customs, traditions, witch-hunts, bride-burning, Sharia laws, genital mutilation, leaving the dead to be consumed by vultures, and in embalming the dead in tombs. The point is that culture, alongside the economic and political, has been the veneer and underside all the time, and in all places, but it was our conceptual preference to see it as being *post-facto*, as *super* structural, and as a *recent* and *new* logic for an *old* economic process called capitalism. The post-Fordist/post-liberalization capitalist city did not choose to be more economic at one phase of capitalism and more cultural at another phase, because use values and sign values have always co-existed to some degree. The spectacular landscapes of the post-Fordist/post-liberalization city allow for an excellent dialectical conceptualization of globalization that transcends the bifurcated base-superstructure, culture-economy, use value-sign value, and modern–postmodern conceptual worlds to indicate how economic and cultural existence are simultaneously resolved around the sacred. The spectacular landscapes of the globalizing city are not just a synthetic veneer of cultural interaction, instead, they are landscapes that metabolize globalization and its economic and cultural angst, and this metabolism evolves and changes daily while the landscapes remain in situ. Fragmenting the sacred into an economic sphere and cultural representation, into use value and sign value, and into modern and postmodern will result in lost reality.

God.com

The information technology revolution has been touted as an important impetus for the current accelerated phase of globalization (Castells 2001). The cyber world of emails, blogs, social media, Skype, electronic banking, credit cards, and cellular technology has resulted, according to Castells (2000a: 10), in a 'technological revolution'. The immensity and impact of the technological revolution over the last two decades is comparable to the industrial revolution, and this revolution has far-reaching implications on social structure. This new social structure is informational, it is global, and it is networked. The generation and processing of vast amounts of data, as well as the consequent decisions to make them accessible or carefully guard them, has become the mainstay of profit accumulation in the new economy. The scope of most activities in this new economy—whether they are financial trading, trading in goods and services, or cable TV—is planetary. Production and circulation take the shape of networks, rather than individual firms working in isolation, and business units come together in groups that share information and collectively work to complete a job before moving on and reconfiguring into a different network of interested parties. The space of flows and the space of places are important topological components of this new economy:

> The space of flows refers to the technological and organizational possibility of organizing the simultaneity of social practices without geographical contiguity. Most dominant functions in our societies (financial markets, transnational production networks, media systems etc.) are organized around the space of flows. And so to do an increasing number of alternative social practices (such as social movements) and personal interaction networks. However, the space of flows does include a

territorial dimension, as it requires a technological infrastructure that operates from certain locations, and as it connects functions and people located in specific places. Yet, the meaning and function of the space of flows depend on the flows processed within the networks, by contrast with the space of places, in which meaning, function, and locality are closely interrelated. (Castells 2001: 14)

My reading of the preceding passage translates as: the networked world of globalization combines the virtual and real geographies of flows and places. Images, capital, financial speculation, and goods are all examples of the space of flows that emanate from the space of places—such as firms, offices, and stock markets—that are located in the globalizing cities of the world. These global cities are the space of places, as they are geographically rooted and yet radiate and receive flows that are not geographically rooted. The flows that emanate from places and go to places transcend geographical moorings by moving quickly across space. It is their ability to rapidly travel, often through cables and wires or through mobile phone towers and remotely sensed technology that all make them fluid, cyber, and space-annihilating. However, they are, at the same time, material, real, and anchored, because we pay for those fast-fluidities, build towers, lay high-speed cable lines, and install satellite discs that harness the waves that are translated into images on our screen. The landscapes of the technological city undergo a material change as the city globalizes and becomes the space of place that anchors a node of the global network, and the city's infrastructural content transforms from laying cables into the deep bowels of the earth to satellite dishes on the roofs, and then to telephone towers that loom large on the city's horizon, creating a technological skyscape that is different from the industrial skyscape of factory sheds and chimneys. This new post-Fordist and post-liberalization city has a deep impact on the social structure of life and livelihood as factory jobs die, sweatshop jobs emerge, call centres flourish, silicon valleys and digital suburbs germinate, and, in India, sparrows and bees disappear due to the electromagnetic radiation of cellphone towers (Kaushik 2011).

In the emerging global city, the space of flows and the space of places create a new cyber-material reality that is as miraculous, ethereal, space-transcendent, and gravity-defying as the images of gods walking on water, floating on clouds, and sleeping on the waves. The space of flows and the space of place allow for levitation and grounding, for local attachment and global reach, and for being everywhere and nowhere at the same time; the Facebook, blogs, YouTube, and twitter representing everywhere while cell-phone voicemail represents nowhere. The city, in the technological age, is almost godlike, and god therefore must be reinvented to be more than a national hero and an international icon. Organized religions, churches, temples, and mosques must keep up with people who are simultaneously everywhere and nowhere, who are parts of networks and almost always transiting through space of flows, and who are *in* one place but plugged-into the other spaces of places. The Internet has provided a cyber-material 'heaven' for re-inventing religion: a plane that is grounded and yet transcends space, is local and yet has global reach, and is everywhere and nowhere. In order to be able to reach out and customize itself to the needs of the immigrants and global diasporas that increasingly depend on technology to keep in touch with their nostalgia, memory, sense of home, and belonging, the Internet and the webpage provide a space for such customization and reinvention. The Internet provides space that mediates between the ethereality of heaven—including the sacred, the unknown, and the virtual—and the materiality of the mundane, including managing donations, providing locators for the nearest church, offering the contact information of priests, and advertising its social message. Religions have always worked hard to be global in their outreach, sending missionaries to far corners; however, in the era of globalization, the Internet provides the space that allows for a globality that is far more transcendental than simply traversing nations across the globe, and it also mediates between the material and the spiritual to produce the 'space of transcendence'. The god of nationally based religions, regionally based religions, and internationally based religions transcends, through the webpages of the Internet, into God.com and appears and disappears at the click of the mouse; it is everywhere and nowhere in the neatly nested tabs and hidden buttons of webpages, and it is local through Google Map's directions to the local church, temple, or mosque and simultaneously global through web-based sermons and online Qurbani (described later).

The US-based National Association of Evangelicals (NAE) includes 40 denominations and thousands of churches. They have a vibrant presence on Facebook, where their members can sign up for email alerts and updates about key themes in the religious interpretation of contemporary global events, ranging from environmental destruction to Syria. Interested parties can join as members by clicking the 'join now' page, old members can renew memberships online and contribute donations via credit card on an electronic page, while sitting at home all the time, they still transcend their earthly abode in their attainment of salvation (National Association of Evangelicals 2014). The Evangelical Lutheran Church in America features an interactive map with yellow dots that indicates the locations of churches in different nations. Clicking on a dot displays a brief blurb that contains information like how many churches belonging to that denomination are located in that country and where and when they were established (ELCA.org 2014). While they are locally placed, it is simultaneously possible for them to be planetary in outreach, and networked and embedded in the 'space of flows' and therefore transcending the mundane materiality of place-stickiness, of the friction of distance, and of impediments to transportation. The YouTube video for the Spanish-American Church attempts to reach out to second-generation Hispanic kids. The promo shows a blue sky filled with fluffy white clouds and Hispanic kids dressed in their Sunday best, smiling and happy popping out from the clouds to send a message: 'No matter what happens, good or bad, I could trust god.' This routine continues for a few minutes with different kids happily delivering similar messages in Spanish and English. The promo ends with a full-screen message showing a toy plane travelling through letters, formed by clouds, that spell out 'Sky' and 'everything is possible with God' as a background voice urges us, in Spanish, to visit the 'Spanish American' Church (Promo Spanish American Church 2014). Newspapers are increasingly reporting that Hispanic churches are finding it difficult to maintain membership, especially among their youth base. Second-generation Hispanic youth find it hard to connect the dots between their present worldviews and the perspective presented by a church invested in old-world Latin and connected to the distant Church of Rome (Jordan 2014). The space of transcendence allows for the mediation of materiality and spirituality in a tasteful fashion; the brightness of the blue sky, the smiles of the happy kids, and the cartoon-like quality of the simple message gives the video the quality and feel of a tourism narrative promoting a beach in the Bahamas. The church is presented as this happy place, with all the fun and freedom of a cloud-filled blue sky, where God simply is a benevolent parent living in the clouds to whom one can run to when in trouble.

The website bahai.org features a webpage that prominently displays a modern, eclectic living room in which a group of mixed-ethnicity youth are sitting in a circle engaged in an exciting fictitious conversation. The webpage efficiently and creatively uses nested boxes to take us through all of the fundamental life questions: from 'What is the purpose of life?' and 'Do Baha'is believe in heaven and hell?' to 'How do Baha'is view the environmental crisis?' The same webpage immediately globalizes and localizes us; visitors can locate children's activities and learn about circles in their area by filling in their zip code, and they can also find the names and contact information for other Baha'is from Angola, to Guam and Ukraine. The webpage can connect a visitor to messages in French, Chinese, Spanish, Portuguese, and Persian, thereby becoming immediately customized to local needs while reaching across half the span of the linguistic planet (Baha'i.org 2014).

The First United Methodist church of Hurst, which advertises itself as a place providing pastoral care and integration for African immigrants makes these claims in their 'youth page':

> Welcome! **Do you know where your third place is?** Home, school—these are the places where we spend the majority of our time, but our third place is like our home away from home. Starbucks pioneered the idea of the third place by creating warm and comfy spaces all over the country; but we don't need coffee. We need a safe place to be our true selves—the people who God created us to be.
>
>   We need friends around who we can depend on and who we can trust. We need space to explore and discover where faith and life intersect. We all have questions, and together we can search for answers.
>
>   **If you are in grades 7–12, let this be your third place. We can't wait to meet you.** Want to meet us online before you meet us face to face? Check us out on *Facebook*. (First United Methodist church of Hurst 2014; emphasis in original.)

'We need space to explore and discover where faith and life intersect'; the church claims to be that safe 'third place' where the materiality of life intersects with the spirituality of faith, and the webpage is a warm invitation, or a precursor or preface, to that 'third place'. The Internet is that space of transcendence, which provides the first window to the African immigrant youth who are new to the cultural context of the US as they struggle in the new economic toils of their studentship, job, or livelihood to make that leap from the virtuality of the webpage to the materiality of the church. The transcendental space of the Internet mediates life and faith, first within the safe third place of the immigrant's computer screen, and then by easing them into the third place of the church. This 'third place' space is proclaimed as better than the favourite iconic youth space, 'Starbucks', because it promises to provide friends and mentors who can be trusted to answer life's confusing questions.

The Dawat-e-Islami describes itself as: 'the international non-political movement for the preaching of Qur'an and Sunnah', and they have a tab on their webpage for 'online Qurbani' (Dawat-e-Islami 2014). Qurbani involves the sacrifice of a goat, cow, or camel on a special holy occasion, with the meat to be distributed to the poor. The online Qurbani allows for the globalization of this tradition, because one can be in Chicago and request a Qurbani be done in a Pakistani town. The site provides a brief description and rationale of this practice:

> DAWAT-E- ISLAMI always arrange collective (Ijthimai) Qurbani for the convenience of Islamic brothers. We have now initiated online Qurbani service with the Niyyath to facilitate its donors and supporters across the world and to ease the logistics and distribution process of acquiring animals and Qurbani/Aqiqa/Charity meat to the under privileged/needy people.
>
> This service will also help those Muslims around the world who have difficulty in slaughtering animals due to infrastructure limitations in their countries.
>
> You can be assured that your Qurbani will be dealt under strict guidance of the Sharia for your assurance we will be sending you an email with:
>
> 1. Receipt of Qurbani payment.
> 2. Confirmation email that your Qurbani has been done (Dawat-e-Islami 2014).

The customer is asked to 'proceed to online Qurbani', agree with a statement of procedure, and then submit the request. A devout Muslim can now transcend the materiality of their existence in Chicago, New York, or Birmingham, as well as the difficulties of carrying out sacred animal sacrifice in those places, by simply clicking a button. The space of transcendence embodied in the webpage allows a devotee to negotiate their unholy materiality and transcend it to achieve a spirituality that they desire. A receipt affirms his spiritual deliverance as Qurbani goes global. The same site provides files on the Hajj pilgrimage. When downloaded, the file provides a step-by-step guide to pilgrims all over the world on what items to carry, what information they should know, and what to expect in the global pilgrimage of Hajj. Therefore, the Internet space not only mediates between materiality and spirituality to allow for space of transcendence but also, in doing so, manages our globality and organizes our everyday globalizations.

The Ahmadiyya Muslim community website has an updated, global appeal. The first click on the site brings up the message 'love for all, hatred for none' with the 'o' in 'love' shaped like a heart symbol. In an effort to adjust to global expectations post-September 11, and probably from a desire to combat general stereotypes, the website offers a customized 'modern' and 'western' version of Islam by emphasizing:

> The Ahmadiyya Muslim Community is the leading Islamic organization to categorically reject terrorism in any form. Over a century ago, Ahmad has emphatically declared that an aggressive 'jihad by the sword' has no place in Islam. In its place, he taught his followers to wage a bloodless, intellectual 'jihad of the pen' to defend Islam.
>
> … the Ahmadiyya Muslim Community is the only Islamic organization to endorse a separation of mosque and state. Over a century ago, Ahmad has taught his followers to protect the sanctity of both religion and government by becoming righteous souls as well as loyal citizens. He cautioned against irrational interpretations of Quranic pronouncements and misapplications of Islamic law. He continually voiced his concerns over protecting the rights of God's creatures. Today, the Ahmadiyya Muslim Community continues to be an advocate for universal human rights and protections for religious and other minorities. It champions the empowerment and education of women. Its members are among the most law-abiding, educated, and engaged Muslims in the world. (Ahmadiyya Muslim Community 2014)

This Internet space becomes a place for transcending the Islamophobic realities of the post-September 11 world, where Muslims all over the world—but especially in the US—must repeatedly demonstrate that concepts like 'jihad' are taken out of context and misused by fanatics. It also allows for a digital transcendence to an updated, 'western' version of Islam that frees up spaces for Anglo-American notions of secularism and democracy, as well as distinctions between the public and private spheres. Here, the Internet provides buoyancy to bubble up from the hysteria of Islamophobia into a web space of contemporary brotherly love and peace. The Internet provides the space of transcendence that globalizes religion by fusing its economic and cultural reality in such a dialectical way that it strikes at the very heart of an analysis that claims social reality is compartmentalized. Memberships are renewed, receipts sent, and new members are anointed as these sites provide digital sermons, gospels and Qurbanis; the economic reality and cultural realities blend into one another to mark a space of transcendence that is modern and postmodern, virtual and yet materially emplaced within the urban technological landscape.

Dialectical Globalization

Globalization is not just a thing or process; it is a way of life. Academics, media personalities, politicians, gurus, and pundits have always attempted to analyse and conceptualize ways of life in order to produce worldviews that can explain the chaos of reality. Modernity and modernism is one such 'way of life', in which the industrial, mechanical age and its convenience, utility, functionality, science, and medicine all define a spectacular industrial city that is thoroughly analysed, described, conceptualized, and circulated as an ideology, as well as imposed as a civilizing mission under the colonial yoke. It is lived as emancipation, while simultaneously struggled against as oppressive, and it involves both an economic reordering from agricultural to industrial and a cultural reordering from religious to secular, as well as a spatial transformation from rural to urban; all of these moments conjoin to create the contemporary social reality. The concreteness of this social reality is conceptually frozen in pages of academic texts that attempt to understand, prescribe, and critique it. Just like modernity, globalization is also a way of life that involves increased mobility, flows, circulation, compression, and borderlessness. In conceptualizing it, pundits have used homogenization, indigenization, time–space compression, deterritorialization, reterritorialization, and hollowing-out, as well as the network, the space of flows, and the space of place as examples of some conceptual categories that can make sense of the chaos of globalization. In doing so, some of these conceptualizations were overwhelmingly economic in their interpretation, while others were overwhelmingly cultural, and yet others political. I have tried to lay down the multi-dimensionality of globalizing reality by indicating that—although these conceptualizations have been rather compartmentalized into economic, cultural, and political categories—these moments are actually untidily imbricated in reality.

Therefore, I have argued that while globalization, in its economic avatar of neoliberalism, causes structural adjustment, enforces deregulation and austerity, and causes city governments to be entrepreneurial, this globalization is also equally cultural, because it emplaces ethnic- and race-specific gentrification, postmodern urban renewals, anti-immigrant hysteria, and at the same time, it is also political as it creates new regimes of visa restrictions for labour. My attempt in this chapter has been to carefully stay away from a compartmentalized analytical approach to globalization, and instead adopt a dialectical stance. This dialectical approach understands the post-Fordist/post-liberalization city in its organic entirety by presenting globalization as the metabolic process that is germane to its existence and evolution. The Fordist city and the post-Fordist city have certain distinctions in their metabolisms, as do the pre-liberalization and post-liberalization city. Fordism entailed a certain economic and cultural form of large factories, gigantic warehouses, organized labour, suburban booms, and mass consumption, while post-Fordism entailed dismantling manufacturing, outsourcing, Sunbelt urbanism, and the postmodern landscapes of gated communities, malls, and enclaves. Similarly, pre-liberalization entailed formal manufacturing, steel and textile cities, and urban re-distribution, while post-liberalization entailed sweatshops, export-processing zones, and gentrified cities of malls and renewed urban retail scapes. These distinctions are by no means homogenously generalizable over space, and ground variegated local and extra-local trajectories.

I look towards Baudrillard, Harvey, and Jameson for conceptual inspiration towards understanding the culture economy inflection in post-Fordist/post-liberalization urban contexts. Baudrillard understands postmodern culture as an ephemeral world of images, identity-enhancing symbols, and proliferation of sign values disjointed from their material moorings, because the distinction between the image and the real is now obscured due to hyper-globalization of the symbolic components of culture. Harvey and Jameson analyse postmodern culture as the proliferation of identity markers, images, differences, and particularisms which late capitalism intentionally manufactures in order to keep itself alive and running. The cultural conditions of postmodernity, or the cultural logic of postmodernity mute the contradictions of late capitalism, therefore, the underside of culture is the deeper, more horrific political economy. There is much to learn from these perspectives, and I will continue to use these ideas throughout the book, but in this chapter, I approach globalization dialectically and hence look towards possible ways of conceptualizing culture not as the horizontal surface of the deeper, vertically embedded economy, but rather, as intertwined with the economy. In doing so, I explore the Internet to show how the cyber world serves as 'a space of transcendence' that negotiates between the materiality of city life and the ethereality of religion to produce a material–virtual sphere that resolves the existential angst of the faithful. Money, credit card, and purchasing power meld political economic reality of urban existence with cultural desires for salvation and deliverance, and hence, the Internet provides the apt space of transcendence for constituting the cultural economic materiality of globalization. Texts on webpages, nested tabs, and a world of 'click here' and 'buy that', 'find the local church', and 'online sermons' constitute the economic and cultural metabolism of globalization and the post-Fordist/post-liberalization city secretes that materiality. Understanding the simultaneity of this culture economy reality, I argue is the very essence of a dialectical approach to globalization. The culture economy dialectics is, however, extremely broad, as it can include anything and everything. In order to meaningfully comment within the scope of a book therefore, I will approach the dialectics of globalization through the city and its sacred (whether embodied in cyber space, in the media, or in the landscape).

Notes

1. Jameson's position is slightly different from Harvey's; I will explore this difference at greater depth in Chapter 5.

2. The term Hindutva is used to refer to political and cultural movements that hold a certain reading of Hinduism as fundamental for its identity. In this reading, India is the land of the Hindus and all the religious groups are invaders who polluted and plundered the sacred land, therefore all religious minorities

in order to be a true Indian must also be Hinduized, giving up their unique religious and cultural attributes (see Shah 2002; Kamat and Mathew 2003).

3. The colour saffron has symbolic importance for all right-wing Hindutva groups, because saffron was the chosen colour of the robes worn by ancient Hindu saints.

4. Oil lamps used in temples and Hindu rituals.

4 Transcendental Landscapes
Akshardham Temples in the US

Young Temples of Yore

Bochasanwasi Shri Akshar Purushottam Swaminarayan Sanstha, or BAPS, is a sect of Hinduism that is popular in the US among Gujarati Indians, who hail from the state of Gujarat in western India. According to the 'who we are' section of the Baps.org webpage, the sect describes itself as 'a socio-spiritual Hindu organization with its roots in the Vedas. It was revealed by Bhagwan [God] Swaminarayan (1781–1830) in the late 18th century and established in 1907 by Shastriji Maharaj (1865–1951)'. Lee (2007) described BAPS Swaminarayan as a sect of Swaminarayan Hinduism, which began as a Gujarati reform movement in the early nineteenth century and now truly exemplifies globalization and trans-nationalism with 600 temples and 9,090 centres in 45 countries around the world. The temples in the US are the 'foreign' brethren of the Swaminarayan, or Akshardham temples near Ahmedabad and Delhi. The Swaminarayan sect swiftly became popular in India and is best known for their imposing and intricately carved complexes, which are replete with sound and light shows, musical fountains, and boat rides. In India, these temple complexes became attractive tourist destinations, along with the likes of the Taj Mahal. In that context, they are the temples of postmodern India, often financed by donations from the Indian diaspora (Lee 2007); in other words, they are very much the products of late capitalism. They are unique, both in India and elsewhere, because of the enormous acreage they occupy, their imposing architecture, and their sudden and almost-unexpected emergence on the semi-urban land on the outskirts of cities. They appear as medieval spectacles superimposed on contemporary landscape, as if a slice of time and space from the past was torn away and pasted into contemporary life, with the intricateness of the temple architecture and the superbly carved marble pillars appearing as an aggressive attack on the starkness and functionality of the modern city. When I interviewed representatives at the Delhi temple, one informant mentioned that modern-day Delhi, the capital city, lacked a sacred space that represented Hindu culture. This angst appeared in Yoji Maharaj's (the leading saint) dream, and he went on to actualize this desire to present Hindu culture in its grandeur and magnificence by ensuring the construction of a temple complex that occupied 100 acres. Therefore, the Swaminarayan temples, also known as Akshardham temples,[1] are, in essence, a modern-day attempt to showcase the hoariness of Hinduism by 'bringing back' the classical style and temple architecture of a grand historic past, from which the 'secular' and 'modern' present-day seems to have been obliterated. Showcasing such 'magnificence' and 'grandeur' would require carving up a slice of life that is the very opposite of the everyday, mundane, ordinary, and functional; the hundreds of acres of Italian marbles and fine carvings accomplish that task. The only element of awe it cannot inspire, however, is the patina of age, the mustiness of history, and the moss-encrusted sediment of time. It cannot claim to be ancient, as it is an imitation of history, a simulated history, and a simulacrum that now supersedes its original relics, the ancient Hindu temples all over the world. Its postmodern newness, the sprawling acres, the glossiness of smooth alabaster, and its urban proximity evoke a 'grandeur' and 'magnificence' of scale, shine, and spatial spread that make up for the lack of age. To that extent, it is an interesting oxymoronic assemblage: a collage of new ancientness where the functionality of parking lots and the precision of LED lights contrast with the over-aestheticized, chariot-like façade that represents the local globality in which an intensely rooted identity is simultaneously transnational.

This format of sprawling acreage, water bodies, and gigantic marble magnificence has been exported to the US as well. The Swaminarayan temple in Atlanta looms large over the mundane landscapes of Lilburn, a suburb about a thirty-minute drive from the Atlanta airport. The Atlanta *mandir* (temple), the largest in the US was constructed in 2007 on 29 acres of land, almost an exact, but smaller, replica of the Delhi Akshardham temple. A representative of the mandir, who volunteers at the gift shop, mentioned that the land for the temple and the cost of construction was entirely funded with donations collected from the Gujarati Indian community in Atlanta. The temple complex is characterized by the main mandir (temple) situated at the centre of a rectangular garden and courtyard. The main temple has a cluster of domes, the tallest of which is designed to look like a mountain peak. In classic Hindu architecture, this peak-like dome is referred to as the *shikhara* (mountain peak) and is curvilinear in outline. Some of the other domes that surround this main shikhara are curvilinear, and some are spherical (Figure 4.1). Sprawled marble staircase leads to the main landing on which the shikhara stands, supported by pillars.

At the very front of the landing is a sign stating: 'No photography beyond this point.' The domes and pillars are intricately carved out of Italian marble. A volunteer at the temple claimed that each piece of marble was hand carved in India and then brought to Atlanta to be assembled like a jigsaw puzzle. Construction workers were brought from India to supplement the local workforce, because the temple needed to be constructed without the inclusion of any metal, in accordance with sacred principles. Inside the temple, under the shikhara dome, is the inner courtyard. The courtyard's canopy ceiling, which is the inner side of the shikhara dome, is held up by intricately carved pillars (Figure 4.2) that are connected by intricately carved arches. LED lights are strategically placed to illuminate the canopy, which is an imposing concave dome with concentric circles, with each circle sporting a theme. One entire circle is devoted to stone-etched men and women dancing, while another circle demonstrates holy men in different poses of meditation.

The perimeter of this inner courtyard is lined by individual cells that house gods and goddesses from the Hindu mythology, like Rama and Sita, and Krishna and Radha, along with Swaminarayan and his various successors, ending with the most recent 'Pramukh Swami'. Each cell has an intricately carved donation chest placed on the front. At the entry to this courtyard is a shoe chamber, where shoes must be removed and stowed away, and another sigh alerts visitors that cameras, food/drinks, and talking on cell phones are not allowed. 'Short sleeve' and 'sleeveless tops' are also not allowed, and volunteers provide shawls if necessary. The temple is surrounded by large reflecting pools, meticulously maintained lawns, and deftly manicured gardens. At the four corners of the garden are four marble-carved umbrellas or *chhatris* (Figure 4.3).

Figure 4.1 Atlanta Temple: Cluster of curvilinear and spherical domes adorned by golden *kalashas*, or pitchers

Source: Photograph taken by the author.

Figure 4.2   Intricately carved pillars at the Atlanta temple
Source: Photograph taken by the author.

Figure 4.3 *Chhatris*, or umbrellas, in the outer periphery of the Atlanta temple
Source: Photograph taken by the author.

A thriving food court exists just beyond the temple gardens, and the volunteers told me that chefs are brought in from India on a five-year visa. The volunteer lamented about the difficulty of procuring visas for the cooks and about the importance of bringing cooks from India, because they are familiar with the sacred traditions of purity and pollution and with the traditional recipes, as well as able to transform the highest quality ingredients that are provided to them into excellent food. The food includes traditional Gujarati sweet and savory snacks delivered in boxes stamped with labels indicating that the food was cooked following the BAPS Swaminarayan codes. The food court is an important source of income for the temple. There also exits a gift shop and an exhibit hall. One bill board in the inner sanctuary displays the price, in dollars, for the intangible ethereal commodities that can be purchased—these include a $5 price for the rite of *abhishek*, which involves a one-to-one ceremony with God in which the devotee is allowed to pour holy water on the idol of Swaminarayan as a boy. The same rite costs $11 as a family deal, and other rates apply for audio-abhishek, in which case the tape can be taken home.

The Houston temple is about 10 minutes from downtown Houston, in a suburban community called Stafford. We drove on a bleak cloudy day and arrived in Stafford at around 4.30 p.m. and branched into a narrow lane bordered with lower-middle-class apartments that were probably rented to first-generation immigrants. I thought for sure that I had taken the wrong turn. Suddenly the white structure of the gigantic mandir loomed on my right. As soon as I walked into the temple complex, however, the world outside washed away. I could have been somewhere in India. Like the Atlanta temple, the Houston temple is made of Italian and Turkish marble, intricately hand-carved into the image of the Dilwara Mount Abu temple in India. The temple brochure claimed that over 38,000 marble pieces were hand-carved by craftsmen and volunteers on a 22-acre plot. So intricate is the work that it seems to be carved out of some soft material, like wood or paper (Figure 4.4). The temple's structure is similar to that of the Atlanta temple, with a peak-like dome surrounded by subsidiary domes. A gigantic array of marble arches marks the gateway to the complex, which is lavishly sprinkled with ponds, waterfalls, reflecting pools, and deftly manicured lawns and bushes (Figure 4.5). Although the weather was extremely cold and windy, devotees dressed in traditional Indian clothes still

Figure 4.4 An intricately carved foundation base at the Houston temple
Source: Photograph taken by Waquar Ahmed.

Figure 4.5   The Houston temple complex consists of acres of manicured lawns and gardens

Source: Photograph taken by Waquar Ahmed.

rippled in to offer their prayers. The inner sanctum has massive tolling bells that hang in front of a light-skinned, androgynous-looking idol of Swaminarayan in gaudy clothes and jewellery.

Two other buildings stand near the perimeter of the complex: an exhibition hall and a gift shop and food court. Exhibition halls and their displays are standard fare in all of the temples in the US. The exhibition hall contains a diorama of handpicked symbols and images representing Indian heritage, culture, science, and technology. The exhibition's posters and dioramas do not just claim pride in Hinduism and its famous members, but also emphasize pride in India; the religion and nation blend into each other to create an interesting assemblage of faith and patriotism presented as Hindu culture. Hindu culture becomes almost synonymous with Indian culture in this heady mix of faith, tradition, culture, and patriotism, even though, while Hinduism is the dominant religion in India, Muslims, Christians, Jews, Zoroastrians, and indigenous peoples account for a substantial percentage of the population as well. The religious minorities and indigenous groups are important components of the tapestry of Indian culture, if there can be such a thing as a national culture. The exhibition hall of the Houston Swaminarayan temple concentrates on showcasing 'Hindu culture'—it is interesting that organized religions find it rather easy to leak out of faith's container-box into the larger realm of 'culture', as if the two are the same. So, the posters and dioramas are not just about the life and teachings of Swaminarayan, which would be normal for an organized religious sect, but also claim and include famous Indian freedom fighters like Gandhi, Nehru, Shivaji, Rani of Jhansi, Netaji, as well as famous poets like Rabindranath Tagore, who had nothing to do with Swaminarayan Hinduism. It also prominently excludes Indian freedom fighters, national figures, and literary geniuses who were not Hindus. A very specific landscape is constructed here; it is a landscape of memory and nostalgia for the homeland, but a selective memory and nostalgia for a homeland predominantly imagined as Hindu. The specificity of Swaminarayan Hinduism is transcended to carefully include non-religious figures, and yet, at the same time, a very specific India is constructed that exclusively speaks only to the Hindu population. For the Gujarati Indian-Americans, transnational nationhood becomes a cultural-economic investment in the specific clan ties of Swaminarayan Hinduism, which is nested within the larger and more general fold of reverence to the memory of the motherland. Globalizing India needs its expatriates to send money to support the construction and upkeep of temples back home while, at the same time, the immigrant Hindu needs to re-negotiate their clan, religious, national, and global identities in a foreign land. Resolving the particularities of sect, clan, traditional rites, and the generality of nationhood, patriotism, national culture, and global citizenship is a tricky task. The exhibit hall, through its careful and selective crafting of patriotism within the container of religiosity, attempts to resolve this struggle between the particular and the general. The invention of zero, the discovery of astronomy, and the practice of algebra among ancient Hindu sages are all highlighted in the colourful life-size posters. As one moves from the ancient period to the present, BAPS is highlighted among the contemporary flag-bearers of Indian culture. BAPS' investment in the environment and community is highlighted through the emphasis on planting trees, donating medicine and blood, and anti-addiction campaigns. A huge poster proudly proclaims the efforts put forward by BAPS in the tribal belt of south Gujarat, where over 300 tribal villages were brought under its socio-cultural civilizing mission. Religion, culture, science, technology, social service, and the environment bleed into one another in producing a cosmology that is larger than religion and almost becomes a way of life in which faith does not have to be anti-science, anti-innovation, or the antithesis to a tribal way of life; it can incorporate each. The universal and global appeal of greenness, sustainability, science, and social and humanitarian relief work appeals to the transnational aspirations of a global Indian community, but membership in this transnational citizenship is earned only within the club of the Swaminarayan sect. The gift shop and cafeteria is teeming with people who drove in for their evening *naasta* and *chai* (snack and tea) and now feast on the traditional vegetarian fare of *samosa* and *dhokla* (Gujarati snack), which are prepared by following the appropriate religious codes. Kids run amok and mommies take a breather after a difficult day as the gift-shop-cum-cafeteria becomes a living and breathing site for re-inventing tradition, community, and network through an interesting assemblage of food and religion. All of the food bears a label stating that it is sanctified by the BAPS.

The gift shop at the Irving temple near Dallas displays a huge wall of CDs containing religious and inspirational speeches and hymns.

Another wall displays a collection of books, ranging from English to Gujarati, on the philosophy of Swaminarayan, Hinduism and women, parenting journals, and women and renunciation. There are also books on tourism in Europe and Africa to appeal to the wanderlust of the nouveau riche Gujarati. Children's books providing pictorial representations of the Hindu epics of *Mahabharata* and *Ramayana* are available for Gujarati children, and textbooks on Gujarati alphabet are also available for sale. Glass, porcelain, and clay models of Krishna, Radha, and Swaminarayan, as well as Gujarati prayer stools and temple furniture are display for sale with the strict instruction 'do not touch'. A large poster just outside the shop provides a menu for the various forms of *seva*, or services, that can be offered to the god. The services include grocery seva, fruit seva, vegetable seva, juice seva, milk seva, and the like, and the menu displays the corresponding weekly and monthly rates, in dollars, for each of these services. A devotee has the option of bringing these goods, or the money amount in dollars, to earn god's blessings, peace, and deliverance from earthly sins. The Irving complex has a huge kitchen in which vegetarian meals are prepared daily, with more elaborate meals prepared for devotees on Sundays. The facility also includes a large dining hall, a huge party hall available for rent, an auditorium with a capacity of 600–1000 that is used for community prayers and hymns on special occasions, and a large basketball court that any university would be proud of. A volunteer explained to me:

> It is very important to teach the children the core values of Gujarati-Hindu culture, especially because they are growing up so far away from Indian tradition. It is really hard for the kids because they negotiate the clash between foreign and tradition every day, they go to American schools, read and converse in English, acquire American taste for music and food, and put in a lot of effort to fit in with their peers. Then they must come home, eat vegetarian meals, converse in Gujarati, and pray to Indian gods. The outside world usually has a greater appeal to them than this private world, because it is more ubiquitous and more vociferous. That is why we ensure that we have special facilities for kids, to encourage them to appreciate their culture. Every weekend we have cultural and sports activity, Gujarati language classes, and *dandia* [Gujarati dance] practice. It is difficult to get kids interested in language lessons and religious education, the sports, dance, and food make it interesting for them. The boys and girls go to separate classes, we keep the genders separate.

The angst of immigration—which involves the tearing away of roots, globalization, and loss of identity—and the need for cultural invest-ment in the next generation is a common theme touched upon by all the temple complexes. A volunteer at the Atlanta temple claimed that the main purpose of the Akshardham temple was to pass down Indian culture to their children and grandchildren. He lamented about the hardships of raising children in a foreign country:

> This country has no culture, it looks great from the outside, very rich and glamorous, but they have zero culture, and do you want your children to grow up with their values—they have no regard for their elders, their children tell their parents 'Get the hell out of here', 'Why have you come to supervise me?' We don't want our children to grow up like that, that is why we built this temple so that they can be in-touch with Indian culture and spirituality. Every Sunday, we have sessions for children, women, and men, there are lectures, training in Gujarati language and spiritual hymns—this is our investment into the lives of our children. What is the point of being rich if your children are disrespectful and mis-behaved? Remember to bring your children to the Akshardham temple, if they come here from an early age they will develop a pride in their culture—why do you think the white folks, the Mexicans come here and bring their kids here? Because they want to partake in our culture and spirituality.

I had been visiting the Swaminarayan temples in the US for some time now, because I felt they represent an interesting interaction between globalization and localisms, tradition and postmodernity, religion and the commodification of religion in unique ways. This interview also made me, for the first time, realize that these spectacular landscapes were not simply geographic sites on which these complex interactions played out, but also an immigrant's narrative of a transcen-dental materialism. The immigrant could transcend the earthly realities of her material displacement (emigration from India and immigration to the US) by re-rooting tradition within the temple complex in this 'foreign' land. The temple complex is an immigrant's narrative of 'true culture' and 'authentic tradition', a safe haven for the pure and sacred in the midst of a sea of 'profane' in the newly adopted country. In this nar-rative, material emplacement of the Swaminarayan mandir complexes allows for a spiritual transcendence that brings solace, a slice of home, a sense of belonging and therefore replaces the angst of displacement (migration) with a feeling of emplacement in a community, a home away from home. The immigrant's dream is to transfer this new narrative of emplacement to her children as well. In her study of Pakistani, Irish, Brazilian, and Hindu immigrants, Levitt (2006) indicated how immigrants bring their religion to the US and transform America while, at the same time, they powerfully transform their countries of origin by maintaining strong ties through advanced information technology and expatriate dollars. She used the metaphor 'global religious citizenship' to explain how religion does not remain discretely contained within the nation-state, but achieves fluidity as symbols, narratives, rituals, and rites travel to new lands, shaping life and landscape there. At the same time, the immigrants return home for important religious ceremonies, developing an intricate global network of churches, temples, and clergies. The American religious landscape is globalized and pluralized, and at the same time, expatriate remittances in the form of money and ideas like individualism and hard work are sent back home. My own effort, in this book, has been to understand the dialectics of globalization by looking at its culture economy metabolism through the lens of the city. I hoped that the religious landscapes of the Swaminarayan sect in the US cities and in India would allow me to do just that. Not only did they not disappoint me in that regard, they also went above and beyond that goal by revealing that this culture economy metabolism simultaneously carves a global reality of belonging and othering, inclusion and exclusion, and integration and marginalization. What is significant in this context and needs to be emphasized is that the Swaminarayan temple complexes in the US represent migrant *landscapes*. As landscapes, they are not just geographical edifices, rather, as discussed earlier they become the very narratives through which transcendence and emplacement is achieved. Therefore, it is imperative that in reading the dialectics of globalization from the temple landscape, we appropriately theorize landscape as a concept. I now turn to that task by re-visiting some of the key ideas in landscape literature.

Theorizing Landscape

In the Saureian humanistic tradition, landscape is a representation of material culture and, therefore, a cultural expression of human habitation (Sauer, 1925; Duncan, 1980; Rowntree, 1996). Space becomes the canvas representing cultural processes. Cosgrove and Daniels (1988) contended that, although landscape is a cultural image, this does not mean it is immaterial. The materiality of landscape may be represented by paint on canvas and writing on paper, and on earth, dirt, and stone, which are material things. In that context, a farm landscape, cityscape, or mining shaft is no more material than a painting or a poem. They further contend that visual, verbal, and built landscapes are interwoven to produce the contexts of social reality. However, these contexts of social reality are not always farm fields, picket fences, and the English countryside; they are sometimes caked by dirt, grime, and sweat in the blind and narrow alleys of slums and favelas, or represent the big holes in the ground produced by drone attacks, or, at other times, the walls constructed to keep whole communities of people out. Therefore, the materiality of landscape produces a social reality that is textured by the grittiness of injustice and exploitation. Gold and Revill (2000: 15) contended that 'landscapes of power and privilege' are the flipside of 'landscapes of exploitation and disadvantage'. Therefore, human geographers have, for some time now, argued for a closer inspection of the landscapes of alienation, exclusion, and injustice (Mitchell 2003; Olwig 1996), in order to reveal what Kirby (2002) termed the more 'gritty' aspects of social reality. Writing about the context following the 2001 Israeli occupation of Palestine, Gregory (2004: 183) borrowed Edward Said's 'imaginative geographies' to indicate how culture and imperialism are stitched together in producing a neocolonial imagination of the 'other' that is not only circulated as ideas and ideologies but is also etched in space in such a way that 'distance folds into difference through a series of spatializations. They multiply partitions and enclosures that demarcate "the same" from the "other", at once constructing and calibrating a gap between the two by designating in one's mind a familiar space which is "ours" and an unfamiliar space beyond "ours" which is theirs.'

Neighbourhoods, places, and landscapes represent domains controlled by 'legitimate' occupants, with legitimacy mostly defined in terms of duration of stay (Nieto and Franze 1997). Any physical intrusion into that domain by socially or culturally distant 'others' is perceived as a contestation to the expression of legitimate identities. Guarding the 'pristine', and 'reclaiming' it, becomes a project that is realized over space by protecting, annihilating, and (re)ordering landscapes (Nieto and Franze 1997). Landscapes are therefore a palimpsest of realization and negation: the realization of identity, ideology, and politics alongside the simultaneous negation of identities, ideologies, and politics of 'others' who could not actualize their realities. When landscapes are negations, they are alienating. When landscapes are realizations, they are the appropriation of land, property, and life. While landscapes embody more than their physical form by encapsulating identities, politics, and ethno-racial discourses, it is also important to emphasize the 'land' in landscape; that is, its material and the physical forms. The material forms, like land use or real estate are just as important as subjective categories like identity, nostalgia, and ethno-racial discourses. Land use represents the supply side of urban development, and serves as a physical resource for developers such as private corporations, local governments, and policymaking bodies (Bourne 1976).

Clearly, landscapes have been conceptualized in a variety of different ways. Landscapes are intensely cultural, political, and economic, and they can embody power, privilege, realization, memory, and nostalgia while, at the same time, representing disadvantage, exploitation, negation, displacement, and trauma. They are geographical and temporal: they are sedimentations of time as well as conglomerations of space. They are a narrative, consisting of a text, picture, and poem, and also simultaneously consisting of land, brick, mortar, and steel. In the interest of a more complete understanding of globalizing social realities, it is important to explore how landscapes are local in their situation, context, expression, and are simultaneously also global. For instance, the Akshardham temples in India crop up in the US, England, Australia, and Belgium. Their cropping up elsewhere on the one hand, signifies globalization of landscape and globalization of culture, but at the same time, for the immigrant Hindu Indian, they provide a sense of community, clan ties, home, and local moorings in foreign soil. It is interesting therefore, that Akshardham temple landscapes *transcend* the contexts of their existence in India and re-emerge elsewhere to produce new global–local contexts of life. In the next section, I hope to theoretically trace this process of *transcendence* and then empirically ground it with some examples.

Transcendental Materialisms

I propose 'transcendental materialism' to understand how material contexts of everyday life that emerge in one place are transcended elsewhere through the production of new meanings and new narratives. Transcendental materialism is inspired by Hegel's transcendental idealism, however, I contend that there are some very basic differences between the two (Albritton 1999; Berger and Pullberg 1965; Hegel 2010). For Hegel, contradictions between ideas produce history, as ideas clash with one another in a battle between thesis and antithesis, it leads towards a synthesis. The synthesis is a perfect combination of the two contradictory ideas and it informs practice and hence the production of history and, if I may add, geography as well. The synthesis is a little more perfect than the thesis and antithesis that it transcended, so the synthesis is an improvement. But soon this synthesis is challenged by a new idea, hence, the synthesis becomes a thesis and this new idea its antithesis, and the process continues. In this way, history progresses towards a perfect, or absolute, idea. The Spirit, in Hegelian 'transcendental idealism', is a larger consciousness that exists above and beyond the idea. The Spirit, informs ideas and is re-informed and enlightened by the process of contradiction. As an idea evolves towards perfection, it informs the Spirit at each stage, and hence the Spirit evolves towards perfection as well. Ideas are the motor of history, as they transcend their imperfect predecessors to move towards perfection, hence 'transcendental idealism'. When an idea reaches perfection, there is no further challenge to it, there is no other antithesis, and there is no more transcendence, as history culminates in perfection. I use transcendental materialism to explain how time and space, geography and history—in other words, contexts of social reality—transcend the conditions of their existence to re-emerge and often be reproduced in other contexts. As they re-emerge they are often reproduced as the new avatar of the older contexts in which they thrived, the old contexts and the new contexts remain dialectically intertwined. I differ from Hegel on three counts. First, unlike Hegel, I do not contend that transcendental materialism results in a move towards a more perfect social reality or an absolute and perfect materiality. Second, I invest importance in materialism, rather than idealism, as the motor of transformation. My emphasis is more on the transforming material conditions, specifically globalizing cities, immigrant temple complexes, and globalizing cyber scapes. This does not mean that Hegel is wrong, ideas always inform the materiality of existence and cannot be artificially separated from reality, but it is my contention that ideas are material too, because they emerge through forms of knowledge production, like research, teaching, dialogue, and the act of labouring, which are all material interactions. Third, I do not engage with the concept of a larger-than-life Spirit or consciousness. In order words, unlike Hegel, I do not assume that a larger force puts ideas in our head. Rather, I assume that ideas emerge out of material interactions. Therefore, for me, transcendental materialism refers to how certain social realities of the globalizing city inform the production and emergence of other social realities, both there and elsewhere—this production or emergence of new globalizing contexts of existence is a transcendence from the pre-existing contexts of material existence that informed its production. Various contradictions—like the culture economy, urban-rural, Fordist-post-Fordist, and pre-liberalization-post-liberalization are the metabolic mechanisms of globalizing cities, and these contradictions continue to be the metabolic force of the transcendent, globalizing realities. This conceptual nugget, I hope, will become clearer and as I explore some examples of transcendental materialism. I provide four examples below and I characterize them as: *Transnational localism-globalism, dollar divinity, the nation in global circulation, and racial disjunctures.*

Transnational Localism–Globalism

The local and the global have become hotly debated in literature. For instance, Swyngedow (1997) argued that it is important to understand that the local and the global are not ontologically given confrontational scales, but rather mutually constitutive of each other in a process he refers to as 'glocalization'. Globalization leads to an erosion of the importance of the national scale that allows cities, the major senders and receivers of flows, to transcend the national scale and become truly global cities (Sassen 2002), in a process of scaling-up that Smith (2000) called 'scale-jumping'. It is not my purpose here to repeat the extensive discussions of geographical scale that already exist.[2] Rather, my objective is to treat the global and local not as scales at all, but rather as constituted materialities of social reality. I am not interested here in their political, spatial, or physiographic expanse, but rather in their material construction through processes. The purpose is to steer clear of Cartesian logics of scale, which understands the 'local' as small, signifying a town or a village, while the 'global' as more continental and transcontinental. Instead, in the context of globalization, where 'space of flows' and 'space of place' are simultaneously co-existent, where time–space compressions are ubiquitous, and where homogenization and indigenization cannot be pried apart from each other, social reality must be understood in newer ways than confining lenses of scales, coordinates, and diameters. The 'local' is local not because it is small or sub-scalar relative to something else that subsumes it, but because it represents a grounding of cultural, economic, and political processes making them familiar, and in-place. However, this does not mean that the local is untouched, or that it is not flowing, homogenizing, or being compressed. The 'global' is global not because it is continental or transcontinental in reach, but because it lacks the familiarity and in-placeness that the local sometimes possess—global is at home anywhere and nowhere.

The Akshardham temple complexes in the US represent a transnational localism for the immigrant Hindu. They are local not because they are smaller than the cities that encapsulate them, or because they represent numerically, a minority religious group in the US. Rather, the Akshardham temple complexes are local in the constituted materiality of the immigrant subject, in this materiality, the temple landscape is a familiar context, a community, and a place to enjoy tea and dhokla surrounded by children who fluently chatter in both Gujarati and English with a hint of a southern drawl. The ornately carved pillars, the reflecting pools, the sprawling staircase, and the displays in the museum are grandiose and magnificent, and at the same time, they re-create the mundaneness of everyday Indian existence that immigrants crave. The spectacle of the landscape is an essential ingredient for recreating the coziness of the distant local in the global immigrant's mind. While being cozy and mundane for the first-generation immigrant, the spectacular landscape is simultaneously awe-inspiring in the minds of the second-generation immigrant children, who are completely unfamiliar with the sense of the 'local', 'community', and 'home' that their parents hunger for.

One interviewee at the Houston temple complex remarked:

> This temple allows us to be who we are, here we no longer have to conform and fit into what others expect us to be. It is like being back home in the same apartment complex if you are in the city, and the same village if you are in a rural area. The temple ensures that sense of community: it

was built on a voluntary basis, men, women, and children contributed free labour and time in polishing the stones, laying the electric cables, planting the trees. It brought us together as a community, like we would be back home. The temple complex feels like home away from home.

In many ways, the Akshardham temple complexes are more local, familiar, and indigenous than their counterparts in India, because the temples in India are impersonally constructed by abundant and cheap wage labour. In the US, however, the devotees and their families pitched in to build the temples, alongside friends who were, in many instances, not even Hindu Indians. The temples were completely built with donations collected from the BAPS Hindu community, and volunteering became the essential route for avoiding expensive labour costs. For a middle-class immigrant Indian who lives in an American suburban—with its cookie-cutter homes, granite counter tops, and strip malls—it is impossible to escape the materiality of their transnational, global existence unless it is through the grandiosity and magnificence of this temple complex. The temple complex constructs an alternative materiality of the familiar in which one can be oneself. Everywhere else, the immigrant subject is a model immigrant who pursues the American dream and aspires for American citizenship, but within the food courts of the temple and its communal vegetarian meals, and in the weekend hymns and prayer rituals, he is Sajjan *bhai* (brother) or Sarla *ben* (sister). However, the younger generation, born in the US, does not relate to the temple complex in the same way as their parents. For them, their suburban home is the safe haven, and the school district they belong to is the 'local', and the 'community'. The Walmarts, the McDonalds, and the neighbourhood bowling alley that they frequent are the happy hunting grounds where familiarity, memory, and nostalgia are produced daily. The grand young temple that has recently come up is a spectacular materiality that inspires awe and curiosity, but not necessarily familiarity and home. A 21-year-old at the Atlanta temple complex remarked:

> We have always been taught about the greatness of India, the richness of its culture, the importance of Hinduism as a religion. We have grown up with it at home, and lived with it through the folktales that were narrated to us, through the prayer meetings we attended. It is so difficult to explain to our American friends who we are. This temple complex solves that dilemma, we have a piece of India's heritage and history in our backyard and we can show it off to our friends as well, this is awesome!

For the transnational, second-generation immigrant youth, their very familiar American neighbourhood is now being transformed by a 'global' and grandiose transnational India and an equally grandiose transnational Hinduism. The youth's local materiality is now re-constituted by the globalizing 'awesomeness' of this Swaminarayan temple complex that has always been very distant. This globalizing landscape, which now exists in the backyard, is something that the second-generation immigrant youth help built, and something they can take pride in. The Akshardham temple complexes in the US are transcended materialisms, because they transcend the Akshardham temples in India, where they are simply grand Hindu places of worship. In transcending the temple landscapes back home, the Akshardham landscape simultaneously becomes a 'local place' for the first-generation immigrant who looks to recreate 'home', and at the same time, it is an exotic 'global place' for the second-generation Indian-American youth who looks to possess and share exotic India. For the first-generation immigrant, American cities represents the global places that they sought to immigrate to for economic opportunities, and so constructing temples that are almost mirror images of the temples they left back home is not just an attempt to replicate a sense of the local in the global, but also an attempt to create the local where it did not previously exist. The Akshardham temples in US cities are not just replicas of their Indian counterparts; they *transcend* them by becoming 'a safe haven', 'a home', 'a community', a space of place, and an indigenized reality in the midst of all the globalizing homogenizations. At the same time, these American-Indian temples also inscribe a globalism for the younger generation who were born in the US Indian heritage and Hindu culture flow through the conduit of the space of flows, to be a globalizing India near the American freeways and industrial parks. The Swaminarayan temple landscapes signify transcendental materialism where the narratives of the local and the global are so imbricated that they remain in dialectical cohabitation.

Dollar Divinity

The Akshardham temples in the US are constructed with funds collected from local congregations. One interviewee at the Irving temple commented that God Swaminarayan had asked followers to donate

5–10 per cent of their income to the upkeep and maintenance of the temples. A DVD sold at the Atlanta temple's gift shop features a Toronto TV news clip in which the newsreader claims that 40 million dollars went into the foundation and construction of the Toronto temple in Canada, all of which came from private sources. Interviewees typically did not provide a figure for the construction and yearly maintenance of the temple complexes, usually claiming that the construction and establishment took millions and that yearly expenses are very high. They also did not know which community member contributed the largest amount, because no one really advertises how much they contributed. If, however, the Toronto temple is a benchmark, then the other temples in North America must amount to more than 40 million, and if the DVDs sold at the gift shop are any indication, then the local Gujarati businessmen that are prominently featured as giving speeches during the inauguration festivals must have important roles as financial contributors. Many interviewees claim that the voluntary contribution of labour has been the mainstay in construction and maintenance of the temples. The DVDs document every step of the construction process, which often starts with the acquisition of the land and includes signing the contract with the local city officials, breaking the land, laying the foundation stone, and then building the temple. The most important aspect of the building process prominently featured is the presence of men, women, and children who are shown carving, polishing, digging, and planting as a background voice narrator explains how the voluntary contribution of free labor made the temple complex possible. While volunteers played an important role, construction workers, engineers, and planners still had to be employed; often, hundreds of construction workers had to be flown in from India. Volunteers continue to play important roles even after the establishment of the temple: they run gift shops, participate in cleaning, run language classes on weekends, and organize various cultural activities. However, in spite of the volunteer's contributions, security personnel must be employed, gatekeepers stationed, cooks brought in from India, and gardeners, landscapers, and custodial staff hired. The interviewees claim that donations from the local community provide enough funds for the smooth functioning of the temple. The point I am making here is that globalization of religion and the reformulation of local geographies costs money and institutional organization, and diasporic communities are happy to contribute labour and dollars. Cultural globalization is therefore intensely political and economic—faith, divinity, spirituality, care, creativity, and artistic splendour require consistent supply of labor and funds. The BAPS group of temples is supervised by a board of trustees for North America, which consists of volunteers who help guide regional temples in their policies and activities. Each city chapter has multiple departments and committees consisting of local devotees who are advised by swamis (saints) who constantly travel in the region, moving from one temple to another and guiding the spiritual and non-spiritual activities.

The temples also raise money on a day-to-day basis from the sale of books, food, religious artifacts, and DVDs from gift shops, which sometimes host special discounts, as well as fresh snacks and tea at the BAPS-sanctified cafeterias (Figure 4.6) and huge ornate chests collecting daily contributions. The Irving-Dallas temple rents out its community hall and auditorium for various occasions, such as marriages and christenings, with a strict list of regulations for maintaining the sanctity of the temple. The various religious and spiritual services that promise peace and oneness with God, cost money. As noted earlier, most temple complexes display menus of sacred services that can be rendered in return for a few dollars. For example, the 'Abhishek' at the Atlanta temple has individual and family rates, and rates for audio recording as well. Grocery seva, fruit seva, and milk seva are popular everyday activities through which devotees can serve the temple's kitchen by actually purchasing the groceries or donating the money equivalent.

Transcendence from the profanity of everyday existence, is a material act that is achieved through the production of sacred geographies, which are expensive. It is also achieved on a day-to-day basis through the material acts of consuming food, DVDs, and religious services, all of which pump capital in the continuous production of the sacred. The production of this sacred is intensely local in its financing and management, because the devotees that donate and form volunteer groups, departments, and committees are drawn from the region. At the same time, however, these local sacred assemblages are produced in the transnational, diasporic contexts of the US in order to allow God, divinity, and salvation to travel from the holy contexts of home (India) to the profane geographies of the foreign land. The established immigrant community's desire for divine connection is actualized through systematic investment in the local community through the material acts of

Figure 4.6 Signs placed at the Atlanta temple's entrance to advertise the temple food court
Source: Photograph taken by the author.

land acquisition and purchase, temple construction, management and committee building, hiring of staff, and maintenance. God goes global, travelling from his indigenous abode in India to be grounded locally in Chicago, Atlanta, Dallas, Houston, and London. This global–local grounding is not a nebulous act in the meditative mind of the devotee; it is material and tangible in the construction of the temple landscape through marble carvings of the stone arches, in the sweet *kaju barfis* (cashew-based sweets) sold in the gift shops, in the meticulously manicured temple lawns, and in the spiritual hymns that emanate when one inserts the temple DVDs into one's computer. The transcendence from the mundaneness, the foreignness, and the profanity of existence into a divine plane of peace and spirituality involves an assemblage of local and global material acts. These sacred acts have an economic metabolism, as they are driven by millions of dollars and they in turn, generate dollars that are re-invested in the production of the divine. In the context of dollar divinity, the transnational global immigrant who carries economic and cultural capital with her does not automatically melt into America's cultural melting pot, becoming homogenized into the predominant protestant Christianity. Instead, the capital is invested towards transcending the materiality of foreign existence by indigenizing the gods brought from home. The gods transcend their indigenous local roots and globalize in Dallas, Atlanta, and Chicago, in the process altering the landscape of urban America. The globalization of the sacred requires an economic engine that is meticulous in maintaining its books, generating funds, forming committees, honouring donors, organizing volunteers, and stocking gift shops and cafeterias. This motor must deal with the many materialisms that spring from the city regulations, visa issues, and producing and packaging religious foods and artifacts. As one volunteer at the Atlanta temple explained:

> The 'do not photograph' sign that you see posted on the main landing applies to the inner sanctum of the temple. This is in compliance with the city regulations. The city wanted us to post it, they did not want people of other faiths—you know, whites, Mexicans, and blacks—from coming in, taking pictures, and misusing them. They did not want bad publicity for their city, we had to comply; this signage is rather expensive, we had to spend valuable dollars that could have gone elsewhere.

Another volunteer, also at the Atlanta temple, remarked:

It is so hard to get a visa for the chef who cooks the daily and Sunday community meals and makes the products for the gift shops. It is hard to get a U.S. visa for working class groups like cooks and construction workers; the immigration authorities fear that they will not go back home. We have to make do with whatever we can get, sometimes the chefs come for five years and they go back, then we have to get another person, this is a big headache!

Culture is not, therefore, a super-structural manifestation of the deeper economic base, or a fleeting and unimportant subsidiary of the sweat, blood, and war that is political economy. Social reality that is inherently society and space—that is, reality in which neither society nor space can hold any meaning if they are analytically separated— is an inherent inflection of culture and economy. Sometimes ties are maintained with home by following the temple construction codes and religious teachings, sometimes they are transcended by forming independent and local congregational boards of trustees, regional bands of travelling saints, and local kitchens and production bases. Globalizing the divine requires an intricate process of dealing with food, architecture, religious customs, and religious artifacts that are predominantly cultural, but also simultaneously involve dealing with supply chains, visa fees, sale and retailing, pricing and listing, city regulations that are also predominantly economic. These simultaneously cultural and economic acts crystallize the materiality, landscape, geography, and narrative of a new city that transcends its earlier more 'profane' version. The many materialisms of dollar divinity allow the immigrant Indian to experience the divine by transcending the 'baseness' of everyday urban life. Therefore, through globalization, the city transcends itself in order to re-emerge in the light of the divine and hence formulate a new and more desirable urban experience for the immigrant.

The Nation in Global Circulation

One of the dominant strands in the globalization debate has been the argument about the 'hollowing out' of nations: scholars (Ohmae 2000; Brown 2001; Strange 2001) argue that, with increased economic deregulation, the political powers of nations will also shrink, giving rise to extra-national entities like region-states (for example, the European Union) and multi-national trading blocs (for example, NAFTA). The

hallowed years of the nation as the supreme political entity, demanding complete loyalty, reverence, and accountability, is on the decline.
Cities, which are increasingly becoming more global, will transcend the
confining holds of their regional and national governments to become
almost like 'city-states' by advancing their own agenda of economic
growth, privatization, and efforts to attract foreign capital (Sassen
2002). Therefore, an important question in the globalization debate
is whether globalization signals the ending of the nation-state. On the
opposite side of the spectrum are scholars who argue that globalization
calls for a re-formulation of the nation-state, but not its erasure (Mann
2001; Slaughter 2001; Hirst and Thompson 2001). The process of economic liberalization, border porosity, and decentralized governance are
not indicators of the disappearance of the nation-state, but rather are
actualized because of the nation-state's willingness to evolve. Brenner
and Theodore (2002) took a middle path by arguing that economic
liberalization does not lead to a standardized, one-size-fits-all transformation everywhere; in fact, the market rationality is very cognizant
of the unique path-dependencies of places, and is hence grounded in
locally meaningful ways. Therefore, in other words, more local variants,
like the nation, have a great deal of agency when interacting with globalization and modifying it according to local and national trajectories.
In the same vein Hobsbawm (1998: 1) argued:

> But a 'nation,' however we define it, is by definition exclusive and particu-
> lar. It is always recognizable by not being another nation. To this extent
> it is by definition not global. This is both objectively and subjectively
> so. From the national point of view, the 'nation' is primary and quali-
> tatively unique. From the global point of view, it is just one component
> among many others of the total system. It may be quantitatively more
> or less important, but qualitatively all nations are equal. The question
> I will discuss today is how the 'nation' fits into, or does not fit into, the
> globalized world of today and the even more globalized world of tomor-
> row. Or, conversely, how that world adjusts to the heterogeneity of its
> components.

Following the same line of argument, he stated (1998: 2):

> But if globalization has to adjust to local particularities, of which 'nations'
> are an important subvariety, particularities are much more powerfully
> affected by globalization and have to adjust to it or be eliminated by it.

These ideas are therefore an attempt to understand how the contradictions between nations/particularities/uniqueness and globalization are resolved, and how to deal with homogeneity and standardization. The Akshardham temple complexes in North America provide an interesting narrative of the nation in global circulation. The temple complexes are not only a sacred space that celebrates, globally and internationally, the magnificence and grandeur of Hinduism, displays ancient Hindu architectural traditions, and cocoons memory and nostalgia for home, they simultaneously become an ad hoc India, a nation away from the nation. Handing down India to the younger generation is the central project among *satsangis* (fellow devotees), and this manifests not just as the need to celebrate Hindu Gujarati culture, but also as the need to celebrate nationalist imaginations and profess patriotism through nationalistic myths, flag, and national anthem. It is taken for granted that the imagination of the nation often becomes conflated with Gujarati Hinduism, which often understands the celebration of religious customs as national culture. As a devotee claimed: 'Performing seva (service) at the temple is performing seva for India.' In this particular devotee's imagination, god and Hindu religion are just extensions of mother India. In the museum, Hindu saints (Figure 4.7) are portrayed alongside Indian freedom fighters, patriots, poets, and artists, as if they are extensions of the Hindu pantheon and hence share the divine project of defining an overarching India. India's rich flora and fauna (Figure 4.8), diversity of language and culture, discovery of zero (Figure 4.9), and contributions to geometry and astronomy (Figure 4.9) are prominently featured and placed within the narrative of a nation constructed with the help of excerpts from high-school history textbooks (Figure 4.10). These displays are not found in Akshardham temples in India; rather, they are special features of the foreign temple complexes: a construction of 'mother India' for the education of the international citizenry through the careful production of a proud nation that can be the 'mother of geometry' and the mother of spirituality at the same time.

A skit organized by the youth members of the Atlanta Swaminarayan community presents a caricature of the tale of Alexander the Great and his aspirations to conquer India. The actor playing Alexander is shown as threatening to plunder India, a country he knows is ridden with many diverse cultural and hence, in Alexander's mind, is easy

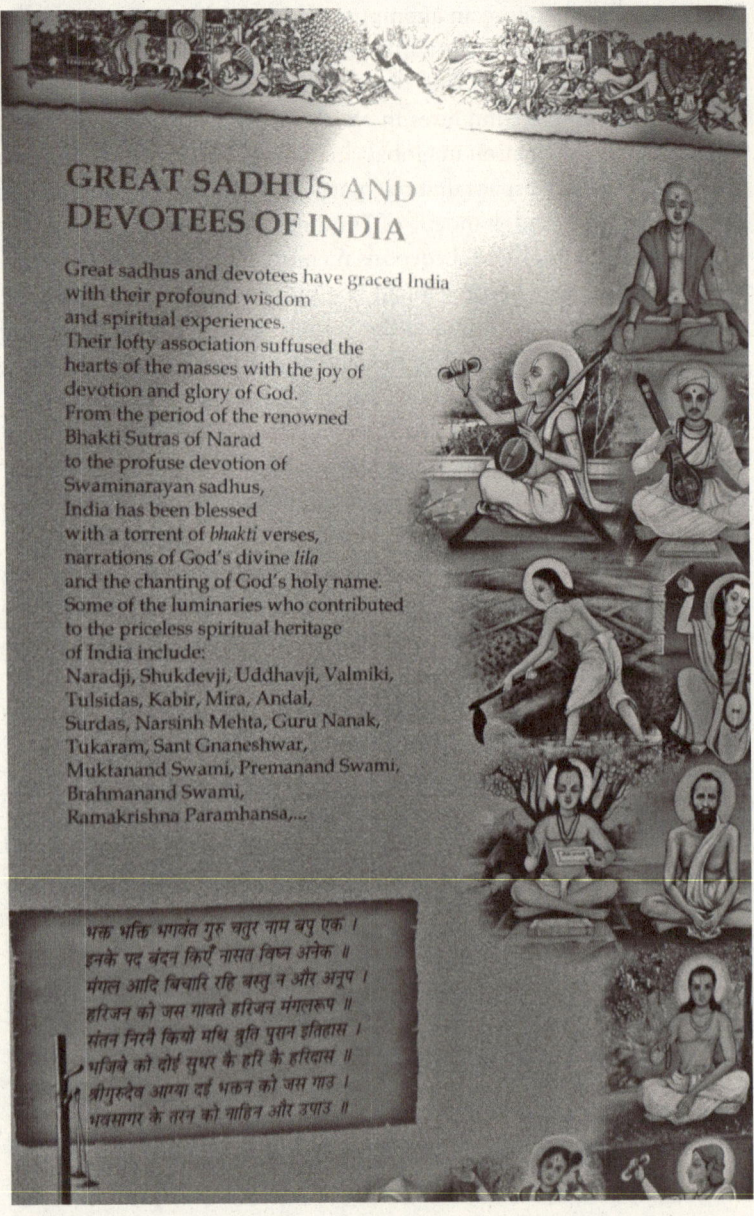

GREAT SADHUS AND DEVOTEES OF INDIA

Great sadhus and devotees have graced India with their profound wisdom and spiritual experiences. Their lofty association suffused the hearts of the masses with the joy of devotion and glory of God. From the period of the renowned Bhakti Sutras of Narad to the profuse devotion of Swaminarayan sadhus, India has been blessed with a torrent of *bhakti* verses, narrations of God's divine *lila* and the chanting of God's holy name. Some of the luminaries who contributed to the priceless spiritual heritage of India include: Naradji, Shukdevji, Uddhavji, Valmiki, Tulsidas, Kabir, Mira, Andal, Surdas, Narsinh Mehta, Guru Nanak, Tukaram, Sant Gnaneshwar, Muktanand Swami, Premanand Swami, Brahmanand Swami, Ramakrishna Paramhansa,...

भक्त भक्ति भगवंत गुरु चतुर नाम बपु एक ।
इनके पद बंदन किएँ नासत विघ्न अनेक ॥
मंगल आदि बिचारि रहि बस्तु न और अनूप ।
हरिजन को जस गावते हरिजन मंगलरूप ॥
संतन निरनै कियो मथि बुति पुरान इतिहास ।
धजिबे को दोई सुधर कै हरि के हरिदास ॥
श्रीगुरुदेव आग्या दई भक्तन को जस गाउ ।
भवसागर के तरन को नाहिन और उपाउ ॥

Figure 4.7   Museum display at the Houston temple listing spiritual leaders from history and proto-history in the different regions of India
Source: Photograph taken by Waquar Ahmed.

Figure 4.8 Museum display at the Houston temple featuring India's diverse flora, fauna, cultures, and languages

Source: Photograph taken by Waquar Ahmed.

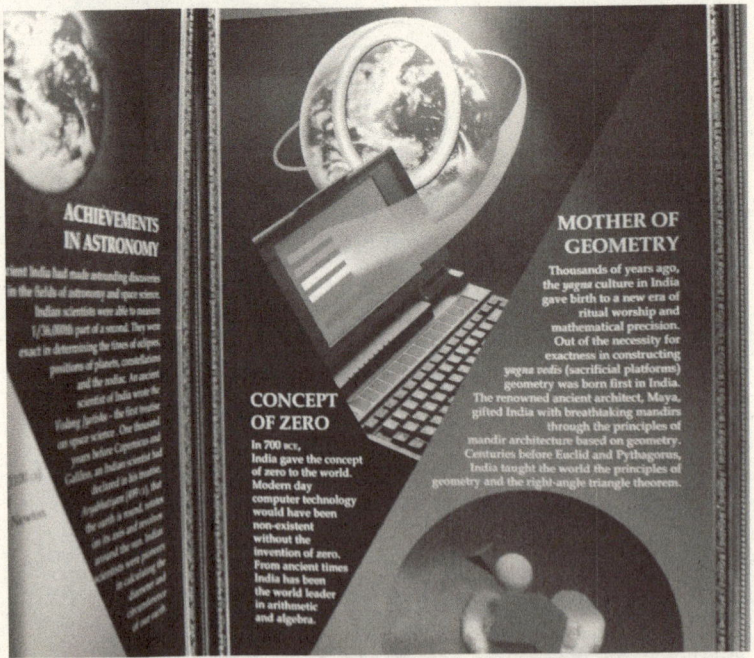

Figure 4.9 Museum display at the Houston temple celebrating India's contribution of the concept of zero and proudly proclaiming its historical lineage in astronomy, geometry, and mathematics
Source: Photograph taken by Waquar Ahmed.

to break apart. He is met by a sage dressed in the saffron garb of an ancient Hindu holy man, who defies Alexander's sabre rattling and humbles him through quotations from the ancient Hindu scriptures of the Vedas and the Upanishads that discuss the insignificance of the human body and the importance of enriching the soul. The sage makes a moot point: Alexander may kill him, but the death of the body will not extinguish the soul of India, which is enriched by its great diversity. Religious nationalism is a dominant political paradigm in India, often taken to an extreme, exclusionist stance against religious minorities in India (Balgopal 2002), where both dangerous and benign conflations between the Hindu and Indian cultures are common among those who ascribe to the majority religious group (Hindus). An important challenge of India's post-independence nation-building project was

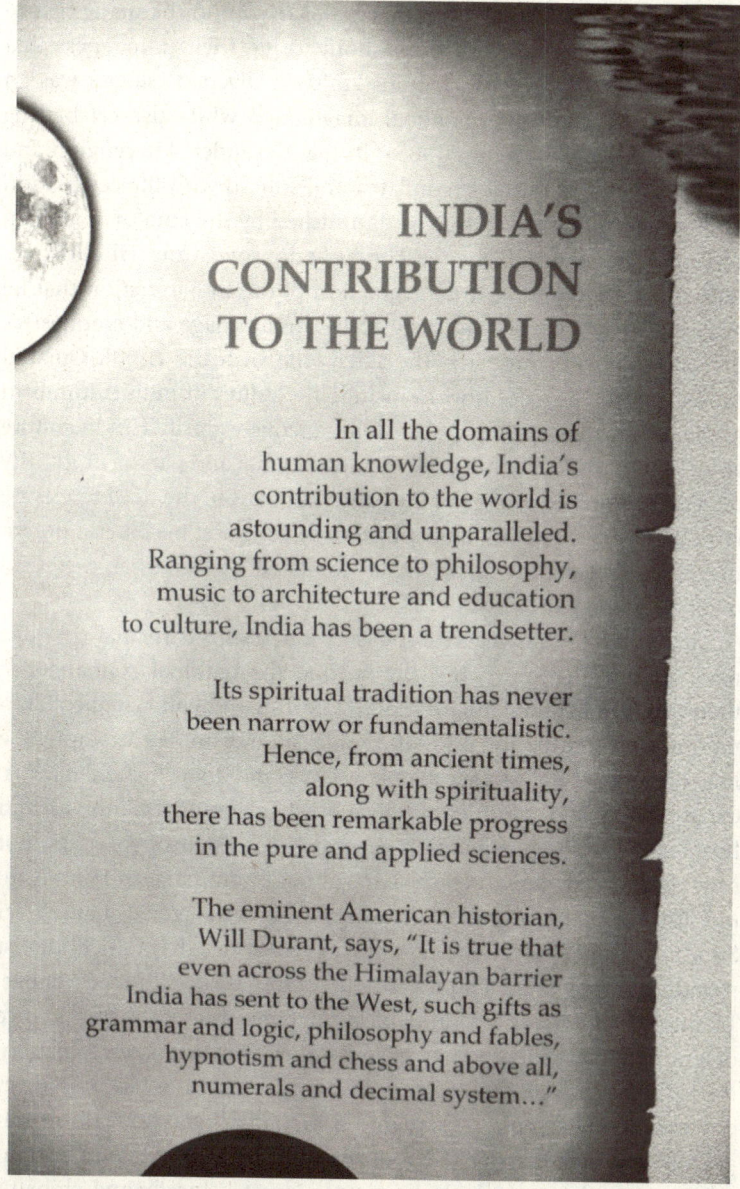

INDIA'S CONTRIBUTION TO THE WORLD

In all the domains of human knowledge, India's contribution to the world is astounding and unparalleled. Ranging from science to philosophy, music to architecture and education to culture, India has been a trendsetter.

Its spiritual tradition has never been narrow or fundamentalistic. Hence, from ancient times, along with spirituality, there has been remarkable progress in the pure and applied sciences.

The eminent American historian, Will Durant, says, "It is true that even across the Himalayan barrier India has sent to the West, such gifts as grammar and logic, philosophy and fables, hypnotism and chess and above all, numerals and decimal system…"

Figure 4.10 Museum display at the Houston temple prominently emphasizing India's 'unparalleled contribution to science, philosophy, architecture, and education'
Source: Photograph taken by Waquar Ahmed.

to find a national imagination that could transcend the many rifts of language, culture, and religion without losing their uniqueness that enriched diversity. Nehru's famous 'unity in diversity' slogan was an attempt to secularize the national imagination while also celebrating its many diversities (Nehru 1985). In the Alexander skit, religion and the nation are comfortably conflated and spliced with the celebration of diversity: Alexander is seen as diminished by the aura of an Indian god man, but this god man is Hindu and quotes from Hindu scriptures. At the same time, the imagination of the Indian nation that he projects extends beyond an exclusively Hindu image and emphasizes the importance of diversity. The skit is rife with the Hindu Gujarati American's dilemma of how to include the values of multiculturalism of the American variety and also simultaneously glorify Hindu culture above and beyond anything else. Being marginal and part of a minority religion within the context of the American nation, the need to elevate Hindu culture through a global history of conquest becomes a potent theme; Hindu culture is of course conflated as Indian culture, and mythmaking replaces history.

Therefore, to answer Hobsbawm's question, particularities like national imaginations, which fly beyond the national containers of their origin, adjust to globalization by existing in hyphenated collaborations with transnationalism and multiculturalism. For example, the inauguration of the Atlanta temple was a grand affair,[3] where mayors, congressmen, and the chief of police brushed shoulders with Gujarati businessmen. The inauguration ceremony consisted of speeches, not only delivered by holy men speaking about Swaminarayan Hinduism, but also by American politicians who waved to the crowds hailing 'Jai Swaminarayan!' The American politicians constructed a multiculturalist narrative of how these temples are sites of India–US cultural exchange. Talking of America as a country of immigrants, and of the importance of immigrants lending vibrancy and innovation to this great nation, the speeches listed the many environmental and social initiatives enacted by the temple. Tree-planting initiatives, anti-addiction campaigns, and post-disaster relief efforts were highlighted as important programmes through which the temple invested locally and globally. These environmental and social programmes were viewed as enhancing both the economy and society, in addition to contributing to the culture and beauty of the suburb of Lilburn, Atlanta. It is as if, by

ascribing to universal goals of sustainability and social betterment, the
temple transcended its cultural particularity, its placial fixity to unani-
mously meld with national and global goals. A congressman declared
26 August 2007 the 'Mandir of Lilburn, Georgia day'. A Gujarati busi-
nessman who probably played an important role in founding the
temple told a cheering crowd who were waving flags with the Indian
tri-colour and US stars and stripes: 'This great nation has given us the
opportunity to embrace our Indian heritage and pass it down to the
next generation.' A choir and orchestra consisting of white and African-
American boys sang the US national anthem, and a Gujarati-American
boy waved a giant US flag. At the end of the song, huge numbers of red,
white, and blue balloons were released. This was followed by a group
of Indian-American boys singing the Indian national anthem and waving a gigantic Indian flag, and then by the release of white, green, and
saffron balloons. The entire inauguration ceremony seamlessly stitched
the particularities of Swaminarayan Hinduism, the celebration of temple architecture, and the emphasis on the greatness of Hinduism with
the globalization of the Indian nation, the pride of Indian patriotism,
and its comfortable cohabitation within the rubric of American citizenship. For American politicians, the Akshardham temple becomes an
important site for the community's 'enhancement', because it attracts
tourists who will consume and spend, and therefore put Lilburn on
the global map. However, at the same time, the temple's establishment
also becomes a caveat in the political narrative of Lilburn, serving as
an example of cooperation, coexistence, cultural exchange, and social
and environmental initiatives between model immigrants and host
communities.

The inauguration festivities, which continued for days, also included
nagar yatra or a tour of the city, during which processions carrying the
temple idols in gaudily decorated chariots were followed by long trains
of devotees, dancers, and children as they made their way through the
city before returning to the temple. In essence, the gods were given a
tour of their new foreign abode before settling into their new home.
The inauguration DVDs begin with a promotional video on the city.
For example, the Atlanta DVD introduced Atlanta as an emerging global
city that has the world's largest aquarium and excellent universities
and convention centres, as well as a state of the art airport, and the
headquarters of 15 of the world's largest multinational corporations.

The Akshardham narratives do not contradict the globalization narratives, and the globalization narratives do not swallow the Akshardham narratives. The global city stays in comfortable cohabitation with local uniqueness, and the transnational nation acts as the linking logic between them. The nation away-from-home is no longer parochial, and no longer inward-looking; it is emancipated from its unique roots and acquires the global stamp of transnational globalism. Such a nation has global purchase, because it transcends the rooted identity of its existence to bring with it many materialisms like exotic foreign culture, interesting myths, age-old traditions, and marble architecture, thus becoming a universal solvent in which global America and local Swaminarayan Hinduism dissolve into an exotic concoction of mandir days, nagar yatras, and patriotic fervour. The global city of Atlanta is marked and charted by an intensely local Gujarati Hindu procession in a 'medievalist spectacle', which does not cause riots or anti-immigrant hysteria, and video footage of the temple inauguration unabashedly promotes and projects the globalness of Atlanta as it spearheads tourism, business, and culture. Such contradictory materialisms are in comfortable cohabitation, because, in the Akshardham narratives, both India and the US are no longer just nations with an inside and an outside, but the insider–outsider and citizen–foreigner dichotomies are now transcended through new globalizing narratives of multiculturalism and transnationalism. Multiculturalism and transnationalism help gloss over the exclusionary Hindu narratives that are produced in the many materialism of the temple's skits and museums. That the Indian nation is actually much more than just Hindu culture is comfortably forgotten, as the 'model immigrant' carefully enables her motherland to transcend its local moorings in India, and dissolve into global narratives of transnational cultural exchange. The city proudly advertises aquariums, airports, corporate headquarters, Hindu culture, and Indian transnationalism as the new artifacts of globalization. As the Indian nation goes into global circulation through a very selective Hindu-Gujarati narrative, it transcends into new materialisms that help calibrate and adjust its particularities within globally acceptable folds of multicultural existence. In its many transcendent materialisms, the nation resoundingly answers Hobsbawm's angst by being simultaneously national and global.

Racial Disjunctures

The Akshardham temples not only attract the local Gujarati community, but also other Hindu Indians, non-Hindu Indians, and other Americans. The temple landscape is so disconnected from the rest of the city that it causes passersby to pause and wonder. Usually, these temples are located in quiet suburbs outside the main city, often close to freeway arteries and sometimes in middle-class, suburban neighbourhoods. They rise suddenly and unexpectedly, towering over strip malls, parking lots, and apartment blocks in their pristine white glory. They have both vertical height and horizontal expanse. The shiny golden pitchers (kalasas) and bright red and white stripe flags that adorn the peaks of the temple dome reach out into the bright blue sky, and the sprawling courtyards and reflecting pools surround, reflect, and reach out into the distant horizons. Religious edifices of such intricacy, expanse, and height are rare in the New World, where churches and other religious monuments are more understated and quiet. The Puritans often arrived in the New World to escape religious persecution in the Old World, and England, where the puritans were protesting against the Catholic Church, the pope of Rome, and the wealth and power it had amassed. The Puritan ethic was therefore a reformation of Christianity from the pomp, show, and grandeur that the European church and Catholicism had come to represent (Peet 1997, 2000). Therefore, the Puritans who settled in the New England region and later spread all over the eastern seaboard to form Protestant churches of various denominations, which were congregational and disassociated from the Church of Rome, and therefore became intentionally austere in contrast to the grandeur and ornamentation of the cathedrals of Europe. In that context, the ornateness and grandeur of the Akshardham temples produced a spectacular slice of the city that is enticing to many. Non-Swaminarayan Hindu tourists quite happily come to the complex to revel in Hindu spirituality in a place so far away from India. Non-Hindu Indians and South Asians visit the complex to marvel at a piece of India so grand and so magnificent, so out of place and yet so appropriate in this foreign land. White Americans, Hispanic Americans, and African Americans come to look at this spectacular landscape as a site of exotic Hindu culture and tradition. Entrance to the temple is free, and people of all faiths and nationality are welcome.

While Swaminarayan Hinduism professes respect for all religions, the Gujarati Indian devotees themselves are quite conservative in how they lead their everyday lives. Most interviewees, both volunteers and devotees visiting the temple, claim that one of the main motivating factors for founding such temple complexes is to infuse a sense of culture among their children, who are growing up in a foreign land. The temple provides a moral mooring against many distractions, like rap and hip-hop music, non-vegetarian food, alcohol, and dating rituals that are all 'foreign' to the Indian way of life. Going out on dates without the presence of elders and pre-marital sex are perceived as ubiquitous among the youth culture of the US and considered to be outside the paradigm of Hindu culture. Romantically interacting with Americans, especially African Americans and Hispanic Americans, is considered a direct violation of the Indian way of life. A volunteer at the Atlanta temple, for example, proceeded to tell me a story of an Indian woman who visited the temple some years ago. This volunteer noticed that she was crying and when he asked why, the woman replied that she was nostalgic for her culture and really sad that her own children had imbibed nothing of it. She was disappointed that her children were dating African Americans and having pre-marital sexual relationship with them (at this point, the volunteer lowered his voice and switched to Hindi to relay this to me, because the cab driver who drove me to this temple, an African American, was standing within earshot). As he proceeded with this story, the volunteer related, in a suspense-filled tone, how he then invited this lady to bring her children to the Atlanta temple and, when the lady visited with her children, this particular volunteer introduced them to the resident monks. The volunteer then paused for effect, and with suppressed jubilation claimed that upon meeting the monks and getting their blessing, the children changed and amended their 'bad' ways. He further qualified with emphasis that the mother was responsible for not inculcating her culture and value system in her children early on in their lives. Such narratives, where the racial other is welcomed to revel in Indian culture and benefit from spiritual guidance, but is not allowed to penetrate the inner sanctum of the Gujarati-Indian community, is quite common among interviewees. Many interviewees claim that Americans of 'other' races frequent the temple complex in search of spiritual purity, which their cultures do not provide. One volunteer at the Houston temple claimed:

This country [the US] looks great from the outside, it is very glamorous, very polished; you can buy all kinds of cars, the best computers, expansive homes and a satisfying lifestyle. But this country lacks a spiritual culture, their only culture is consumer culture. We want our kids to be worldly wise and economically self-sufficient, but we don't want them to lose our culture in the process. We don't want them to be drinking and driving, doing drugs, shouting at their parents, going to jail, or carrying on with Blacks and Hispanics. We want them to retain their Indian ways. Children are our biggest investment: we have to ensure that we are enriching their souls so that they can reject the materialism, the consumerism, sexual promiscuity especially of the inter-racial kind. Mexicans, blacks want to partake in our spirituality, because they have none in their culture, we welcome them to the temple, but they are not like us.

These narratives should not be confused with the narratives that are materialized in the public sphere. In the public sphere, all races and colors are to be tolerated and welcomed and all faiths are to be respected. The inaugural ceremonies of the temples included white, black, and Hispanic public figures. These individuals are blessed by the Pramukh Swami (leading saint), garlanded by him, taken to the inner sanctum of the temple, and fed with food cooked in the temple kitchen. Within the private sphere, the temple functions as a community centre, teaching the Gujarati language, hymns, and organizing cultural activities and play groups in order to maintain a thick community network within which babysitting duties are swapped, marriage alliances made, and business deals sealed. In this inner sanctum of the Swaminarayan Gujarati community, critical perceptions and narratives about 'others', the 'foreign', and 'the different' are forged in the context of nested worlds of 'we', 'the satsangis', 'the Gujaratis', 'the Hindus', and 'the Indians'.

These narratives are mostly racial narratives in which the various materialisms of public life in a foreign land also call for a transcendence into a very private world of 'us'. However, this transcendent materialism is disjunctured, cleaved, and messy; it does not present, in a simplistic broad stroke, the racial hatred towards the homogenous others. The racism materializes differently in different spheres of existence, and so people of all colours and races can imbibe the spirituality of the temple complex; there exists an element of racial pride in being able to provide spiritual transcendence to those who are viewed as 'culturally bereft'. Therefore, the Akshardham temples are not landscapes of exclusion in the sense that they do not physically keep anyone out, but the act of welcoming-in is born out of a racial-disjuncture, a perception that the 'vacuous other' needs to be culturally and spiritually filled. While politicians and public figures of all colours are welcomed—and such meetings become symbols of inter-cultural exchange, co-existence and multiculturalism—private liaisons with the sons and daughters of 'Americans', particularly African Americans and Hispanic Americans, are not encouraged. While the US is viewed, as a 'great' country, there exists a disjuncture between 'their ways of life' and 'our way of life' in which 'their way of life' is often a racial extrapolation and selective reading of the 'crime alert' section of the local news. Materialism, consumerism, social dysfunction, and anomie become important lenses for viewing the 'other', while the 'we' becomes a culturally deep and spiritually rich community that must be protected from the sea of depravation that lies beyond the temple's walls. The Akshardham landscape allows the immigrant to transcend the imagined debauchery and cultural poverty of her chosen land and materialize a safe haven of cultural purity that can be passed down to future generations.

The City as Transcendental Materialisms

I have, in this chapter, attempted a dialectical approach to globalization using the Akshardham temple complexes in Houston, Irving-Dallas, and Atlanta as slices of social reality. The purpose here is to understand how globalization is grounded in the US, a country assumed to be the very site from which flows of economic and cultural globalization emanate. The importance of the Washington-Wall Street alliance in influencing the World Bank and International Monetary Fund, and hence in shaping neoliberal policies that define the contours of market liberalization and globalization, has been well documented (Peet 2003; Stiglitz 2002; Harvey 2005). The importance of American corporations vociferously pushing McDonaldization in the rest of the world has also been well documented (Ritzer and Malone 2000; Barber 2000). My intention here is to indicate that globalization, as a process, does not unidirectionally emanate from the First World to the Third World, even though this trajectory may be the most prominent. My intention here is also to emphasize an approach to cultural globalization that understands culture not as a discrete thing isolated from the economy, society, and landscape and treated as a manifestation, reification, superstructure, and an echo of the economy. I attempt to understand globalizing social reality as transcendental materialism in which the metabolic processes (both economic and cultural) of the city undergo changes. The city therefore transcends itself to evolve into a new globalizing avatar (re) constituted by many material acts like, temple construction, immigrant re-imagination of home and community, racial imaginations and othering, ideas about patriotism, the nation, and multiculturalism, and acts of grounding the gods in a foreign land. Transcendental materialism is a take on Hegel's transcendental idealism, in which Hegel contended that history progresses through contradictions between ideas. An initial idea or thesis is contradicted by another idea, or antithesis, to evolve into a new synthesis that influences human action and transforms the world. Ideas therefore produce action, each synthesis soon becomes a thesis and is once again challenged, and civilization proceeds towards the perfect, or absolute, idea. Each synthesis transcends its more imperfect predecessor to move history towards perfection, hence transcendental idealism.

In this chapter, I, unlike Hegel, emphasize the changing material conditions as the driving engine of globalization by arguing that ideas cannot be artificially separated from the materiality of existence because they are materially produced as well. Using transcendental materialism as my philosophical backdrop, I explore globalization through the Akshardham landscape. It is important to understand that landscape is not only understood as built geographic forms, but also as narratives, perceptions, texts, speeches, stories, and oral histories that flesh out the landscape as much as the marble and concrete. Therefore, the temple landscape becomes an important canvas on which to read the texts of globalization as they play out in some US cities.

In Chapter 2, I laid out the conceptual backdrop for this book, which I had proclaimed would be an attempt at a dialectical approach to globalization. I argued that the city would be a great microcosm of social reality for understanding that dialectic. A dialectical approach understands social reality as an organic whole in which the relational context of distinct elements in the social totality is emphasized. Although the relational contexts may be opposed to each other, or co-aligned, they exist in unity, and the context of relations that make up this whole are not imposed from outside, but are rather integral and organic to it. In the spirit of that conceptual backdrop, here I have treated the Akshardham temple complexes not just as cultural land-scapes produced on the surface layer of society, but rather as represent-ing the social totality of globalization. The city encapsulates this totality through many transcendental materialisms which are the metabolic processes of this globalizing reality. These transcendental materialisms include transnational localism–globalism, dollar divinity, the nation in global circulation, and racial disjunctures. For many first-generation immigrants, a single city landscape becomes an intensely local space, a community, and a home transcended from the original version in Gujarat, while for the sons and daughters it becomes, at the same time, a transnational reality of a globalizing India. This transcendental mate-rialism depicts a dialectic of globalization that turns the local–global ontology on its head by indicating that the local and the global are not fixed, pre-given containers. In the relational cultural-economy of glo-balization, landscapes can be simultaneously local and global depend-ing on who constitutes this materiality. Dollar divinity indicates how the production of the sacred is an expensive political–economic process of negotiating visa issues for god-men and cooks, keeping the books, collecting donations, and dealing with city regulations and the law. It also indicates how the sacred produces itself through food courts, gift shops, and rental spaces that are important income producers. Spiritual transcendence therefore demands meticulous materialisms involving land acquisition and titling, managing supply chains of food and holy artifacts, forming committees, and pricing and valuing sacred encoun-ters with God. These many cultural economic materialisms of dollar divinity allow the immigrant Indian to transcend the foreignness of everyday urban existence and chalk out a 'sacred' globalization. The for-eign city, as it globalizes, is touched by the divine and hence transcends into a new avatar. Globalization has always been assumed to be a chal-lenge to the nation's existence as an identity, but the section 'The nation in global circulation' indicates how the Akshardham temple simulta-neously becomes an extension of Indian nationhood and American multiculturalism. The pride and patriotic fervour of the American Indian is inscribed in national anthems, skits, and flag waving. The Indian nation transcends its place of origin to circulate through mate-rial acts of inter-cultural exchange like mandir days and nagar yatras carried out in American cities. A globalizing nation forms the linking logic between the 'global' America and the 'local' India to allow for the co-adjustment of these opposing forces within the social totality of the city. The Akshardham landscapes also materialize several racial disjunctures: Indian immigrants often depend on this temple landscape for their transcendence, and hence deliverance, from a 'foreign land' that is imagined as culturally weak, often morally degenerate, and socially dysfunctional. The racial 'other', is welcome to the temple, and is certainly respected when she arrives in the public space as a politician, judge, or policeman, but she simultaneously becomes a disjuncture, a world apart, when she attempts to penetrate the private sphere of the Gujarati-American community. The materiality of the globalizing city is often seen through a racist lens through which the American 'other' becomes synonymous with cultural depravity, promiscuity, and drunkenness from which the temple landscape offers protection and solace. Globalization is fraught with many such racial disjunctures, where the distant 'other' is brought within the realm of familiarity but, doing so makes her simultaneously desirable and deplorable. Globalization needs a dialectical approach that can reveal these many materialisms (sometimes contradictory and sometimes compatible) that constitute it. In revealing some of the transcendental materialisms of the city, I hope, that the dialectics of globalization becomes clear.

Notes

1. The Swaminarayan temples are sometimes called Akshardham temples, because Bhagwat Swaminarayan (the god of this faith) was born in Akshardham, near Ayodhya in Uttar Pradesh, India.

2. For an extensive discussion on scale read Marston (2000) and Marston, Jones, and Woodward (2005).

3. Based on archival work examining audio-visual recordings of the entire 14-day inauguration ceremony, held from 16–30 July 2007.

5 Mapping the Fantastic
Akshardham Temples in India

Escaping the City

The twentieth- and the twenty-first-century 'western' city is an awe-inspiring spectacle for urban planners, architects, and academics of all sorts, because it immediately materializes the gritty reality of every-day existence and the fantastic unreality of an imagined utopia. I am referring to the emergence of what has been called the Disneyization of urban landscape to produce theme parks (Bryman 1999) and fantasy spaces (Hannigan 2002) of consumption. For the un-initiated, the Disney Corporation imagined Disneyland as an alternative to New York's Coney Island, which was viewed by Disney as dirty, inefficient, and garish (Weinstein 1992). Disneyland was conceived in the 1930s and, in the 1950s, Disneyland was developed in southern California. Disney's images, cartoons, and characters had become larger than life and entered into ubiquitous circulation, and their inscription on urban space, within the theme-park context, reproduced urban space in a revolutionary way, as a space where dreams were never fleeting and transient, but always tangible and available. The Disneyland theme park spread from its original location in California to other parts of the US, Japan, and Europe to encompass a global spatial fantasy. Its aura, argued Sorkin (2002: 335) transcends its specific geographic location to become an all-encompassing urban ideology:

> But the empire of Disney transcends these physical sites; its aura is all-pervasive. Decades of films have furnished a common iconography on

generations. Now there's a television channel too. And years of shrewd
and massive merchandising have sold billions of Disney things—video
cassettes, comic books, pajamas, paper cups, post-cards, and mouse
eared coin purses—which vaunt their participation in this exponentially
expanding system of objects. The litter of Disneyland is underfoot in
streets from New York to Shanghai. More people know Mickey than Jesus
or Mao. Who doesn't live in Disney World?

Industrial modernity, it has been argued, introduced a banal functionality into urban space stripped of embellishment, iconography, and
ornamentation, creating a utilitarian space that was cost-effective and
efficient (Gottdiener 1997). The warehouses, factory sheds, and mills
were functional landscapes connected by arteries of roads, highways,
and freeways that linked with docks, freight yards, and airports. Rows
of working class and middle-class housing would be interspersed with
markets, stores, and bus stations that defined the non-descript geography of urban living. Planned urban parks would provide the occasional
and brief green respite from the ubiquitous beige, gray, and glass morphology of city living. The industrial cities were a sharp contrast to the
ancient or medieval cities of Athens, the Vatican, Beijing, and India's
Banaras, Ajmer, Agra, and Mahabalipuram. The modern, mechanical
way of life ushered a need for the standardization of taste, preference,
and consumption habits that also simultaneously resulted in the stripping away of signification, often because of the secularization of aesthetics (Hannigan 2002). Industrialization meant a day-to-day reliance
on machines managed by humans, rather than on nature, as was the
case in agricultural and hunting and gathering societies. This disenchantment with nature (Weber 1992) paved the way for urbanism and
secularism, as nature no longer needed to be pacified for sustenance.
The aestheticization associated with the worship of the elements of
nature, animism, and celebration of the harvest gods could therefore be
discarded. Factories and warehouses became the temples of the modern industrial landscape, replacing the ornate cathedrals, synagogues,
and mosques and, in turn, creating an urban modernism devoid of
signification, symbols, and ornamentation. This stripping of signification was most profound in the New World, because of the immigrant
puritan ethic of austere, hard work that was invested in materializing
the New England textile industrial revolution (Peet 1997). It was also
most profound in the US, because the puritans, pilgrims, and pio-
neers encountered a vast wilderness that was minimally modified by

the original inhabitants of the land, the Native Americans, and also because, the new immigrants were able to erase older edifices with an aggression that the Native Americans could hardly match. Elsewhere, the imposition of industrial modernity on the ornateness of ancient and medieval life produced collage-geographies of a schizophrenic variety in which ancient and historical sites, cathedrals, amphitheaters, great walls, monuments, forts, and temples collide with modern-day malls, factories, and bus stations in places like Rome, Beijing, Delhi, Agra, and Jaisalmer.

The late twentieth and the twenty-first centuries have been hailed as the postmodern era (Baudrillard 1981, 1994), the post-industrial age, or the post-Fordist age, during which the secularization of industrial modernity was replaced by a religion of signification and semiotics. The circulating images, symbols, and signs thickly penetrated into the very private sphere of everyday existence through the advancement of telecommunication, information technology, and the World Wide Web. Our reality is no longer defined by the flows of commodities from warehouses and shipyards, but rather by the flows of images from high-speed Internet cables to our bedrooms. In other words, according to Baudrillard (1981, 1994), the hyper-circulation of fantastic images through advertising, aggressive market research, and blogging has resulted in sign value's enhanced importance over use value. Therefore, the defining character of postmodernity is that our material realities are no longer constituted by the uses and functions of the commodities and spaces we consume, but rather by the identity-enhancing properties they possess: a car is no longer a vehicle of transportation, but instead an extension of our image; a house no longer serves just as a roof over our heads, but also defines our soul; and the city is no longer a conglomeration of life and livelihood invested in the non-descript beige and grayness of mill towns, factories, and warehouses, but also a fantasy and utopia, conglomeration of all the signs and images that transport us into a world of themed pleasure and entrainment. The postmodern city must embody sign value, and it must embed spaces that allow, above all else, the emancipation from the ordinary and an escape from the grayness, banality, and grittiness that is the very essence of the urban condition. A Las Vegasesque spectacle must be so commonly circulated that Las Vegas no longer remains an outlier as a fantastic city of lights, gambling, booze, and sex where pyramids and sphinxes brush shoulders with Eiffel Towers and plastic tropical jungles. A little Las Vegas must be present in every city. Sociologists and urban planners have debated this ideological shift from planning spaces for the purpose of emancipation from poverty, inequality, and racial marginality to planning spaces for the purpose of emancipation from boredom. The ideological shift produces a city that makes 'escape', a real, tangible destination.

The Logic behind the Fantasy

I have earlier (in Chapter 3) alluded to Harvey's and Jameson's argument that late capitalism produces the material conditions of postmodernity (Harvey 1989a), and that postmodernism is the cultural logic of late capitalism (Jameson 1984), let me re-visit their arguments here in order to understand this new religion of semiotic aestheticization and the fantastic Disneyfication of urban materiality with a little more clarity. Harvey (2000: 164–65) refers to Marin's (1984: 240) intriguing concept of 'degenerate utopias':

> The example that Marin used [for degenerate utopias] was Disneyland, a supposedly happy, harmonious, and non-conflictual space set aside from the 'real' world 'outside' in such a way as to soothe and mollify, to entertain, to invent history and to cultivate a nostalgia for some mythical past, to perpetuate the fetish of commodity culture rather than to critique it. Disneyland eliminates the troubles of actual travel by assembling the rest of the world, properly sanitized and mythologized, into one place of pure fantasy containing multiple spatial orders. The dialectic is repressed and stability and harmony are secured through intense surveillance and control ... All of this is degenerate, in Marin's view, because it offers no critique of the existing state of affairs on the outside. It merely perpetuates the fetish of commodity culture and technological wizardry in a pure, sanitized, and a-historical form.

Harvey argues that the problem is, utopianism, once materialized in a spatial form, cannot be anything but degenerate. Utopia destroys itself as it becomes realized. Other examples of the nostalgic realization of utopian visions in spatial form include, according to Harvey, the classic shopping mall, an urbanism designed to reproduce the small-town America of the past. The shopping mall is a fantasy world ruled by the commodity, a fantastic, non-conflictual, pleasant, and well-organized environment that sells real commodities with the promise of the unreal: the fairest skin, the spotless face, and the softest mattress. The new urbanism in the US has the single-minded spatial ideology of reinventing the community by getting 'the spatial play right' (Harvey 2000:169). The alienation and inauthenticity of the American city would be overhauled through high-density living, sidewalks, cafes, markets, and bakeries that reinvent the nostalgia of the village community in a series of 'urban villages', that are neat, pretty, and environmentally conscious, and by creating environments in which neighbours know each other and, if they do not, housing associations would ensure that they got to know each other through choreographed activities. For Harvey (following Marin), the spaces of utopia are steeped in irony, because they attempt to reproduce a space, an era, a memory, and a community, but only succeed in producing a caricature that is a commodified version of it. Harvey explained (2000:173):

> But who is at fault here? ... In practice, most realized Utopias of spatial form have been achieved through the agency of either the state or capital accumulation, with both acting in concert being the norm ...The failure of realized utopias of spatial form can just as reasonably be attributed to the processes mobilized to materialize them as to failures of spatial form per se ... But there is a more fundamental contradiction at work here. Utopias of spatial form are typically meant to stabilize and control the processes that must be mobilized to build them. In the very act of realization, therefore, the historical process takes control of the spatial form that is supposed to control it.

For Harvey, the materialization of either a utopia or degenerate utopia is its spatial form, which helps stabilize the contradictions embedded in the processes that work to build it. Free market capitalism is a form of utopianism that Harvey examined: free market capitalism, according to Harvey (1978), is ridden with contradictions that, if not managed, can lead to catastrophic crises that in turn lead to its own demise. Therefore, the free market utopian vision materializes a certain space—which allows it to function and to mitigate its contradictions for the time being—resulting in the production of a space, landscape, or geography in its own image at a particular point of time, which will only be destroyed at a later point in history. The production and destruction of space was essential for managing contradiction, and hence allowing for the continuous accumulation of capital. Capital passes through different circuits of production, creating and destroying spaces in each. In the primary manufacturing sector, the surplus value extracted from the industrial working class through various forms of exploitation—such as lengthening the workday, reducing wages, and replacing labour with machines—is accumulated by the capitalist. A part of this accumulated capital is plowed back into the production process, and the scale of production expands. This circuit is ridden with contradictions because, while the scale of production must expand, the majority class in society—namely, the working class—must be paid low wages, which means that they have low purchasing power and that, as a result, the bulk of society has low purchasing power. In other words, society cannot absorb the continuous expansion of production in addition to the constant lay-off of the working class as technology improves, as this results in a further cut in its purchasing power. The result of these contradictions is a falling rate of profit, which causes capitalists to reduce or stop plowing back profit; when investments stop, capital lies idle and is devalued. In essence, the capitalist class is hit hard and, because of low plow back or low investment, new jobs are not created, resulting in the working class being laid off and the economy facing staggering unemployment. Instead of dealing with the contradictions of continuous expansion and working class exploi-tation, capitalism manages these contradictions in the short term by producing new spaces and new landscapes for productive investment that can end the crisis and jumpstart the economy. Investment in the secondary sector—that is, in the urban built environment—becomes the new arena of capital accumulation. The old industrial landscape, the factory sheds, warehouses, and working-class living quarters of an industrial city must be overhauled, and new condos, apartment blocks, and suburban homes must be constructed to renew the city in the accordance with the image of capital during the contemporary stage in history. This switch from primary to secondary is not automatic and seamless, because a state that is pro-capital must create the institutional structures necessary for smooth transfers by aiding and relaxing its banking and mortgage lending regulations and by guaranteeing and financing projects involving the urban built environment. The appear-ance of crisis in the secondary sector manifests through the overpro-duction of housing stock, malls, and office blocks that lie vacant and unused, leading to a further relaxation of mortgage-lending regulations that often lead to housing market bubbles that eventually burst. Capital then moves to the tertiary sector, in the interest of managing the crisis that has surfaced in the secondary sector. The sectorial shift of capital leaves its own trail of destroyed spaces, which were either overhauled to free up the flow of capital or produced to absorb new investments. The geography of destruction and creation becomes essential for managing the contradictions of capitalism. Therefore, for Harvey, the spaces of utopia are always attempting to 'stabilize and control' the contradictions embedded in the processes that made them. Hence, they are no longer utopian, no longer pure, and no longer perfect, because their materialization involves the destruction of everything utopic. They are degenerate utopias, because they function not for themselves but rather for the purpose of the unhindered accumulation of capital. They are hence unabashedly the projection of efficiency, fantasy, awe, and pleasure. In a similar, but not identical, vein, Marin (1984: 240) claimed:

> Disneyland is the representation realized in a geographic space of the imaginary relationship that dominant groups of American society maintain with the conditions of existence, with the *real* history of United States, and with the space outside of its borders.
>
> This function has an obvious ideological function. It alienates the visitor by a distorted and fantastic representation of daily life, by a fascinating image of the past and the future, of what is estranged and what is familiar: comfort, welfare, consumption, scientific and technological progress, superpower, and morality. These are values obtained by violence and exploitation; here they are projected under the auspices of law and order.
>
> All ideological pressures are brought to the fore here. All forms and aspects of capitalist alienation and of modern imperialism are represented. Disneyland is the representation of the makeup of contemporary American ideology. Because this place of projection where we can view and test out ideology of the dominant groups in American society.

For Marin, Disneyland is not an innocent space, a fantasy world, or a spectacular nostalgia; it is the ultimate materialization of the American empire and the actualization of the corporate colonization of other national economies, of nature, and of people's culture. Mickey Mouse is not just a happy mouse who is angelic, funny, and cartoony; he is also the forbearer of corporate mergers and takeovers, because he eradicates folk artists, indigenous fairytales, and local heroes, as well as destroys local environments through the steamrolling effects of rollercoasters and fantasy castles that leave the stamp of American cultural economic imperialism. He is part of the pantheon of symbols produced by the global elite, and therefore, in the war over worldviews, he is a semiotic imperialism that allows the bourgeois to impose their cultural economic ideology on the world. In this semiotic imperialism, folk tales, indigenous cartoons, and indigenous fairy tales are lost and the Disneylands of the world become the metropolitan centres and colonial headquarters of semiotic control. Disneyland symbolizes class warfare: the ideological and material contradiction between those that have the ability to disseminate their semiotic worldview and those who do not (I. Chatterjee 2009).

Unlike Harvey's critique, Marin's critique of the Disneyland utopia is not a detailed exploration of the mechanics of capital exploitation. Rather, it is an exploration of American capitalist power as an economic, political, and cultural assemblage that has acquired imperial proportions in the contemporary stage of history. For Marin, Disneyland is a metaphor for the contemporary post–World War II neocolonial history of American global dominance. For Harvey, there exists an economic logic to the aesthetic and semiotic production in the postmodern age. The many contradictions of capitalism that lead to its own demise because of the falling rate of profit, devaluation, and unemployment are mitigated in the postmodern age through the production and consumption of the fantastic. The ruthless logic of capital accumulation hides behind the veneer of cultural and aesthetic production and consumption. Semiotics, images, and fantasy projects solve imminent crises of capitalism by absorbing investments and bringing idle capital into the circuit of production and consumption, thus fueling employment and giving a fresh lease on life to late capitalism. Therefore, cultural goods like Disneyland are the glossy veneers that mask the deeper complexities of a contradiction-ridden economic system. These glossy objects penetrate every aspect of life and every inch of land in this world to completely commodify the very conditions of our existence, leaving nothing outside the realm of aesthetic production and capital circulation. To convey the intensity with which commodification proliferates, Harvey (1989a: 336–37) claimed:

'Once the poor become aestheticized, poverty itself moves out of our field of social vision', except as a passive depiction of otherness, alienation

and contingency within the human condition. When 'poverty and home-
lessness are served up for aesthetic pleasure', then ethics is indeed submerged by aesthetics, inviting, thereby, the bitter harvest of charismatic
politics and ideological extremism.

   If there is a meta-theory with which to embrace all these gyrations of
postmodern thinking and cultural production, then why should we not
deploy it?

The postmodern condition, according to Harvey, is a historical material
realization of late capitalism in which capital deploys aesthetic production and leaves nothing outside its circuit, even poverty. This intense
commodification (cultural production) is a necessary condition for the
survival of late capitalism (economy). Therefore, post-industrialization
does not mean the end of the economy or class exploitation, but rather
that, as material consumption (the consumption of goods) reaches
new levels of saturation, capital reinvents new forms of consumption:
the semiotic consumption of aesthetic goods like fantasy, utopia, and
the spectacular. The meta-theory that can conceptualize this postmodern cultural production is the meta-theory of capital's re-invention and
penetration into these new avenues for greater capital accumulation:

> It is conventional these days, for example, to dismiss out of hand any
> suggestion that the 'economy' (however the vague word is understood)
> might be determinant of cultural life even in (as Engels and later Althusser
> suggested) 'the last instance.' The odd thing about postmodern cultural
> production is how much sheer profit-seeking is determinant in the first
> instance. (Harvey 1989a: 336)

Furthermore, again:

> Cultural life is often held to be outside rather than within the embrace
> of this capitalistic logic. People, it is said, make their own history in
> these realms in very specific and quite unpredictable ways depending
> upon their values and aspirations, their traditions and norms. Economic
> determination is irrelevant, even in the famous last instance. I hold this
> argument to be erroneous … Precisely because capitalism is expansion-
> ary and imperialistic, cultural life in more and more areas gets brought
> within the grasp of the cash nexus and the logic of capital circulation.
> (Harvey 1989a: 344)

Therefore, to reiterate, the point that is being made here is that there is an
economic rationality behind the postmodern cultural production—the

economy that determines culture—and it is possible to explain it with a general meta-theory of the circulation of capital and its built-in contradictions. Let us hold this thought for a moment, because there are some brilliant conceptual nuggets here.

I now revert to an additional elaboration of Marin's ideas, in order to bring out some of the similarities and differences in these arguments. Disneyland, according to Marin, is a utopic space. A utopic space, according to Marin, is an ideological discourse where certain systems of ideas, modes of beliefs, and worldviews (ideologies) are put into play. Utopia appears in history only when capitalist production emerges because, according to Marin (1984:198), at this moment in history, the possibility of a 'theoretical (or scientific) universality' comes into existence. This theoretical universality is the possibility of material and epistemological rupture within an existing society, because of the contradictions that exist within it. This rupture is a material–intellectual revolution that actualizes because—within the existing, contradiction-ridden society—there are material–intellectual seeds of conception for a new society, a utopia that can resolve the contradictions of the existing society. At this juncture, Marin differentiated between the material revolution that occurs in the economic conditions of production and the ideological superstructure in which humans become aware of the material contradictions. At the discursive level, the superstructure, or utopia, raises consciousness and indicates how these contradictions work in the economic base, as well as how we can think of them, theoretically or conceptually. The utopic discourse is therefore critical and ideological, because it explicates the contradictions of existing society while allowing us to conceptualize a new one. A degenerate utopia, according to Marin, is one that would lose its critical quality and become a watered-down product of the very ideology that produced it. Therefore, instead of explicating the material contradictions of society and providing the conceptual tools for understanding it, a degenerate utopia becomes an extension of the dominant ideology of a given society interested in keeping these contradictions hidden. More specifically, utopia emerges with the capitalist mode of production, and has the ability to anticipate, in a theoretically universal way, the scientific history of a society. Therefore, it has a great critical edge and revolutionary potential. However, a degenerate utopia becomes an extension of the dominant ideology; in the case of a capitalist society, it simply represents the dominant class, obfuscating the true contradictions in which humans are embedded. Disneyland is a degenerate utopia, as it represents, in all its aesthetic and semiotic might, the importance of the consumption of the unreal, in which Sleeping Beauty's castle, the pirate ship, and Winnie the Poo's private quarters all become unreal real spaces that must be purchased. The ideology of consumption is pushed by the dominant class in order to make consumers of us all, so that the real contradictions of profit accumulation and exploitation are materially and conceptually subverted. However, the beauty of Marin's analysis is that he did not treat the participant as a mere dupe who consumes this degenerate utopia in a mind-numbing stupor. Because utopia always contains within itself the conceptual seeds for the critique of the society it is embedded in, Marin (1984: 241) contended:

> We can examine how the visitors' tour becomes a narrative, how their itinerary becomes a narrative, how their itinerary becomes 'lexical', revealing a reading for the picture as a whole. The divergent systems then emerge, pitted one against the other, and their correlations can be examined. Thus the backstage workings are revealed, and their ideological meanings and repercussions can be pinpointed. It is at this point that a degenerate utopia, changed into text and image, can start to produce. It should tell us what we have known since the development of theory of political economy and ideology.
>
> In other words, the visitors to Disneyland are put in place of the ceremonial storyteller. They recite the mythic narrative of the antagonistic origins of society... Their path through the park is the narrative, recounted umpteen times, of the deceptive harmonization of contrary elements, of fictional solution to conflicting tensions. By 'acting out' Disney's utopia, the visitor 'realizes' the ideology of America's dominant groups as the mythic founding narrative of society.

Therefore, for Harvey, the cultural production–consumption of postmodernism hides the true logic of late capitalism and its contradiction. For Marin, the cultural production–consumption in Disney's utopia, or in a degenerate utopia, reveals the contradictions of capitalism. Here 'correlations can be examined', 'backstage workings are revealed', and 'ideological meanings and repercussions pinpointed' when the visitor becomes embedded in the narrative. In becoming the narrative, or becoming 'lexical', the visitor becomes aware of the deceptive harmony that binds contradictory elements and realizes the fictional solutions that are proposed for real contradictions. In 'acting out', the visitor is no longer 'acting in' a play by merely speaking rehearsed script; she demystifies the ideology of America's dominant class—the mythic narratives of the 'American dream', 'social mobility', 'freedom', and 'democracy'—that is constructed to hide the contradictory elements of poverty, inequality, privatized health care, torture, drone attacks, and the support of dictatorial and fascist regimes.

Marin made no attempt to separate culture from economy and politics, or from space and society. The conceptual tool that is used to relationally bind all these elements together in an organic whole is 'utopia', which is simultaneously envisioned as a place, a discourse, and a practice. Marin's is a dialectical attempt to understand capitalist society—and, in some places of the book, American imperialism and hegemony—through the philosophical lens of utopia. Ideology becomes the glue that is implicated in 'acting out' (to borrow Marin's phrase) utopia. Unfortunately, this dialectic is rudely interrupted when he, in one instance, reverts to the dual model of 'economic conditions of society' and the 'ideological superstructure'. He is, of course, quick to point out that this superstructure, or the conceptual domain, is inseparably tied to the material conditions. Utopic space/utopic discourse actualizes this co-imbrication of the material and ideological, thus bringing together the economic condition–ideological superstructure divide. This dichotomy is so fleeting that I intend to give Marin the benefit of doubt, and instead agree to read his work as a dialectical analysis of capitalism's spectacular geographies. Bringing Harvey's analysis of capitalism back in, it should be noted that Harvey, like Marin, considered the capitalist mode of production as foundational for cultural production–consumption under postmodernism. However, the difference is that Harvey states categorically that the economic base determines the cultural superstructure in a particular stage of history called late capitalism. To emphasize this, let me reiterate a sentence from the text I quoted earlier: 'It is conventional these days, for example, to dismiss out of hand any suggestion that the "economy" (however the vague word is understood) might be determinant of cultural life...'(Harvey 1989: 336). For Harvey therefore, even though it is unconventional and out of fashion, it is important to emphasize that in the first and the last instance, the meta-theory of postmodern cultural production-consumption is *produced* by the economy.

Jameson (1984) contended that postmodern theorists have been vociferous in their ideological claim that this postmodern era of art, architecture, technology, media, and aesthetics signifies a break from the laws of capitalism, specifically the structures of industrial production and class struggle. Therefore, according to postmodern theorists, this era is post-industrial and post-economic; it does not put forward an agenda for revolution or a blue print for change, but rather is purely cultural. This cultural turn is for its own sake in the here and now, and not a means for any larger end. Jameson, however, took a different view, aligning himself with the dominant Marxist position (for example, Harvey's and Marin's) that postmodernism is actually a return to a purer stage of capitalism and not a break from it. Like Harvey, Jameson believed that the economy does form the underlying base for cultural production. For example, he states:

> What has happened is that aesthetic production today has become integrated into commodity production generally: the frantic economic urgency of producing fresh waves of ever more novel-seeming goods (from clothing to airplanes), at ever greater rates of turnover, now assigns an increasingly essential structural function and position to aesthetic innovation and experimentation. Such economic necessities then find recognition in the institutional support of all kinds available for the newer art, from foundations and grants to museums and other forms of patronage. Architecture is, however, of all the arts that closest constitutively to the economic, with which, in the form of commissions and land values, it has a virtually unmediated relationship: it will therefore not be surprising to find the extraordinary flowering of the new postmodern architecture grounded in the patronage of multinational business, whose expansion and development is strictly contemporaneous with it. (Jameson 1984: 56–7)

However, instead of referring to this culture–economy dialectic as the new economic rationale for cultural production, he preferred to emphasize the 'cultural dominant', claiming that postmodernism provides the cultural logic for innovative ways in which multi-national capital is re-inventing itself:

> I have felt, however, that it was only in the light of some conception of a dominant cultural logic or hegemonic norm that genuine difference could be measured and assessed. I am very far from feeling that all cultural production today is 'postmodern' in the broad sense I will

be conferring on this term. The postmodern is however the force field
in which very different kinds of cultural impulses—what Raymond
Williams has usefully termed 'residual' and 'emergent' forms of cultural
production—must make their way. If we do not achieve some general
sense of a cultural dominant, then we fall back into a view of present history as sheer heterogeneity, random difference, a coexistence of a host of
distinct forces whose effectivity is undecidable. This has been at any rate
the political spirit in which the following analysis was devised: to project
some conception of a new systemic cultural norm and its reproduction,
in order to reflect more adequately on the most effective forms of any
radical cultural politics today. (Jameson 1984: 57)

Therefore, Jameson, like Harvey, ascribes to the broad Marxist position
of an intertwined economy-culture base-superstructure model. Unlike
Harvey, he prefers to emphasize that there is a cultural logic to late
capitalism, rather than the reverse. According to Jameson, postmodern capitalism is a simulacrum for which no original exists, and it is
a society rendered deeply cultural because of the circulation of image
over object, the copy over the real, and the exchange value over the use.
This cultural turn is not benign and coincidental. It did not just happen, and it provides a new system of signification and a new world of
semiotics through which globalizing multinational capital can invent
new strategies of exploitation and accumulation by remaining faceless.
Out-sourcing, sub-contracting, the global disaggregation of labouring
groups, rebuilding war-ravaged economies, and financing environmental catastrophe all provide new cultural tool-kits for exploitation and
accumulation beyond the 'classic', factory-style, worker–versus–capitalist models. In that context, the cultural logic is so ubiquitous, all-pervasive, and penetrative that a critical rupture is almost impossible:

No theory of cultural politics current on the Left today has been able to
do without one notion or another of a certain minimal aesthetic distance,
of the possibility of the positioning of the cultural act outside the massive Being of capital, which then serves as an Archimedean point from
which to assault this last. What the burden of our preceding demonstra-
tion suggests, however, is that distance in general (including 'critical distance' in particular) has very precisely been abolished in the new space of
postmodernism. We are submerged in its henceforth filled and suffused
volumes to the point where our now postmodern bodies are bereft of spatial coordinates and practically (let alone theoretically) incapable of dis-
tantiation; meanwhile, it has already been observed how the prodigious

new expansion of multinational capital ends up penetrating and colo-
nizing those very pre-capitalist enclaves (Nature and the Unconscious)
which offered extraterritorial and Archimedean footholds for critical
effectivity...What we must now affirm is that it is precisely this whole
extraordinarily demoralizing and depressing original new global space
which is the 'moment of truth' of postmodernism. (Jameson 1984: 87–8)

The dominance of the cultural logic is so profound and spectacular
that our 'postmodern bodies' are completely submerged in it, and our
postmodern consciousness is so stupefied that we are incapable of critiquing this cultural logic of late capitalism in spite of the ubiquitous
geographies of exploitations, colonizations, and devastations in which
we are steeped. However, Jameson, like Marin, believes that demystification, achieving 'critical distance', and finding the 'Archimedean point'
for critical assault is a dialectical process. Like Marx, he encouraged us
to think of this cultural dominant as both positive and negative. It is
negative because it is all-penetrative, mind-numbing, ubiquitous, and
allows the absolute seeping of multination capital everywhere, therefore creating a 'demoralizing and depressing original new global space'.
It is also positive, because it may contain within it the seeds of its own
critique and the conditions for transcendence, and hence emancipation from the very structures of exploitation that render it culturally
stupefying. Therefore, the cultural logic of late capitalism may allow the
'postmodern bodies' the ability of 'acting out' and disrupting the semiotic ideologies that multinational capital has inscribed everywhere.
Such disruption will occur, according to Jameson, through a project
of *disalienation*, which involves a new aesthetic of cognitive mapping.
Therefore, in his own words:

> In a classic work, *The Image of the City*, Kevin Lynch taught us that the
> alienated city is above all a space in which people are unable to map (in
> their minds) either their own positions or the urban totality in which
> they find themselves: grids such as those of Jersey City, in which none of
> the traditional markers (monuments, nodes, natural boundaries, built
> perspectives) obtain, are the most obvious examples. Disalienation in
> the traditional city, then, involves the practical reconquest of a sense of
> place, and the construction or reconstruction of an articulated ensemble
> which can be retained in memory and which the individual subject can
> map and remap along the moments of mobile, alternative trajectories.
> Lynch's own work is limited by the deliberate restriction of his topic to

the problems of the city form as such; yet it becomes extraordinarily suggestive when projected outwards onto some of the larger national and global spaces we have touched on here. Nor should it be too hastily assumed that his model—while it clearly raises very central issues of representation as such—is in any way easily vitiated by the conventional poststructuralist critiques of the 'ideology of representation' or mimesis. The cognitive map is not exactly mimetic, in that older sense; indeed the theoretical issues it poses allow us to renew the analysis of representation on a higher and much more complex level. There is, for one thing, a most interesting convergence between the empirical problems studied by Lynch in terms of city space and the great Althusserian (and Lacanian) redefinition of ideology as 'the representation of the subject's *Imaginary* relationship to his or her *Real* conditions of existence'. Surely this is exactly what the cognitive map is called upon to do, in the narrower framework of daily life in the physical city: to enable a situational representation on the part of the individual subject to that vaster and properly unrepresentable totality which is the ensemble of the city's structure as a whole. (Jameson 1984: 89–90)

Disalienation involves disruption and demystification from the aura and stupefaction that is produced by the spectacle of cultural production–consumption, while the alienated city is a place in which the stupefied subject is unable to map her position in the totality of urban existence. Disalienation involves the ability to recapture this lost sense of place in the world, as well as the ability to hold it in memory and then represent it through maps. A cognitive map, according to Jameson, is not a simple imitation of coordinates, grids, and objects in space, but also an ideological link between the subject's experiential position and the abstract, conceptual scientific knowledge that emerges from it. Ideology, therefore, represents a subject's 'Imaginary relationship to his or her *Real* condition of existence'. The cognitive map is that ideological representation. What utopia does for Marin, cognitive mapping does for Jameson: they are ideological in the sense that they represent someone's sense of place as she imagined it to be in the context of the toils or comforts of existence. An exploited subject's ideology, or the working class' scientific abstraction, is different from a ruling class' conceptualization, because they are steeped in different experiential contexts: the working class is exploited, the ruling class is not. Experience and its rendering into scientific abstraction that enables knowledge, is an ideological act. An ideological act is always steeped in a representational dialectic, because ideology is always the act of representing someone's experience. A cognitive map allows for a 'situational representation', rather than an abstract representation, because it presents the particular nitty-gritty of someone's sense of place in the context of the larger totality of existence. Therefore, disalienation or disenchantment from the spectacle of postmodernism's cultural production–consumption will be a political act of global cognitive mapping in which the global exploitative geography of multinational capital will be represented in a new way. In this new representational dialectic, people will re-gain their individual and collective (class, gender) sense of place, situated within the global. The new representational dialectic will be a new ideological project that will break through the stupor of cultural stupefaction, actualizing disalienation.

A Cognitive Map of the Fantastic

The Akshardham temples in India[1] (located in Ghandinagar, Gujarat, and New Delhi) embody all the ornate white grandeur of their counterparts abroad, with hundreds of acres of lawns, gardens, huge reflecting polls, beautifully paved garden paths and courtyards, exquisitely carved domes, pillars, arches, and beautifully decorated Hindu idols in gold and gaudy colours. However, they are different from the temple complexes abroad, in the sense that the Indian temples go all out to reproduce Disney's theme park; if Disneyland sold religion, it would look like the Akshardham complexes in Ghandinagar and New Delhi. A temple representative in the New Delhi temple mentioned:

> It is very important to give concrete shape to the mystical abstractions of religion and spirituality, so that people who don't know us can understand us. Special core group of saints were sent all over the world to see and study spectacular representations of space, search for the technology that is out there so that they could have a global perspective on how to organize space, design the architecture, and conceptualize Akshardham as an awe-inspiring site for the display of Indian culture. The water show was started in 2010, a French architect having a global reputation of designing water shows in Las Vegas, Paris, Singapore, and Tokyo, was commissioned. This sound and light water show is the first of its kind in India, and visitors can experience it after sunset for a nominal fee of seventy-five rupees.[2]

Visitors of all religions are welcome, and no entrance fee is charged. Cameras and mobile devices are to be left at the gate at the temple entrance, and visiting the inner chamber and viewing the idols are both free of charge. However, beyond this spiritual moment of one-to-one connection with God, the rest of the temple space is a schizophrenic diorama of exhibition halls, theatres, water shows, and boat rides, each of which is a packaged landscape sold separately for a price that varies between adults, children, and senior citizens. The star attractions are the water and laser-light show that features after sunset and the mystical boat-ride through 'Vedic India'. Themed spirituality is elegantly, efficiently, and meticulously managed. Visitors first follow a spotlessly clean and rationally organized garden space leading into the temple complex and, as they exit from their spiritual moment with the gods, they are automatically guided into a series of themed exhibition halls and movie theatres leading to the indoor 'cultural boat ride'. The boat ride culminates into the 'garden of India' and the 'lotus garden', and then the visitors finally find themselves arriving at the laser and musical fountain show.

The exhibition halls are a spectacular array: they pack the surprise and awe of Madame Tussaud's, natural history museums and planetariums all rolled into a single hall. Audio-animatic technologies are used to simulate mystical conversations between Lord Swaminarayan and the other ancient sages, transposing the visitors into the fantasy world of a proto-historic forest replete with life-like plastic trees, realistic moss hanging from the branches, the sounds of a trickling stream, and visions of sparking water splashing over fake rocks. It is an echo of a Vegasesque spectacle—in Las Vegas, one easily slips from the Arabian deserts to the depths of the Amazon forest while moving from the hallway of one hotel to another. It is a Disneyesque spectacle—in Disneyland, as one lowers one's head to enter the neat little home in which Mickey and Minnie Mouse dwell, one is led through the quaint kitchen with fake cupcakes baking in a fake oven before stepping out into a fake vegetable garden where a sign indicates the way to the Pirates of the Caribbean ship. The Akshardham temples borrow the spirit of Vegas and Disneyland and use it for a spiritual organization of space and time. The exhibition halls at Akshardham not only sell fantasy and awe, they also culturally produce India within a subset of Hindu mysticism where spirituality, saffron clad saints, and philosophical prose from ancient books like the Vedas and Upanishads become the sign value of cultural production and consumption. The abstract history of India becomes coterminous within the plastic concreteness of a very specific Hindu lens, in which Muslims, Sikhs, and Christians are non-existent, the grotesque stories of oppression of some of these religious minorities are un-mentioned, and the horrifying saga of caste exploitation, the casting-out of forest and indigenous peoples, and the marginalization of women are sanitized to present a diorama of a very patriarchal Hindu narrative. Such a narrative may or may not be conscious of what it erases, but it is intensely aware of the importance of packaging and theming its mystical spirituality so that the path to *nirvana* (salvation) becomes a cultural product that is almost vaguely attainable by being present in this synthetically produced space–time. The visitors 'act out' their fantastic presence in fantasy time–space to consume a spirituality that makes God attainable just like the tangible touch of Mickey's gloved hand as he stands at the doorway shaking hands with every visitor.

From the depths of a proto-historic forest, one disjunctures into a black space filled with gleaming stars and planets shining with a greenish-blue radiance. One transcends their earthly abode to be placed in the centre of space as the Milky Way washes visitors in a violet glow of focused lighting. As the eye adjusts to the contrasting waves of darkness and bedazzling neon glow of stars and planets all around, one faintly perceives Lord Swaminarayan's image slowly descending from the heavens on to the polished metal surface of a glowing earth as a flood of happy music fills the visitor, earth, and heavens. The awestruck audience, in a dazed stupor, silently follows into the carefully simulated slopes of the mighty Himalayas, where Lord Swaminarayan's idol is depicted as meditating, standing on one leg on the banks of Mansarovar Lake. Backdrops of artistically created caves and rope-bridges hanging over fake lakes that are beautifully encrusted with pebbled beaches combine to create a swift disjuncture from real life: the audience is immediately transported from their daily mundane world of negotiating their city, job, kitchen, and school to an adventurous spiritualism that no tourism agency can provide. Not only are they standing within an extreme mountain scene that, in reality, could only be accessed by the most professional of mountaineers, they are also forming the narrative within which an incident of spiritual enlightenment is being attained. For a little bit of money, themed spirituality allows a drive-through version of a spiritual high, a happy combo of witnessing salvation while also being part of it, very briefly and fleetingly, before the halls, scenes, and themes change, leaving the audience desiring more and, hence, wanting to return and drive through the spiritual journey again. A dazed audience not only consumes the aesthetics of religious production, it simultaneously becomes a part of it: the exhibition halls and their dioramas are a simulacrum, an identical copy for which no original actually existed. The images of the artificial lakes, the fake rocks, and the imitation bridges all create a spectacle, a fantasy that becomes the momentary reality that the audience can purchase for a price. Images replace reality, as salvation and spiritual purification become the exchange value that transcends their use values. From the Himalayan Mansarovar, a visitor is taken to the moist jungles of Cherrapunji in Assam. Extreme environmental impediments are exaggeratedly simulated in order to communicate to the audience the earthly difficulties that Lord Swaminarayan encountered in his path to nirvana. Rain-making machines and pumps continuously shower water droplets in the midst of a foggy green tropical forest to cleverly simulate the humid environs of northeast India. Electronically operated plastic owls sit on plastic trees intermittently hooting and eerily rotating their heads a full three-hundred-and-sixty degrees, and plastic snakes with gleaming red light-bulb eyes hiss. Fake clouds float over fake springs that ripple with fake rapids to complete the wonderland of pleasure and pain.

The dioramas of pleasure and pain are interspersed with auditoriums featuring, at regular intervals, an enticing combo of video, sound, and light shows, and fibre-optic cosmos depict the story of child Swaminarayan in a 45-minute movie titled 'Mystique India'. Real actors trace the life of the saint from childhood to adulthood as background narrators explain—in English, Hindi, and Gujarati—a story set two hundred years ago, now carefully reconstructed through emotive acting and a deeply authoritative narration of a picture of India steeped in spirituality and godliness. The audience is extolled to experience pride in the mysticism, sacredness and metaphysical qualities of their nation—qualities that cannot be earned or produced, but must be bestowed by the divine when he is pleased with the sacrifice, spirituality, and enlightenment of his male saints, who gave up their wives, families, and the comforts of their homes to be one with nature and with the divine. However, as soon as the film ends, the spiritual tension that holds the audience's gaze is snapped, and the crowd jumps out of their seats like children wanting to catch the next carousel ride, running to the door in order to get the best seats in the next themed space in anticipation of the next round of entertainment.

One star-attraction is the 15-minute, indoor boat ride over a synthetic stream, which takes the visitor through a simulated version of the Saraswati River and 10,000 years of Vedic India. For a little money, with special concessions for children and adults, the peacock-shaped boats carry the audience through a selective mystical history of Hindu India, extolling its ancient greatness in the spheres of science, technology, education, and politics. A background voice and Vedic chanting give context to the life-like collage of displays along the banks, and the ceiling light-up in a bright firmament of stars and planets. Themed settings, replete with Madame Tussaud–like figures, depict scenes from the past, showing the first bazars, markets, and global hubs of trade and economics, therefore grounding a political economy of global mercantilism in a mythical India. The town of Lothal is depicted as the world's oldest commercial port. The prestigious historic university of Taxila, which is an archaeological site in the northwestern part of undivided India (now in Pakistan), is shown in real-time as a thriving global educational center with wax figures that depict international students entering the university as a background voice proclaims that its global appeal was so profound that students came from Greece and China. In another scene, advancement in medical science is displayed in the first Vedic hospitals, where Vedic priests are displayed performing everything from brain surgery to plastic surgery, Vedic dentists attending to teeth, and Ayurvedic doctors dispense medicines. Scientists and mathematicians are displayed as they discover zero, study the eclipse, and calculate the circumference of the earth, and geoscientists are shown calculating the laws of gravity thousands of years before Newton. Other settings focus on the Vedic exercise of yoga and the Bharatnatyam dance form as indigenous art forms invented in India, along with the game of chess, which is emphasized as the 'intellectual game'. Political scenes depict the first elections and, hence, depict India as the first nation to give birth to democracy. Hindu epics and religious figures from different parts of India are shown weaving the indigenous spiritual-cultural fabric of the nation. The ride concludes with the background voice concluding that India is a 'land of enlightenment' while a mass of men, women, and children, all adorned in prominently Hindu clothing, stand at the bank of the river carrying the Indian flag. The boat transports the visitors from a very particular fantasy of Lord Swaminarayan's life and the evolution of Swaminarayan Hinduism to a more national and global fantasy of India's place in the world. Interestingly, instead of looking into contemporary India, the fantastic travel through time goes back to a partial past that is a combination of fantasy, history, mythography, and proto-history. In a fascinating post-colonial saga of re-inventing the great nation before it was defiled and deformed by foreign influence and British imperialism, the selective construction of India takes a mystical form. A glorious history of science, technological, and cultural achievement is presented like a picture book with many pages missing. The arrival of the Aryans and the establishment of Vedic culture through the conquest of indigenous people, and the marginalization of indigenous culture, technology, civilization, and history is untold, as if Vedic culture was founded on a vacant land and started as a clean slate. The process through which the indigenous people of India became outcasts through the creation of a caste system and, therefore, the institutionalization of a racist order of purity–pollution (Srinivas 1962,); the Mughal (Muslim) influence in art, architecture, science, and in the creation of fantastic urban landscapes like the Taj Mahal; the marginalization of women from education; and bride burning, or *sati* (Chakravarti 1962), are some of the missing pages that form the dark underside of this golden history. A postmodern subject capable of wresting the 'Archimedian point' and 'critical distance' is forced to reckon with the ideology of selective narration and erasure. Of course, one understands that the purpose behind this aesthetic production is an intelligent business of conducting religion in which accumulation and cultural production are dialectically intertwined, but the visitors want to consume a sense of place in the world that they can be proud of, and they are not interested in being shocked out of this aesthetic gratification by jarring notes of critical self-reflection; where is the fun in that, and why would they pay for it? Therefore, the fantasy land must carefully protect the visitor from the jarring edges of cultural production, and the 'other' in history, the 'different' in mythography, and the 'darkness' in the narrative must always be cast as the villain, the monster, and the decline of the golden age. The mystical boat ride must not feature the villain, monster, and the decline of the golden age; that is not what spectacular fantasies are built upon. The purpose of this spectacle is a continuous circulation of spirituality, mysticism, and wonderment that ensures the spell is never broken. It does not matter if Swaminarayan Hinduism slips into Hindu nationalism, because even as that myth becomes history, the story becomes fact, and the gaps and erasures stand prominent as missing pages, it is through carefully, dazzlingly, and efficiently managing these slippages and transitions that the postmodern schizophrenic spectacle is predicated. The more partitions, breaks, and seams, the prettier the vision that is seen through the kaleidoscope, as long as the partitions, breaks, and seams do not jar the viewers from their cultural stupefaction.

The sound and light show, replete with laser beams, is a Bellagioesque spectacle that is touted as the first of its kind in India. Visitors can spend some time in the gardens enjoying the herbs, the statues of idols, and the reflecting pools, and children can hop on the various rides while they wait for the sun to set and the light and laser show to begin. Once again, the visitors must pay an additional charge to partake in the experience of the Sat-Chit-Anand water show, with its 130-foot-high and 70-foot-wide water screen, 4,000 nozzles, 2,000 lights, 100 pumps, and 160-foot-long 'sea of fire' spectacle, during which fireballs dance and spread over water as 7.1 surround sound system plays. The fountains twirl, rise, spread, and dance to create a flurry of rainbows and spirals. The water synchronizes with the music and engages with the fire, and the elements dance alongside the music, with a voiceover telling stories from the Hindu scriptures, the Upanishads. One would think they were standing in front of the Bellagio in Las Vegas or Versailles in France, but for the spiritual underpinnings of the tale of Nachiketa, the little boy who confronted the god of death. However, the purpose is the same: to cast a spell, weave a fantasy, produce a spectacle, and provide entertainment worth the audience's money. Just as a gambler in Las Vegas, standing in front of the Bellagio fountains, is happy even though he has lost a lot of money, and just as the tourist in Versailles is ecstatic even when she is tired, the devotee in Akshardham experiences the height of this crescendo of entertainment even though she was visiting for a humble spiritual cleansing. The utopia that is Akshardham in India is the grounding of theme-park globalization, a cognitive map of spiritual fulfilment that presents a representational dialectic between who we are and who we become as cultural consumers.

The Dialectics of Globalization and Disalienation

Globalization, I have argued, is complex. There is a lot of truth to the homogenization argument, which states that the era of multinational capital (that is, McWorld) will commodify the un-commodifiable and hence ultimately homogenize all of the unique and traditional forces that are opposed to the logic of accumulation (Barber 2000). There is also a lot of truth to the argument that complete homogenization is never a reality, and that globalization is grounded in accordance to pre-existing path dependencies that often produce completely new modes of interaction (Appadurai 1990). It is also valid that as time and space are compressed (Harvey 2001) due to the increased intensity of spaces of flows (Castells 2000a, 2000b)—such as flows of money, ideas, images, and goods—spaces of places emerge as new local–global hubs that both send and receive globalization. Vasquez and Marquardt (2003) are also accurate in arguing that the deterritorialization of religions from their places of origin, their reterritorialization in new spaces, and their new interaction with the technological world of the media and the Internet produce new hybrid forms. Kamat and Mathew (2003) warned that the hybrid multiculturalisms born from re-rooting in new spaces can be dangerous, because culture becomes de-contextualized, ahistorical, and a kitsch that is innocently disconnected from the havoc and mayhem that produced it. All these ideas speak to the fantasy spaces of the Akshardham complexes in India (the Ghandinagar and New Delhi temples). Mickey Mouse and his corporate entourage makes commodities of the sacred so that it becomes a product that is efficiently organized, rationally managed, and technologically re-produced into a fantastic array of sounds, lights, and simulations. It does seem that 'Mcworld' forces will iron out and overpower the inward-looking 'jihad' forces of tribalism, religiosity, and difference. A new McReligion is in the making, in which Mickey Mouse deftly hands out McSacred on a plate as devotees become consumers in the-drive through alleys of the McTemple. It also seems that this McDonaldization and Mickey-Mouse monopoly is not a one-way process of standardization. The 'local' actively rears its head to mould McDonaldization and Disneyization, indigenizing them enough to become 'native' without going 'too native' (Ritzer and Malone 2000). The Bellagio's fountains tell the tale of the Upanishads. The fibre-optic displays, the fog machines, rain-makers,

LED lights, and the schizophrenic hallways of fantasy re-produce Hinduism, Swaminarayan Hinduism, and the Indian nation. Mickey Mouse is not the idol here; in fact, Mickey is thoroughly converted into his many new avatars as he narrates the tale of Vedic India. It is indeed the time–space compression of globalized reality that has allowed the saints of the Swaminarayan order to visit these themed entertainment-spaces of the world and bring back ideas of the fantastic. It is also this compression that has allowed expert groups, engineers, and the technological knowledge from the Disneylands of the world to travel to Akshardham. The Akshardham temple complexes are indeed 'spaces of places' that transcend their local existence to transmit global flows of religious fantasy: the volume of tourists, web pages, and brochures are all testimony to how far the outreach has extended, and they willingly absorb and ground the global flows of Disneyesque spectacle in order to, as a volunteer described, 'give concrete shape to the mystical abstractions of religion and spirituality, so that people who don't know us can understand us'. They represent a spectacular combination of traditional-technological, Vedic-mediascape, and sacred-cyberoptics into a unique, postmodern hybridity. Of course, the danger of such hybridity is that they are decontextualized from Florida or California, and from their function of producing 'the happiest place on earth' (Disneyland website), and instead channelled into producing 'the most sacred place on earth'. For devotees who have not experienced the entertainment of a Disneyesque theme park, this themed sacredscape is probably a fantastic reification of the divine, and the only way in which the presence of the divine can be experienced. The irony of cultural consumption, of the aesthetiziation of spiritualism, may or may not be revealed here. However, if critical distance is attained, and the 'Archimedean point' is achieved, then such a critical 'revelation' is not impossible.

However, is it necessary to assume that critical distance? Why is it that religious sects cannot present and represent themselves in any way they want? Is the production of fantasy somewhat profane if it is engaged in the business of religion, rather than in the business of Disney Corporation? In answering these questions, it is important to point out that the Akshardham maps are simply a metaphor for the larger global postmodern narrative of aesthetic production and consumption. A religious sect can present and represent themselves in any way they want, but how they are perceived, analysed, and dialectically approached is not in their control. Such a perception, analysis, or dialectics is not a critique of the religious sect and their worldview, but rather a critique of the postmodern reality. A critical stance cannot be escaped, because it is the second nature of a thinking human who wants to understand the complexity of globalization. The last question—that is, whether the production of fantasy is more profane if it is engaged in the business of sacred—is probably the most difficult to answer, and that is where I turn now.

In answering the above, I would like to contend that there is a need to go deeper than the ephemeral conceptualizations of globalization. By ephemeral, I am referring to the formulations discussed earlier (time–space compression, McDonald versus jihad, indigenization, and spaces of flow and spaces of places). Ephemerality is not a bad quality to possess, because it demonstrates the surface appearance of processes and hence provides an important glimpse of what lies beneath. However, what lies beneath must be conceptualized along with the surface occurrences. It is important here, however, to be very clear that, by suggesting a surface–undersurface analogy, I am not referring to a base–super structural model of globalization. Instead, I am calling for deep theories that bind all layers of social reality into an organic whole and encapsulate their complexity in a totality, because such a theory does not—in vertical, horizontal, scalar way, or any other way—fragment reality and, therefore, is true to the dialectical approach that is my agenda.

For Marx and Engels (2002), production is what separated humans from animals: the ability to add labour to matter and transform it into useful forms that can meet sustenance requirements is the inherent genetic code of society, history, and geography. The problem arises when the means of production—or the tools, raw material, and technological knowledge—are forcibly cornered and contained within laws of private property by a few, preventing most others to produce from their own ability as humans. Alienation results because most humans are then separated or estranged from their own labour and forced to sell it for a wage to a class of people who have cornered the means of production. Therefore, production is an inescapable part of existence, but the context of production determines whether the resulting history–geography, or the resulting social reality, is exploitative or not. Alienation is bad, because it is the precursor to exploitation:

humans lose their sense of place in the world as they lose the ability to produce their sustenance, or, in other words, the ability to produce themselves. This means that the alienated human must engage in wage relations to earn sustenance. Wage relations are exploitative, because the class that owns the means of production will, in a capitalist social reality, want to extract more value from the labour than they give to the labour in wages. Therefore, the value produced by labour must be stolen by the owners of the means of production (capitalists) as profit. Profit represents the accumulated stolen value from labour, as well as the material representation of the exploitation of labour. Capitalists must continue to accumulate and re-invest profit in the production process to grow, if they want to stay competitive with other capitalists. Therefore, capitalism is both expansive and inherently global. As local markets are exhausted, local labour is also exhausted and pushed to the level of near-sustenance existence as local raw materials are stripped, and, as a result, capitalism will encounter a crisis. Capital must find spaces outside of itself to mitigate this crisis, and this translates into the globalization of capital in various imperialistic ways (Lenin 1999). This globalization can be in the form of old-style imperialism, such as acquiring colonies, or new-style imperialism, such as multinational corporate penetration, mergers, and takeovers. New-style globalization encapsulates the latter. This part of Marx's work is a deeply dialectical theory of social totality that does not fragment or stratify reality into scales, orders, base–superstructure, or the culture-economy. In my approach towards fantasy, I find this starting point quite useful.

If production is an all-pervasive aspect of reality, then the commodities that emerge from the production process are also an all-pervasive aspect of capitalist social reality. Therefore, commodification, like production, is all-pervasive. In that context, a computer, wheelbarrow, painting, gown, sculpture, building, formal education, physiotherapy, and psychiatry evaluation are all commodities. Religion, belief systems, customs, and traditions are also produced through scriptures, holy books, religious schools, families, and movies, and, although they are intangible, they therefore are, and always have been, within the realm of production; the priests, popes, monks, and sages who have to eke out their sustenance from religion and cultural production understand the importance of commodities quite well. In that context, salvation, confessions, purification of the soul, baptisms, and abhisheks are all commodities that come at a price, and the profit accumulated from the sale of the sacred must be re-invested into expanding the aura of the sacred so that the market is protected and the customer base expanded. Religion has always been global, as is seen in the cultural logic of imperialism, which was often about missionaries saving the souls of heathens. In the capitalist–imperialist era, religious missionaries went global to spread the aura of the Christian God. In the postmodern era of multinational capital and its globalization, religion has also demonstrated a spirit of global production–commodification in the form of the online 'spaces of transcendence' that have allowed for global devotion that not only laterally transcends nations and regions but also creates a fantastic mediation between the grounded materiality of everyday existence and the technological ephemerality of cyber scapes, so that the global devotee spiritually transcends her material existence at the click of a mouse.

The problem is that religion, like capitalism, is fraught with contradictions: it must produce and consume, but the cultural production–consumption must be mediated by the divine. This larger-than-life force—the god and his avatars and saints—that humans have produced, imagined, and worshipped have a greatness and potency that lie in their ability to transcend the 'basest' material forms, money, property, and profit. This is what every religion has in common: the greatest gods, messiahs, and prophets must shun their earthly desires and, in order to do so, separate themselves from the masses. It is in their denouncement of matter that their aura, enigma, and charisma rest. It is in their self-inflicted alienation from the material that they assume greatness and immortality. Alienation is not imposed, but rather self-imposed, and it is a good and divine thing. How to resolve this basic contradiction between the moral need for alienation from the 'material' in order to produce an aura that leads to the accumulation of the 'material' through churches, temples, and synagogues? The survival of religion depends on the production of sacred commodities that are consumed by devotees within the circuit of religion, allowing it to further invest the profit accumulated from the production and consumption of the sacred, and again further expand its aura. However, this production–consumption must be premised on the fundamental principle of alienation from accumulation. How, then, to continue a global multinational business of accumulation if alienation from accumulation must be the very motor on which such a production–consumption system is based? The spectacle of fantasy allows for the momentary resolution of this contradiction. Fantastic spaces, fantastic landscapes, and fantastic cities will enable the production of the divine aura that will preach the value of alienation from accumulation, the spirit of austerity, and sacrifice in a more profound way than ever before. The fantastic city and its themed temple complex will spend millions of rupees to dazzle the devotee, penetrate her soul, cast a spell, and create mixed emotions of pleasure and pain through the use of fibre optics, fireballs, and synthetic streams. The production and consumption of fantasy will enhance the aura of a divine that has self-alienated itself from material wealth. The fantastic production of an efficiently managed, million-dollar spectacle will urge the devotee to alienate herself from a portion of her material accumulation through the purchase of tickets and donations given to the temples in order to be one with god. The contradiction between alienation from the material and the need to accumulate it, is resolved in a more profound way through globalization. Globalization allows the sacred to find an 'outside' of itself in the 'profane' and supremely materialistic worlds hungry for spiritual consumption, and hence a way to open up new spaces for expansion into new markets and new consumer bases within faraway immigrant communities. It also allows for the exploration and mining of new raw materials, like the technology and knowhow of theme-park entertainment from California and Orlando, that can then be extracted and brought within the sphere of sacred production–consumption, so that contradictions can be temporarily resolved.

The visitor/the devotee who enters the fantasy temple produces cognitive maps of fantasy that presents her sense of her material world through the haze of spectacular commodification. Globalization therefore represents a new dialectics of representation in which mapping fantasy creates stupefaction, awe, and hence, prevents disalienation from the spectacle. Disalienation would mean a break, stoppage, or disruption of production–consumption because the global subject has reached her critical distance, an Archimedian point from which she discovers her sense of her material world as a mother, immigrant, or labourer and is able to cognitively map her position in the city, globe, and the social totality. Such a disalienated being does not need the divine to arbitrate the production–consumption of her existence, spectacle loses its appeal, and the devotee no longer feels the spiritual need to donate, contribute, and buy religious artifacts. Her sense of place in the material world is secure, the dialectics of representation between who she really is and what she wants to become is no longer ideologically mediated through the cognitive maps of fantastic spectacles and, if they are, she is able to achieve a critical distance and disrupt that ideology by critiquing it. A critique would mean that the production–consumption of spectacle comes to an end, because the spectacle loses its appeal and its ability to hypnotize the visitor's gaze. As the visitor 'acts out', the utopia reveals its ideology and is rendered degenerate, unspectacular, and profane. Therefore, disalienation is dangerous, and globalization and capitalism must prevent disalienation through the continuous mapping of fantasy.

The business of religion straddles an uncomfortable existence in all of this. It must invest capital in the production of fantasy, but that very investment in megalomaniac spectacles must teach its followers the value of sacrifice, austere living, and alienation from worldly wealth. In other words, all the mystifications of fantasy must teach its followers how to demystify commodification. Therefore, the followers of religion must produce, but they must also resist consumption, save, and siphon large parts of their accumulated gains back into the religious sphere. This plowing back of profit allows an organized religion to spend large portions of its accumulated revenue on cultural-aesthetic production–consumption in society. Therefore, while religion must preach a delinking of consumption from production as a way of life, it must also do the opposite and *produce* fantasy and *commodify* itself in order to mesmerize a general mass of followers. This opposition between what religion must preach and what it must become in order to capture the visitor's gaze is what Marin would claim, is the ideological element of utopias. The concretization of this ideology involves production of utopic landscapes and then their consumption through the sale of the spectacular. It is in this contrariness that the production of fantasy in the religious sphere becomes more problematic than Disney Corporation. Disney Corporation is blatant in its production of fantasy, and in the deep level of commodification in its agenda, because the mantra of such multinational capital is the deep believe that happiness is attained through material consumption; this is why Disneyland is touted as the 'happiest place on earth'. On the other hand, the business of religion must be covert in its production of fantasy, and the biggest spectacle must renounce base attachments, even as those base attachments—money, profit, and private property—are the essential elements that allow religion to survive. Globalization creates a dialectic of representation between who we are and the fantastic 'utopias' that our religions have mapped for us, that prevent our disalienation, and allow the continuation of capitalism/religion. However, if, in 'acting out', the ideology of this utopia is somehow revealed, the fantasy loses its mystique and is rendered profane, disalienation can then emerge as a social totality that challenges multinational capital and multinational religion.

Mapping Fantasy

It is impossible to escape a spectacle today; in fact, spectacles have become the ultimate escape from the boring, mundane, and banal: our everyday landscape is formed by the spectacular mall, the spectacular office building, the spectacular resort, the spectacular convention centre, the spectacular theme park, and the spectacular temple form our everyday landscape. The spectacular landscapes weave fantasy into our daily lives as a dialectic between who we are and what we would like to become. The Cinderella, the Mickey, and the pirate inside us come out in gay abandon as we step into a theme park. The theme park was conceived as the ultimate space of fantasy, where the irrational would be beautifully presented, efficiently managed, and meticulously organized. The post-industrial age called for a respite from the grayness, starkness, and darkness of the inauthentic industrial city through its production–consumption of fantastic goods in places other than factory sheds. Cultural critics have argued that this represents a postmodern era of intensive production and consumption of sign values, which are consumed not for their use, but because of their identity-enhancing properties. Globalization, technological mobility, the easy flow of images and ideas allowed for an even deeper penetration of cultural production–consumption in this postmodern age.

In this chapter, I use the example of theme-park entertainment to conceptually understand cultural production–consumption in postmodern urbanity. In that context, Harvey claimed that there exists an economic rationale behind postmodern cultural production–consumption. The postmodern penchant for an analysis that is non-economic, ahistorical, and non-structural actually serves the interest of capital, because the economic contradictions of accumulation and exploitation underlie the production–consumption of spectacular fantasy that allows multinational capital to render exploitation invisible. Marin focused on Disneyland as a site for aesthetic production–consumption while also arguing that they serve the interest of capital. However, Marin attempted a less deterministic and more dialectical analysis than Harvey. For Marin, utopia, which is a space, discourse, and practice, emerges in history as capitalism emerges. Utopia is so dialectical that it contains within it the possibility of a critique of the very society that has produced it, and is therefore an ideological-material space. A utopia becomes degenerate when it loses out the possibility of this critical exploration. According to Marin, theme-park spaces like Disney World are utopias that present the ideology of the dominant class, as well as the dominant imperialistic nation, in a neo-colonial world. They have become degenerate, because they have lost the ability to critique the exploitation that exists in aesthetic production–consumption. However, according to Marin, it is possible that a visitor in this utopic world becomes a part of this narrative of commodification and, instead of following the lines of the script, actually 'acts out' and reveals the very ideology that produced this narrative; thus, there is hope that a critique may emerge from degenerate utopias. Jameson (1984) argued for a cultural dominance in the postmodern era of multinational capital. He believed that this intense circulation of images, signs, and symbols represents an aesthetic production–consumption that allows multinational capital to continue its accumulation in a very profound way. Therefore, postmodernism is a cultural logic of capitalism. This cultural logic, according to Jameson, is deeply dialectical, because it is simultaneously positive and negative. It is negative because it produces a spectacle that is so shiny that it can create cultural stupefaction, but at the same time, it can engender seeds of critique. A cognitive map, according to Jameson, is akin to Marin's utopia, because it is an ideological representation (representational dialectic) of the postmodern subject's imagination of her place in the world. A representational dialectic is this ideological link between what a postmodern subject imagines herself to be and what she represents herself as being. This dialectic is represented in a cognitive map that a person draws. Alienation occurs when postmodern subjects are so stupefied by the dazzle of aesthetic consumption that they unable to map their position in the city and in the social totality. Alienation therefore, produces cognitive maps of spectacles or utopias that are degenerate. Disalienation involves the ability to once again cognitively map one's place in this city, class, and social totality, and therefore, achieve a critical distance from the aesthetic production–consumption that resulted in alienation in the first place.

I produce a cognitive map of the Akshardham temples in Ghandinagar and New Delhi, India, specifically a cognitive map of the spectacular, themed landscapes that are sold to audiences. I juxtapose the spectacles of Vedic boat rides, mystique India dioramas, and Sat-Chit-Anand water-and-laser shows with the themed spaces of Disneyland. The cognitive map that emerges, reveals a blatant consumption of the spectacular through themed spaces of religious consumption. Globalization therefore, creates cultural stupefaction through dazzling arrays of spectacular consumption and hence, prevents disalienation. Boundaries between religion and capitalism become blurred: like capitalism, organized religion becomes a site where accumulation takes precedence over everything else. But herein lies the contradiction: religion needs donations, contributions, and worldly wealth to survive and expand its reach, but at the same time, it must preach the opposite, that is, renouncement from wealth and worldly desires. An organized production of fantasy, or what I call 'mapping fantasy', provides a temporary resolution from this contradiction. Capital extracted from devotees and visitors are invested in producing spectacular fantasies that allow accumulation to proceed unhindered while, at the same time, these fantastic spaces are themed to teach the values of alienation from accumulation. Globalization—with its ability to circulate technology, engineers, ideas, funds, and themed spaces—creates a dialectic between what a postmodern subject is and what her religion has mapped for her. It is in our ability to 'act out' this ideology of cultural production–consumption that a critical distance may be achieved and disalienation may result, disrupting the sphere of stupefaction so that we can produce alternative maps of who we are and our position in the city, therefore producing an alternative globalization. Such an alternative globalization, or a project of disalienation would constantly demystify spectacles like, Vedic boat rides, water shows, themed temple complexes, and Disney's fairy-tale castles to reveal the ideology of multinational religion and multinational capital so that the distinction between economy and culture disappears.

These spectacles like Disneyland and Akshardham temple complexes are 'degenerate' to the extent that they are complicit with the ideology of multinational capital and multinational religion, but they also hold within them the possibility of achieving a critical distance, a possibility of acting out, a possibility of shaking the stupefaction. In accepting that dialectic between utopia and degenerate utopia, I hope to steer clear of logics that may assign economic causality to postmodern culture, or treat culture as the dominant logic of late capitalism.

Notes

1. The examples in this section are based on fieldwork observations in Akshardham temples of Ghandinagar and New Delhi. No photographs could be provided because taking photos is strictly forbidden within the Akshardham complexes in India.

2. Approximately $1.20.

6 Subjecting Globalization
The Class and Gender of Globalization

Is Globalization on Auto-Pilot?

The city constitutes the materiality of globalization. Globalization, as I have argued, is not just a set of flows (of commodities, people, information, and so on), a set of spatial configurations (networks, nodes, supply chains, and so on), or a set of cultural changes set in motion by a set of economic policies; it is more than that. Globalization involves the reconstitution of the materiality of everyday existence, and the city is the cell in which this reconstitution is brought to fruition. The city synthesizes the culture economy, society–space, and production–signification dichotomies of globalizing reality into an indissoluble synthesis. Therefore, a city is not just a site, but also a concept that explicates the dialectics of globalization. However, this dialectics is not a super-organic machination, a divine plan, or a pre-ordained cosmic ordering, but is driven and shaped by subjects who are agents in constituting the materiality of their existence and whose subjectivities are, in turn, shaped by these materialities. People, therefore, constitute the materialities of globalization: the architectural intricacies of the American Swaminarayan temples, or the Indian flavours in the samosas sold in these Indian-American temples constitute the materiality of globalization. Similarly, the background narration of the Vedic boat rides and the construction and maintenance of laser-and-water shows in the Indian Swaminarayan temples constitute the materiality of globalization. These people, or agents, are not just subjects producing and shaping objects on a material stage called the city. These people are simultaneously the subjects and objects that form the constituted materiality of the city. The city is understood here as a concept that synthesizes the materiality of globalization, and must transcend the object–subject/mind–body dualism, along with all the other dichotomies (society–space, culture–economy, and production–signification).

The classic Cartesian (Descartes 1969) dualism, in which body is material and subject to the laws of physical science while the mind is immaterial and not ruled by the laws of physical science, so deeply permeates our conceptual faculties that it becomes easy to fragment whole realities into agents acting on objects, rather than understanding agents as material-subjects. Merleau-Ponty (1962), in an effort to disrupt the classical Cartesian dualism, referred to agents, or subjects, as 'body-subjects'. According to Crossley (1995), Merleau-Ponty rejected the mechanistic division between mind and body, and instead argued that the human body, as an effective agent, is the very basis of subjectivity. The body, therefore, simultaneously *embodies* both an objective side (or a tangible side, for example: the skin, hands, and eyes) and a subjective side (or an intangible side, for example: the senses and interpretations of those senses). The tangible and intangible are at once aspects of the same being. Embodiment is the basis of experience, consisting of our being in the world and our point of view of the world. Everybody is an embodied subject, and this embodiment is always a position from somewhere, and is never nowhere. The mind–body/object–subject dualism was challenged not only in phenomenological traditions of Merleau-Ponty, but also within the historical materialism of Marx. According to Marx (1970), it is not the consciousness of human beings that determines their existence, but rather, it is their social existence that determines their consciousness. Existence signifies the transformation of the material environment through the act of labouring, and it is through interpreting these acts of labouring that consciousness is informed. Consciousness, mind, and subjectivity are not in a delinked opposition to the body and the material/physical world as Descartes would have us believe; they are dialectically conjoined with it. In that context, consciousness, subjectivity, and the mental are as much a material product as is the act of labouring. Existing is at once both a material and subjective act.

For Marx, this had larger social implications, because act of labouring was never an individual act but always consisted of work done in the social context. Marx was particularly interested in the context of class society. Existing in the working-class context would mean a very different life-world than existing in the bourgeois context. Working-class subjectivities were structured by the conditions of exploitative existence, while the ruling class subjectivities were structured by a need to exploit. Subjectivities are therefore not individualistic, but rather the constituted materialities of a classed existence (Marx and Engels 1975). This is where the historical materialistic version explicitly differs from phenomenological traditions. Phenomenological traditions acknowledge that the body is an embodiment that is positioned somewhere, and this positioning is in relation to the embodiments of other bodies (inter-subjectivity). However, phenomenologists do not explicitly claim that this embodiment and its inter-subjectivity are produced through acts of labouring. Furthermore, phenomenologists do not explain societal subjectivity in the context of an exploited class and an exploiting class. Instead, they focus on perception as the central axis for understanding the constituted materiality of the body–subject, and they are therefore more interested in the discrimination resulting from how one is seen and how one sees.

If the city synthesizes the constituted materiality of globalization, then understanding globalization would require understanding the embodied subjects whose labour shapes the city. To understand globalization as more than just a set of spatial configurations, cultural change, and economic policies, or, in other words, to understand its constituted materiality, it is imperative that we understand the constituted materiality of the subjects that shape globalization and are shaped by it. If globalization is not an abstract, super-organic, cosmological certainty, then it is driven, informed, and shaped by people. This chapter hopes to understand globalization by understanding the subjects that make it and are made by it. These subjects and their subjectivities, as discussed so far, are not to be understood in a mechanistic, Cartesian way as delinked from the materiality of the city, but rather as embodied in it. This chapter hopes to query these subjects and subjectivities in order to understand if and how their embodiment is classed and gendered. In other words, I intend to bring phenomenological notions of embodied subjects together with Marxian notions of labouring and consciousness to understand the subjectivity of globalization.

The Gendered Subject

Women have had a contentious relationship with globalization, especially in the sphere of work. The flight of capital from First World economies to the Third World brought many informal jobs in sweatshops
and export-processing zones, ranging from the Bangladeshi garment
factories to the maquiladoras of Mexico. Ong (2000) argued that this
informal wage work represents curious tropes of exploitation and liberation. On one hand, the proliferating sweat shops, garment-assembly
sites, and industrial homework allow rural women to free themselves
from the traditional patriarchy that exists at home and seek out an
independent, self-sufficient life in the cities where they not only earn a
wage but are free to make decisions on what kind of haircut they want,
and they are even able to save enough to send back to their villages.
However, at the same time, the traditional patriarchy seeps into the
workplace in the form of managers and middlemen who use village
ties, kinship, and clan connections to create new narratives of gender
stereotypes, intimidation, and sexual harassment. The 'new' urban,
global woman, freed from the paddy fields, must learn to negotiate
new forms of patriarchy and frame new kinds of resistance. Ong argued
that, in this complex and nebulous terrain of post-industrial informal
sector exploitation, class struggle is replaced with a cultural struggle
in which gender and kinship often become new sites for launching
covert and subtle forms of resistance against the patriarchy present at
the workplace. These everyday forms of resistance may not bring about
overarching structural transformations, which are often the aim of class
struggles, because they instead struggle over meanings, values, and
goals that play an important role in reshaping everyday attitudes and
norms. Pratt (2004), in her investigation of Filipina nannies in Canada,
used Foucault, Haraway, and Buttler to understand how discourses produce the globalizing women subject in the context of Vancouver. She
also indicated how discourses serve as enabling sites for resistance. Like
Ong, Pratt is grounded in post-structural theory in her attempt to bring
out the multiple subjectivities that make up the gendered geography of
globalization. Discourses are not, according to Pratt, abstract linguistic
formulations, but rather reflect the world while simultaneously constructing it, and therefore are as abstract as they are concrete. In many
ways, they are like the embodied subjects of phenomenology, in that

they simultaneously inflect both the tangible and the intangible aspect of our being in the world and our point of view of the world. For example, the gendered globalized discourses like 'women's nimble fingers' (Fernandez-Kelley 1983) are discourses that are produced by flexible capital to create a subject, but, simultaneously, many women try their best to fit into these discourses in order to be able to make a living. The nimbleness of fingers and docility are not inherent genetic propensities of women, but rather a process of situated discursive production. These discourses are situated because they are locally, geographically, and placially emplaced; the construction of subjectivity is a material process and the embodied subject is located somewhere, because discourses may lose meaning beyond the materiality of their production. The discourses of 'nimble fingers', for example, will have no meaning within the gendered context of the army, where subjectivity of women in the military need not be constructed around nimbleness, because this is not a necessary quality that the patriarchal geopolitics of the military is looking to exploit.

In her study of the Filipina nannies in Vancouver, Pratt (2004) demonstrated how registered nurses from the Philippines are deskilled through immigration. Globalization, therefore, leads to a complete negation of the years of training and the skills accumulated as a nurse. The Filipina leaves her family to participate in the Canadian caregiver programme, under which she must work as a nanny and live in her employer's home for full two years before she can apply for an open visa and invite her family to join her. In participating in that programme, the Filipina becomes a nanny who must live in her employer's home, a new situated practice that creates a new embodied subject emplaced in multiple discourses like: 'being docile', 'eats almost nothing', and 'is non-intrusive', but simultaneously also a 'husband-stealer', and 'less erudite than Eastern European nannies'. These disabling discourses serve as sites of exploitation, and nannies learn to understand the global context of their exploitation by sharing their experiences with other nannies. Therefore, Marx's argument fits here—the consciousness of the nannies is shaped through their working class existence. Pratt argued that these disabling discourses become enabling sites as Filipinas try to produce contra-discourses of feminism, class exploitation, and imperialism that critique the exploitative sites of the employer's home and question the very logic of oppressive institutional programmes like the caregiver programme. These discursive critiques are grounded in the situated practices of exploitation and allow for a 'discursive disruption' of the logic of exploitation. Therefore, the globalizing women subject is not just an unconscious dupe, because her embodiment in the world produces a view of the world that is its very antithesis. It is in imagining this antithesis that a real revolution starts. The question is whether this revolution is a cultural struggle and discursive disruption, or a structural transformation of society. A Marxist approach to globalization tends to focus more on the structural aspects, whereas a more post-structural analysis, like those of Ong and Pratt, tends to focus more on the everyday forms of resistance that may not visibly change structures but are nonetheless grounded in the formation of a subject that critiques global capital. Post-structural feminists like Ong and Pratt share their penchant for embodied subjectivity with phenomenologists: the subject, the agent, is an important component in framing an alternative to exploitation. There is a diversity of opinions in terms of what this alternative is; for example, as discussed earlier, Ong argued for a cultural struggle in place of class struggle. On the other hand, those like Pratt, view all kinds of nested possibilities in which cultural struggles are not separate from a discursive struggle against class and imperial exploitation. The only difference from a more explicit Marxist formulation is the plea for understanding multiple subjectivities like race and gender, as well as how they shape, and are shaped by, discourses. The argument seems to be that without a firm grasp of discursive deconstruction, it would be impossible to understand the complex terrains of exploitation eked out by contemporary globalization. In a world of disappearing factories, growing informalization, flight of capital and proliferation of sweatshops, global migration of labour, and gender-, race-, and ethnic-specific exploitation of immigrant labour, a singular model of class exploitation and labour-union politics falls far short of comprehending reality.

On the other hand, socialist feminists like Eisenstein (1999) and Fraser (2009) argued that subjectivity, identity, and recognition often lead to exploitation's complete de-centering from class. The result is a cry for identity validation around race, sexuality, and ethnicity that leads to an identity politics with absolutely no vision for political–economic emancipation. Culture and economy are severed into two separate worlds, with cultural validation taking precedence over questions of redistribution. What results is communitarian, tribal, indigenous, and gay-lesbian movements for identity validation that leave global capital unscathed. Globalizing multinational capital is particularly willing to grant concessions for multiculturalism, sexual freedom, and women's freedom from both the village and factory, because these struggles distract from the fact that global capital actually uses these freedoms for ever more virulent forms of commodification and exploitation. Fraser (2009: 108) commented:

> Neoliberalism's rise coincided with a major alteration in the political culture of capitalist societies. In this period, claims for justice were increasingly couched as claims for the recognition of identity and difference. With this shift 'from redistribution to recognition' came powerful pressures to transform second-wave feminism into a variant of identity politics. A progressive variant, to be sure, but one that tended nevertheless to overextend the critique of culture, while downplaying the critique of political economy. In practice, the tendency was to subordinate social-economic struggles to struggles for recognition, while in the academy, feminist cultural theory began to eclipse feminist social theory. What had begun as a needed corrective to economism devolved in time into an equally one-sided culturalism. Thus, instead of arriving at a broader, richer paradigm that could encompass both redistribution and recognition, second-wave feminists effectively traded one truncated paradigm for another.

Therefore, for Fraser, the 'cultural struggles' that Ong referred to are not an effective and impactful critique of globalization and multinational imperialism, but simply a coopting of gender, racial, clan, tribal, and indigenous subjectivities within the insidious forms of flexible accumulation. Middlemen, managers, and subcontractors use village, clan, and tribal ties to stereotype and exploit women workers at the behest of a neoliberalism that has learned to use identity politics to its advantage. The result is a 'feminist romance', an almost 'false consciousness' that, in a haze of stepping out of domestic patriarchy, misidentifies patriarchy at work as the new global vantage point from which economic emancipation would be launched. It is Fraser's (2009: 111) contention that

> the feminist romance attracts women at both ends of the social spectrum: at one end, the female cadres of the professional middle classes, determined to crack the glass ceiling; at the other end, the female temps, part-timers, low-wage service employees, domestics, sex workers, migrants,

epz workers and microcredit borrowers, seeking not only income and
material security, but also dignity, self-betterment and liberation from
traditional authority. At both ends, the dream of women's emancipation
is harnessed to the engine of capitalist accumulation.

In other words, multiple subjectivities, and the discursive production
and disruption of those subjectivities, are all very well and good, but
somehow the analysis of global capitalism loses its edge because of
an emphasis on a purely cultural subject who is unable to discern the
economic aspects of exploitation. The new wave of 'global' jobs that
proactively seek women either in the form of call-centre jobs, sweat
shop jobs, sex work, or in product-assembly plants all seduce women
workers into believing that globalization economically emancipates
women. In reality, however, globalization preys on women, this time
by not excluding them from the job market, but rather by ghettoizing
them through flexible forms of exploitation. Eisenstein (1999: 511)
echoed similar sentiments:

> A World Bank official noted that 'women remain a "huge, untapped"
> resource in the Middle East and North Africa, where more women work-
> ers are needed to transform economies that must depend increasingly
> on private-sector exports to compete worldwide.' This, however, goes in
> tandem with the other orthodoxies of neoliberalism, which require the
> state to withdraw funds and institutional support from the services most
> required by women.
>
> The workings of international capital, then, systematically dis-mantle
> the structures, however inadequate, that protect women and their chil-
> dren—ranging from health care, education, housing, to affordable food
> and fuel—thus creating intensified poverty, disease, and unprecedented
> levels of wealth polarization. But they simultaneously invite women
> into the market economy, arguing that this is the path to liberation and
> equality (Chossudovsky 2003, 67–8). The legitimization of feminism
> masks the radical restructuring of the world economy, and the glitter of
> economic liberation disguises the intensification of poverty for the vast
> majority of women.

Both Eisenstein and Fraser emphasized the need for a nuanced
understanding of the economic devaluation of the economic–cultural
subject, women, and therefore implied that a critique of neoliberal globalization cannot just be a subversive cultural struggle or a discursive
disruption, but rather must be a concerted struggle not only for cultural

affirmations (recognition), but also for economic emancipation (redistribution) as well.

I have in the past (I. Chatterjee 2012) tried to bring these divergent understandings of women subjectivity into conversation with each other by arguing that women's embodiment in the context of globalization should be conceptualized using Marxian and Gramscian notions of false consciousness, rather than merely understood as co-optation. I quote an excerpt from my earlier work here, because it seems pertinent to the discussion:

> False consciousness indicates moments when structures of exploitation have not been identified, or have been misidentified by the exploited. Co-optation, however, signifies moments where the exploited intentionally partake in exploitative mechanisms lured by promises of personal gain. There exists a conceptual difference between the two. False consciousness holds possibilities for change from 'within', and hence holds possibilities of civil hegemony when structures of exploitation are organically demystified. Co-optation, on the other hand, is a theoretical closure to all resistance, because the co-opted woman is understood as a mere dupe choosing to extend exploitation for short-term 'gains'.
>
> ... Gender exists in a complex assemblage of class, ethnicity, religion, and caste to produce multi-dimensions of 'actually existing women' and 'actually existing feminisms'. Feminist consciousness is therefore indissoluble from an assemblage of other forms of consciousness... (I. Chatterjee 2012: 795)

My argument is for a dialectical understanding of the woman-subject in which her cultural being is indissolubly inflected with her economic being to produce the person as she actually exists. Some facets of this person may not recognize the real contexts of exploitation as she embarks on becoming the 'women temp' and the sweatshop worker, but not all of her personhood is mystified by false consciousness. There may be aspects of her that are intensely critical of a neoliberal system that is dismantling health care, food stamps, and unemployment compensations that benefit women. Therefore, the same person is an assemblage of false and real consciousness; she is not always all cultural, she is not always all identity politics. If globalization is producing her subjectivity, if she is shaping globalization, if globalization as a social reality is simultaneously economic and cultural, and if subjects are not piecemeal beings with separate economic and cultural compartments, then there is no reason to assume that a conscious, embodied subject cannot, at some point, conceptualize the economic with the cultural. In my attempt to bring a more post-structural analysis, which draws on Ong 2000 and Pratt 2004, into conversation with a more Marxist analysis, which draws on Eisenstein 1999 and Fraser 2009, I am agreeing with some aspects of both strands of literature while also disagreeing with some aspects of both. I agree with Pratt that multiple discourses produce a person, but disagree with her emphasis on discursive disruption as the basis for resistance. I wholeheartedly agree with Fraser and Eisenstein that the economy is important and redistributive justice should be one of the major axes of resistance, and that neoliberalism finds it easy to harness liberal feminism's penchant for work outside the home, but I disagree with their bifurcation of social reality into cultural and economic spheres of recognition and redistribution. If existence is at once a material and subjective act, as Marx claimed, and if existence is not an individualistic practice but always a social practice, then existence is always already classed and gendered, and both class and gender are subjectivities that are economic and cultural. Therefore, there is no academic purpose in creating that distinction in the world of intellectual journals. The point of our intellectual endeavour should be to render explicit that which is implicit in the consciousness, or false consciousness, of the embodied subject of globalization. If the cultural aspect of class position is implicit, it must be intellectually queried to better understand globalization. If the economic aspect of gender exploitation is implicit, it should be rendered explicit in order to better understand globalization. However, the point remains that the person who has a class and gender position is always cultural and economic, and is always being exploited by globalization both culturally and economically, simultaneously. Therefore, we should be analysing her exploitation as a whole, rather than her exploitation bifurcated as cultural devaluation and economic marginalization. In an attempt towards that end, I now turn to the gendered subject who is also always embodied in a class context.

The Subject of Class

The impact of globalization has largely been studied, at least in the academic left, as class analysis, although it has not always been explicitly couched in those terms. For instance, Neil Smith (2005) understood globalization not only as a geo-economic project that enables multinational corporations by opening up the globe, but also as a geopolitical project in which the US pushes its post-September 11 foreign policy at a global level in order to consolidate its position as the supreme global state. Globalization, therefore, is a consolidation of the economic and political elite's class power over the working people of the world. Harvey (2003) focused more on the economic aspect of globalization, attempting a historical-material analysis of neoliberalism in which he indicated how trade liberalization, privatization, the removal of subsidies, and other aspects of deregulated, free-market capitalism involves the accumulation of capital by the capitalist class through dispossessing workers, women, peasants, and indigenous people from their labor, their forests, and their resources. Mike Davis conceptualized this class exploitation in the urban context, arguing that free-market globalization produces a new marginal class of urban proletariats who represent the unemployed, the partially employed, and the informal workers. The new structures of free-market globalization push Third World nations away from poverty alleviation, slum revitalization, home subsidization, and employment generation, and instead force them to become competitive through privatization. Privatization aids capital and not labour, and the cities of the world are therefore overflowing with a heterogeneous urban informal class. Many other scholars took a closer look at the class context of globalization through case-study-based approaches to informalization (Roy 2005), slum eviction (I. Chatterjee 2014), bourgeois urban renewal targeting the poor through gentrification (Baviskar 2003; P. Chatterjee 2004), the dissolution of social safety nets like food stamps and subsidized food distribution systems (Ahmed and Chatterjee 2013), and exploitation in sweatshops and export-processing zones (Guha-Banerjee 2011; Fernandez-Kelley 1983). The general theoretical position of these case-study based approaches is that the neoliberal policies that have defined globalization work in ways that have disenfranchised the poor as a class; the term 'class', however, is understood as the context of poverty defined by the lack of access to capital, private property, and employment. The conceptualization of the heterogeneous, urban proletariat is therefore a bit different from the classical notion of the industrial working class defined by depressed wages, horrible working conditions, and long work hours on the factory floor. Globalization has altered the context of class exploitation. The working class has gone from being defined by exploitation on the factory floor, where value was extracted from the lifeblood of the worker and converted into profit for the capitalist class, to now being defined outside the factory floor in the myriad contexts of the informalization of work, subcontracting, sweatshops, and slum evictions, because deindustrialization and the decline of the factory floor is rampant both in the First and Third Worlds.

Existing in globalization means producing a class-consciousness that can no longer be defined within the realm of the factory floor. Harvey (1996: 359) therefore suggested that class is a process: 'a situatedness or positionality in relation to processes of capital accumulation'. Situatedness and positionality are understood as an embeddedness in the process of accumulation while acknowledging that, although embeddedness can often be multiple (sometimes as a sweatshop worker, at other times as a slum dweller), this multiplicity does not deter from the possibility of a coherent politics in the world stage of capitalism. Therefore, it can be interpreted that in the context of globalization and deindustrialization, Harvey (1996: 363) made a conceptual shift when he described class as positionality with respect to capital accumulation rather than the ownership (or lack thereof) of the means of production, and then replaced class struggle with 'social action'. It can be inferred that—although factories die and labour unions fade— struggles over jobs, livelihoods, and resources still exist. For Harvey, this changing reality is best conceptualized by re-envisioning class as positionality vis-à-vis the process of accumulation. This positionality is the lack of control over the use of surplus value, or over the conditions in which it was produced. For Harvey, therefore, the dialectics of globalization is shaped by an urban underclass that is broader than Davis's informalized proletariat, in the sense that it not only includes the unemployed, underemployed, low-paid, and informally employed, but also those who are regularly displaced by slum eviction, the eminent domain wreaked by bourgeois urban renewal, and various other forms of foreclosures.

Marcuse (2009) added another dimension to the subject of class when he contended that the deprived social class is not only economically determined through conditions of poverty and unemployment, but also determined by cultural marginality. In other words, deprivation should

also include race, gender, and ethnophobic exclusions. Patriarchy, racism, xenophobia, and homophobia define real contexts of cultural
alienation, and those who are marginalized by these cultural variables
constitute a class of the exploited, even if they are not in any way economically marginalized. Carroll and Ratner (1994) attempt to render
porous the fixed productionist notion of class, and they try to bridge the
economy culture divide by insisting that the new global under-class is
defined by its resistance to capital. In other words, women fighting patriarchy are often fighting capitalist patriarchy, gays, and lesbians fighting
homophobia are fighting a homophobic capitalist state. Therefore, one's
class position is also one's cultural position, and globalization is, by
nature, simultaneously economic and cultural. E.P. Thompson (1978),
in his work on the English working class, brilliantly opened up class as a
category, and I find the Thompsonian dialectic to be particularly useful
in querying the class subject in the context of globalization.

According to Thompson:

> Class *eventuates* as men and women live their productive relations, and
> as they experience their determinate situations, within 'the ensemble of
> the social relations', with their inherited culture and expectations, and
> as they handle these experiences in cultural ways. So that, in the end, no
> model can give us what ought to be the 'true' class formation for a certain
> 'stage' of process. No actual class formation in history is any truer or
> more real than any other, and class defines itself as, in fact, it *eventuates*.
> (1978: 150; emphases mine)

For Thompson, class, in existing within the material conditions of life,
therefore emerges dialectically as people struggle within structures of
productive relations, while simultaneously interpreting these struggles;
the material and subjective, existence and consciousness, are always
already dialectically conjoined. There is no pre-given pure class category into which subjectivities can be shaped, class is a spontaneous
evolution into a historical-geographical moment, and, as people are
always emplaced within ensembles of 'social relations', their class
subjectivities are inflected with these social relations, like race, gender,
religion, sexuality, clan, tribal, and other relations. Therefore, class is as
much economic as it is cultural. Class is always contextual, because it
is embodied in a historical-geographical moment and it is inflected in
certain ensembles of social relations. Therefore, it cannot be aspatially
and a-historically generalized. Since it emerges dialectically (eventuates

itself), it is always the last stage, not the first, in a historical geographical process. There can be no classic formula or social experiment that can freeze a ubiquitous imagination of class, for any attempt at such un-dialectical orthodoxies is, according to Thompson (1978: 148), fraught with 'endless stupidities'.

Eisenstein (1999), in her socialist-feminist approach, contended that class relations that eventuate in the realm of production are not disconnected from the class relations that emerge within the family in the realm of reproduction. Thus, ensembles of social relations always define the multiple contexts of subjective existence. Drawing upon Marx and Engels' ideas on the sexual division of labour, Eisenstein pointed out that Marx and Engels were aware that reproductive work at home like childbirth and caregiving, and domestic chores were sexually defined, making women the first working class. Marx and Engels did not go quite far enough in indicating how this sexual division of labour within the family also impacted and structured the division of labour outside the family, in the realm of production. A socialist-feminist approach, according to Eisenstein, is a synthesis that makes the relationship between class relations at home and class relations at work explicit. A socialist-feminist approach begins by understanding the sexual division of labour within the family:

> It is the biological family, the hierarchical sexual division of society, and sex roles themselves which must be fundamentally reorganized. The sexual division of labor and society expresses the most basic hierarchical division in our society between masculine and feminine roles. It is the basic mechanism of control for patriarchal culture. It designates the fact that roles, purposes, activity, one's labor, are *determined* sexually. It expresses the very notion that the biological distinction, male/female, is used to distinguish social functions and individual power. (Eisenstein 1999: 202)

Deviating from Marx's and Engels' analysis, which presented the family as the superstructural manifestation of the deeper economic base, Eisenstein argued that the family does not simply reflect the conditions of production or class relations in the economic realm, but rather it is the patriarchy within the household that determines the class relations outside of it:

> The point to be made is not that the family does not reflect society, but that through both its patriarchal structure and its patriarchal ideology

the family, and the need for reproduction, structure society as well. This reciprocal relationship, between family and society, production and reproduction, defines the life of women. The study of women's oppression, then, must deal with both the sexual and economic material conditions if one is to understand oppression rather than merely understand economic exploitation. (Eisenstein 1999: 201)

Oppression is more complex than exploitation. Exploitation is encountered in wage work and signifies the theft of labour power from labour through the mechanisms of depressed wages and long working hours. Women experience exploitation *and* oppression, because they not only contend with capitalist exploitation at work, but also patriarchal oppression based on the sexual division of labour at home. Oppression works through a larger assemblage of social relation than class, which also includes gender. Therefore, in the social order of contemporary capitalism, capitalism and patriarchy work together to create contexts of oppression. For Eisenstein, capitalist patriarchy signified the inflection of reproduction and production, and class and gender relations, to constitute oppression:

> Power, or the converse—oppression—derives from both sex and class, and this is manifested through both the material and ideological dimensions of patriarchy and capitalism. Oppression is inclusive of exploitation but reflects a more complex reality. It reflects the hierarchical relations of the sexual division of labor and society.
>
> This system of oppression, which connotes the *mutual dependence* of capitalism and patriarchy as they are presently practiced, is what I have chosen to call capitalist patriarchy … Capitalist patriarchy, by definition, breaks through the dichotomies of class and sex, private and public, domestic and wage labor, family and economy, personal and political, ideology and material conditions. (Eisenstein 1999: 203–4)

Capitalist patriarchy is the conceptual synthesis of oppression in a contemporary capitalist society in which class is understood as an assemblage of social relations that are simultaneously cultural and economic. It encapsulates the economic position of exploitation and the cultural position of oppression.

In my analysis of the dialectics of globalization, I argued early in the chapter that it is my intention to understand the constituted materiality of globalization as it is brought to fruition through the city. In doing so, it is important to emphasize that globalization is not a super-organic machination, a divine plan, or a cosmic ordering, but is rather shaped by agents who are also shaped by it. Therefore, I intend to understand the globalizing subject as an embodied position and a body-subject, and phenomenology allows for this co-existence of subjective-material worlds. However, phenomenology does not extend this understanding beyond the individual, while Marxist analysis does. Herein is the opportunity to bring phenomenology into conversation with a Marxist analysis, because the latter provides a sophisticated understanding of group subjectivities by way of the conceptual entry point called class-consciousness. Class-consciousness is embodied subjectivity that emerges from labouring in a group, and understanding how this happens in the context of globalization can help us understand how globalization is classed. I also bring gender into my discussion here because, in my interactions in the field, I encountered numerous gendered spaces, gendered subjects, gendered landscapes, and gendered narratives that I am convinced constitute the materiality of globalization. In attempting to understand the gendered-classed subject that shape and are shaped by globalization, I argue, following Eistenstein, that the structures of reproduction and production must be understood as co-dependent, that gender is always already a class position, and that a class position is always already gendered. Therefore, I also agree with Thompson that class eventuates as a gendered moment in particular historical-geographical circumstances, because it is indissolubly cultural and economic. I am critical of Fraser's attempt to conceptually divide emancipatory politics into 'redistribution' and 'recognition', and I am also critical of Pratt's emphasis on discursive disruption as a revolutionary moment. It is my argument that if capitalist patriarchy forms the context of this historical-geographical moment of globalization, then the globalizing subject who is classed and gendered must resist structures of oppression not as separate moments of redistribution and recognition, because reproduction and production are so enmeshed that, in reality, they must be *totally* opposed. In other words, while it may be theoretically lucid to talk about redistributive justice and the politics of recognition, these 'conceptual boxes' do not *actually* exist. Reproduction is always part of production and separating them into two struggles, against cultural marginalization (struggle for recognition) and against economic inequality (struggle for redistribution), is a prescription for a revolutionary praxis that may work well conceptually, but is meaningless practically. In the interest of a dialectical understanding of globalization, I hope to therefore approach capitalist patriarchy in totality, encompassing the structures of reproduction *and* production in an indissoluble whole. Discourses are indeed important in understanding how the globalizing subject is shaped and how she shapes globalization, but I am less optimistic than Pratt in imagining that discursive disruptions would lead to enabling moments launch critiques against patriarchy, capitalism, or imperialism. My engagement with globalizing subjects indicate that discursive disruptions may be few, if any appear at all, and even then, they may not always become enabling sites for a critique of oppression. What that portends for globalization, and what that means for my globalizing subjects, is worth exploring.

Religious Patriarchy, Capitalist Patriarchy

As I walked through the hallways of the Swaminarayan temple in Irving, a volunteer stopped me at a point where a large sign read: 'No women allowed beyond this point'. The volunteer explained that the living quarters of the saints were located beyond the sign, and some of them never interacted or came in contact with women. The temple landscape is visibly gendered. Weekend classes for children are segregated by gender. The saints are all men, there is no possibility of a woman becoming the lead saint, or even joining the sub-hierarchies of *swami*s (saints) that form the entire personal entourage of Lord Swaminarayan. Women participate in the celebrations and rituals, and contribute labour to the temple construction. However, the priesthood is a prized patriarchal enclave whose sanctity and purity must be preserved by a strictly gendered ordering of life. This is not something unique to the Swaminarayan Hinduism, nor is it unique to Hinduism per se. In Catholicism, for instance, the elaborate bureaucratic organization of the papacy is completely male-centric. There has been vigorous debates on the ordination of women into the priesthood, however, an overwhelming amount of media space has been occupied by 'experts' who claim that women's ordination as priests is impossible within Catholicism, because of 'differences between men and women, which the Church insists are irreducible; men and women, by their natures, are suited to different, yet complementary, roles and functions' (Richert 2014). These irreducible differences are given historical validity by indicating that the Lord Jesus himself was male, and that he chose a college of 12 apostles, all men.

If capitalist patriarchy has used the sexual division of labour, or reproduction, as a site for working class exploitation, then religious patriarchy has entrenched it by giving it a divine sanctity. Hindu women have had a particularly unruly relationship with religion, because, on one hand, the Hindu pantheon is replete with multifaceted goddesses who are symbols of strength, warriors, slayers of demon, givers of wealth and knowledge, and protectors of men and children. However, the celebration of their multifaceted, divine qualities has always traditionally been supervised and organized by male priests who belonged to the uppermost caste in society. Therefore, religious patriarchy organized reproduction and production in such a way that, in the context of the sexual division of labour within the household, women were allowed to carry out private religious rituals for both male and female gods but, outside the home in the context of the realm of production, the priesthood and business of praying were a gendered profession. Only upper-caste men were allowed to conduct prayers in arcane Sanskrit verses, a literary skill from which most women and 'low' caste men were systemically deprived. In the private sphere, religion was almost like caregiving: a women's job that was unappreciated and unpaid. In the realm of the public sphere, however, religion became a business of accumulation and, like all other forms of accumulation, a top layer of upper-caste men controlled it. All women, and all lower-caste men, were considered too 'impure' and 'polluting' to partake in religion as production. Religion, in the realm of production, did produce a great deal of tribute, both in cash and in-kind, for a whole class of male priests whose livelihood depended on this gendered and classed exclusion. Chakravarti (1993) contended that the transition from a hunting and gathering economy to a more agricultural society (which occurred from 800 BC to 600 BC) led to this stratification of caste, gender, and class in India. She argued that, in the hunting and gathering economy, women participated in both production and reproduction, and that reproductive duties were particularly valuable because the survival of the community depended on it. Such a society, according to Chakravarti was one in which there was no evidence of women being subjugated by men or other women. The arrival of Aryans into India, and their disdain for the dark-skinned indigenous races led to conquest and plunder, as well as to the emergence of the Vedic period. The Vedas mention the existence of *dasis*, or conquered indigenous women, who were kept as slaves after their menfolk were slain. Agriculture production occurred outside the household, and dasis were enlisted to assist other men in this process. A class division therefore emerged among women, in which assisting in production became the occupation of lower-class women. Upper-class Aryan women were left to attend only to their reproductive duties at home. With the solidifying of the caste system, women's sexuality became a prized possession that needed to be constantly safeguarded in order to ensure caste purity. Chakravarti (1993: 579) states:

> In the theoretical explanations for the proliferation of caste the most pol-luting and low castes are attributed to miscegeny, i.e., the mixing castes ('varnasamkara'). Most polluting are those castes which are the products of reprehensible unions between women of a higher caste and men of a lower caste.
>
> … The safeguarding of the caste structure is achieved through the highly restricted movement of women or even through female seclusion. Women are regarded as gate-ways-literally points of entrance into the caste system. The lower caste male whose sexuality is a threat to-upper caste purity has to be institutionally prevented from having sexual access to women of the higher castes so women must be carefully guarded. (Ganesh 1985: 16; Das 1976: 129–45).

Religious patriarchy in Vedic Hinduism meant a strong control over women's sexuality through the meticulous monitoring of their movements and the strict guarding of the private sphere of reproduction, because the 'innate nature' (Chakravarti 1993: 580) of women was their lasciviousness and promiscuity. The sealing-off of caste categories required the gendering of spaces and of livelihoods, which meant that a certain class of women could no longer access public spaces and public activities, like production. Slave women continued to lend labour to production under exploitative relations, without any control of the accumulation process. Being outside the realm of the caste system, their reproductivity had no impact on the accumulation process. Since caste mobility was impossible, the slave woman's offspring would be positioned in the lowest caste order, unable to control capital or accumulate it by the unfortunate accident of their birth.

The gendering of religious spaces—such as through signs proclaiming 'no women beyond this point' or separate classes for boys and girls—must be understood in the context of the caste-class-gendering of Vedic India and its trickling down over time and space. The subject of globalization is not a value-neutral, a-spatial, and ahistorical agent that cranks the levers of global flows; the sedimentation of socio-geographical subjectivities is resilient, and they interact in unruly and uncomfortable ways as they inflect the dialectics of globalization. In *Renunciation and Reform and Women in Swaminarayan Hinduism*, the author, Professor Suresh Raval (2012: 87–8) of the University of Arizona, interprets the *Shikshapatri* (SP), a code of conduct laid down by Lord Swaminarayan:

> … it [SP] asks them [male householders] not to remain alone in a solitary place even with their young daughter, sister, or mother … Further on married women are advised to serve their husbands in all conditions (SP:159). They are also asked to avoid close contact with unrelated males, dressing immodestly, watching vulgar shows, and the company of depraved and morally corrupt women (SP:161). They are cautioned to be discreet when their husbands are abroad.

In interpreting the gendered norms of the SP, the author explained that the most important function of these codes of behaviour was to protect women from the exploitation of men. The regulation that the monks and priests should avoid contact with women is to ensure women's protection from the exploitation of religious authority. The importance of the separation of spaces within temples is explained as a necessary safeguard from 'mutual sensual temptation and to help achieve spiritual progress' (Raval 2012: 89). Celibacy is considered to be the ultimate aspiration of a Swaminarayan ascetic, which is difficult to attain because the mind is not innately pristine but still worthy of pursuit, and even attainable if a strict moral regimen is maintained and if the ascetic can be constantly vigilant against impure thought and action. In that context, Raval (2012) asserted that the derogatory statements made against women in Hindu texts should not be taken literally; rather, such texts were inserted to provoke a sense of revulsion for sexual desires in the new initiates. The renunciation of women is the ultimate test of an ascetic's purity, because women, like other worldly possessions, are a hindrance against and a competition for the attainment of true spirituality:

> It is not that women are irredeemably marked by carnal longings and men are somehow free of such proclivities until they come in contact

with women. The highly negative characterizations of women are meant
to convince potential spiritual aspirants that avoidance of women and
gold (*Kamini* and *Kanchan*) is central to asceticism. (Raval 2012: 143–4)

These interpretations stand in sharp contrast to the feminist deconstruction of religious patriarchy as an ideological narrative that treats
women as objects in space that are so overtly sexualized and steeped
in carnal attraction that their entire subjectivity is reduced to the sole
function of being a sex-object, a vessel for man's reproductive desires.
All other subjectivities—like being a daughter, sister, or mother—fade
into insignificance when they are in isolated contact with a man who is
a son, brother, or father, because of the innately objectified portrayal of
women. Therefore, for a male subject, a woman is preeminently a sex
object, a *maya* (a material attraction) and an *apsara* (a demonic woman
possessing sexual charms), particularly in spaces of isolation, and therefore she must be secluded for her own protection. Gendering space is
not an act of confinement, but rather an act that 'liberates' women from
the impure gaze, and the benevolent act of patriarchal protection from
itself. It is not that women are 'irredeemably marked by carnal long-
ings',—they are capable of purity and chastity—but their inability to
escape their innate womanhood that makes them the site of an impure
societal gaze from which they must be protected. Emancipation will not
come by challenging the perception or gaze that objectifies women in
the first place, but rather it will be attained by a chosen few who muster
the art of refusing to look. By refusing to look, the ascetic will be cured
from his 'addiction' towards alluring things like gold and women. The
emancipated man will transcend worldly desires for a transcendental
spirituality. Women, of course, are not candidates for such emancipation, because they are simply a test or hurdle to be passed by 'great' men
who are capable of great things. The gaze that objectifies a woman is
never critiqued, because the gazer simply cannot help it and patriarchy
is never socially produced in the eye of the patriarch, but rather is the
normal course of life. The patriarch can protect both himself and her
by separating the realms of reproduction and production and, if he is
lucky, by following the strict rules of celibacy through which he attains
emancipation; there is no attempt to conceptualize women's emancipation. The best a woman can do is to 'serve her husband', be 'discreet'
when her husband is not around, cover herself up, stay away from male
relatives, and, if she is widowed, shave her head to look as unattractive

as possible—all these strategies if deployed carefully, will make a truly pious woman that facilitates male emancipation.

A woman devotee and a volunteer at the Atlanta Swaminarayan temple insisted that the separation of the social activities of women and girls is not novel:

> Most religions of the world have spaces delineated by gender within the temple, mosque, and church. This is as much a civil way of controlling the crowd, as much as it is to allow women and girls the space they need is public places. In the eyes of God everyone is an equal, but the sanctity of the temple may be violated if there are any untoward incidents. Plus, women excel in certain activities and men in others, their potentials can be best extracted when they are allowed to flourish in separate spaces. BAPS women also undertake several rituals, fasts and celebrations that, according to the scriptures, are just for women, because under Hindu religion women are assumed to have great strength, patience, and forti- tude, and social communal gatherings and worship at the temples allow women to have the spiritual support they need. This is not an example of exclusion of men from these activities, but rather, creation of supportive spaces for women.

It is important to be clear here that the volunteer is not exaggerating: it is true that the creation of gendered spaces, the exclusive right of men to the priesthood, gendered spiritual activities, and gendered religious roles are not exclusive to Swaminarayan Hinduism. It is indeed not my objective here to amass evidence to prove otherwise. Rather, in my exploration of the dialectics of globalization through the lens of spec- tacular urban landscapes, I am simply using the temple complexes as sites to understand the gendering of globalization. Therefore, this is an attempt to take globalization away from its sterile networks and flows, spaces, and atom-like imagination to a place where its DNA is formu- lated and reformulated by subjects who are a complex assemblage of subjectivities and consciousness. In that context, my interviewee is asserting that allowing the sexual division of reproductive spaces to bleed into productive spaces, thus creating gendered public spaces, is enabling for women as well as men. The Swaminarayan temple com- plexes in American cities signify an entrenched grounding of globaliza- tion and, at the same time, allow for a grounding of religious discourses away from the spaces of their origin. The purpose behind god going global is to allow a flow of religious subjectivities to spaces that are foreign and alienating, thus allowing the global migrant to experience spirituality away from their home. God, in its global travel to new host societies, must assimilate, but not completely so; it must go native but never completely Americanize. The spiritual appeal must be retained by holding on to 'scriptures', traditional mode of architecture, and traditional norms of the gendered division of labour; however, at the same time, its global appeal must be broadened to include global subjects in the global cities of the world and their migrant lives. Therefore, it would be 'out of place' to say that BAPS women in Atlanta and Houston should serve their husbands, stay away from young male relatives, and shave their heads in widowhood, because such readings would be out of context and impossible to observe in Dallas, Houston, and Atlanta. The subjects and subjectivity of globalization must allow for a dialectical process of gendering in which patriarchal norms must be opened to some discursive disruption through re-interpretation. While it will be impossible to retain the scriptures' codes of conduct for women in their entirety in those moments of disruption, it will still be possible to retain some of those codes by ways of gendering classes and activities, and restricting women from certain secluded spaces in the temple complex. For my woman volunteer, who was engaged in discursive disruption, these instances of gender segregation are not an issue of confinement or of the sex-selection of men and women's spiritual roles, but simply an extension of the safe-space of the home into the public domain, so that the activities women can do at home can be done as a community outside the home. They can better conduct such activities among their own sex, because men and women have sexual proclivities to excel in different activities. In her reinterpretation of religious patriarchy, she pried it open, loosened and softened it, and made it go global. However, in her discursive disruption she never problematized the production of the sexual discourse per se: that the sex-division of reproductive roles that happens at home (the realm of reproduction) is itself problematic. The long list of rituals and fasts that women must undertake for the well-being of men, and the lack of such rituals that men must undergo for women, is problematic, as is the sex selection at home that assumes women are 'normally' good at certain roles—like cooking, cleaning, and child-rearing—while men are good at running the household and the economy. When the gendering of reproduction, or the sex divisions within household, is not critiqued, the same sex division will bleed into the sphere of production, thus extending patriarchy outside of the household. Hence, the separate classes for boys and girls learning Gujarati, the separate scheduling of basketball games that allow girls and boys to play separately, the fasting meetings that women meet and organize for the longevity of their husbands, and the greater number of men than women serving as treasurers and members of the board of trustees for the temple. This is not unique to BAPS Swaminarayan, but what this example helps to elucidate is that, in subjecting globalization, we become aware of the discursive disruptions that are happening to soften and pry religious patriarchy open. However, these disruptions are unfortunately not enough to strike at the core of the oppressive structures of reproduction and production.

There is, of course, plenty of evidence of the religious patriarchy being chipped away and softened as it is subjected to globalization. For example, the Dallas Swaminarayan temple website advertises: The '7th Annual BAPS Women's Conference' (BAPS Swaminarayan Sanstha), which was held in March 2014 and attended by prominent women professors, entrepreneurs, and charity and community workers of the Swaminarayan sect who gave speeches and sat together in panel discussions on topics involving leadership. A YouTube video of the conference displays women in traditional Gujarati sarees registering for the conference and attending meetings and discussions, which are interspersed with images of Lord Swaminarayan from the temple's inner sanctum and of girls performing traditional Indian dances. In a moment of introspection, one woman entrepreneur remarked:

> I had two different sides, where my mother was always trying to do charity outside and help women and children, and my dad was on the other side saying charity begins at home, when you take care of your home, you can always take care of others ...

The women's conference is an interesting example of discursive disruption. Many women from the Swaminarayan community are second generation immigrants, born and educated in the US. They speak with impeccable American accents and have professional jobs, they run charities and small businesses or teach, and they simultaneously value their spiritual connection and the networks of their religious community. They are subjects of globalization, simultaneously cultural and economic beings, spiritual and rational, Indian and American, and simultaneously localizing and globalizing Swaminarayan Hinduism. The women's conference is a site of this simultaneity, and an attempt at chipping away the religious patriarchy by showcasing women who are in charge of both reproduction and production, who are leaders and role models, and, most importantly, who have not, in becoming all of those things, transcended their Gujarati-Indian culture; the beautiful sequin crusted sarees and the Indian dance interludes are supposed to create the seamless assemblage of a global subject who pursues economic emancipation by retaining her cultural-spiritual core. This woman need not be discreet, because she can protect herself from the lascivious gaze of men and hence does not need to remain undercover, and she is capable of serving society even while serving her husband. When the temple uses cyberspace to put out this new narrative of women 'out there', it shapes a new globalization in which gender subjectivities are in a state of transformation, disruption, and porosity relative to the patriarchal 'code of conducts' laid down in the *Shikshapatri*. In that context, the globalizing Swaminarayan Sanstha is attempting a revolutionary discursive disruption by celebrating women's role in production, and choosing key figures who are educators, entrepreneurs, and social workers, and posting them on cyberspace under its own banner. Globalization fashions a women subject in a very different manner than what traditional patriarchy intended for her. However, this discursive disruption falls short of critiquing the patriarchy at its core. The middle-class woman subject does not quite deconstruct the structures of oppression as Eisenstein would want her to do. She is economically emancipated but culturally oppressed, because she easily quotes her father in emphasizing her mother's, and hence her own, exclusive role in caregiving. If her mother could be an excellent caregiver at home, this reproductive role would naturally extend into the public sphere. Her father's role in caregiving is not part of this new global introspection at all, because fathers are not assumed to have a genetic proclivity towards caregiving, and hence not expected to participate in it in any way. If the mother wanted to be a good caregiver in society, she must first demonstrate that she was good at providing care at home and, under no circumstances, let her household duties suffer for her larger calling, because the father would certainly not have the time or inclination to subsidize her absence from home. Other introspections followed similar narratives of the true leader who is able to balance the multiple roles of motherhood and wifehood along with her career. The core of these narratives being: economic freedom is a good thing, especially as women subjects become global, but this emancipation should not be launched by disrupting patriarchy at home. The women's conference softens religious patriarchy while staying within the rubric of capitalist patriarchy by choosing not to disrupt the structures of reproduction. The dialectics of globalization is shaped by a new realm of production that can function in alignment with the exploitative gendered roles of reproduction without ever disrupting them. Separating the economic and the cultural into questions of redistribution and recognition will not, as Fraser suggested, be very helpful here, because the globalizing, gendered subject, as well as the kind of globalization she shapes, is structured in such a way that capitalist and religious patriarchies dovetail in strange and unruly ways. Therefore, an emancipatory dialectics cannot deal with culture as separate from the economy because, in this case, it would mean separating the sphere of reproduction (cultural) from the sphere of production (economic). Oppression will lose its context, and hence its meaning, under such an un-dialectical segregation.

The globalizing women that shape globalization by tempering religious patriarchy while preserving capitalist patriarchy in Houston, Dallas, and Atlanta are simultaneously engaged in a 'class act'. The softening of religious patriarchy and the preservation of capitalist patriarchy, as well as their participation in the production in ways that do not disrupt reproductive roles, are not individual acts. Rather, they are gendered, middle-class acts. Marx contended that the seeds of class-consciousness lie in material existence, and that in existing, we either labour as a class or extract labour time from another class. Middle-class women, in my analysis, are therefore not just individual phenomenological subjects who embody a personal worldview, but also represent a gendered class that embodies a group consciousness in the context of accumulation. Most of my interviewees in the US cities belonged to the Patel community, which is traditionally the landowning, upper castes in Gujarat, India. In the context of their immigration to the US, they are mainly positioned as small-business owners within the realm of accumulation, and hence within the US middleclass. Class 'eventuates' in cultural ways, that is, the American Indian woman immigrant engages in a gendered class act: while embracing her role in the economy (production), she never really criticizes a capitalist patriarchy that encourages her to manage both production and reproduction, while her husband and father is absolved from caregiving and reproductive duties. In fact, she easily glosses over the cunning of capitalist patriarchy by extolling the super-heroic abilities of the modern Gujarati women who can easily juggle both production and reproduction; she therefore, preserves capitalist patriarchy, which serves her middle class interest. These women are mostly second-generation immigrants from families that come from a layer of entrepreneurs, mainly the owners of hotels and motels, Indian grocery stores, Indian clothing boutiques, and jewellery stores, as well as CEOs of medium-level firms.[1] Generations of accumulation shaped an entrepreneurial Gujarati middle class in India, who could then migrate to the US and other cities of the world and use their accumulated capital to start businesses in foreign land. Indian contexts of traditional patriarchy allowed accumulation to proceed as husbands, brothers, and fathers worked capital while the women worked at caregiving.[2] This sexual division of labour was traditionally normalized and sanctified by religion. This traditional religious patriarchy is slowly softened through globalization, with priests, volunteers, and devotees interpreting and translating it in ways that allows for discursive disruption and porosity. Therefore, when in Atlanta, Houston, and Dallas, women were allowed to contribute labour for temple construction, participate as volunteers, organize celebrations and anniversaries, give speeches, and even have their own conferences on leadership. However, these discursive sites do not launch an incisive critique at the very heart of capitalist patriarchy. The women who are entrepreneurs, educators, and CEOs repeatedly emphasize the need to first 'attend to the home' and 'balance duties as mothers and wives along with their careers'. They do not expect any such balancing act from their fathers and husbands, whose only calling is to go out and earn a living that would continue to sustain a middle-class existence. In this class act, women balance reproductive roles along with their entrepreneurial duties in order to aid accumulation and sustain class position, while simultaneously keeping the sexual division of labour intact at home. Women's participation in production, leadership, and the economic sphere does not alter the context of oppression in the reproductive sphere. The softening of religious patriarchy shapes a globalization that preserves capitalist patriarchy. As temples increasingly celebrate middle-class women through conferences, 'open up' their translations of gendered scriptures, and allow women to get ever closer to, but never quite in, the inner sanctum, they produce a class consciousness and an embodied subject of globalization that rationalize their exclusive role in reproduction not as patriarchal oppression, but as a skill that a true woman leader must possess. Eisenstein argued that family and society are co-dependent, that is, production and reproduction are co-depended—capitalism and patriarchy depend on each other to create the context of women's oppression. The globalizing subject shapes the dialectics of globalization by engaging in a class act that allows capitalist patriarchy off the hook, leaving sexual division of labour undisturbed at home. Many women allow for it and consent to it, as they derive consent from the benevolence of a new religious patriarchy that now accepts and rewards their productive roles outside the home. Religious consent buys a ticket to participation in production, even if this means that women must now do double the work, reproduction and production. This is all good, because this ultimately aids accumulation, and accumulation is always a class act—the globalizing subject shapes globalization through a co-dependence of religious and capitalist patriarchal oppression. Thompsonian Marxism made us aware of how important culture is in eventuating class, and yet, in the final analysis, we often segregate questions of redistribution from questions of recognition, or we interpret production and reproduction, as well as exploitation, in the purely economic terms. In an effort to keep culture intact within the economy of globalization, and to keep the economy as eventuating through culture, I hope to reiterate that capitalist globalization is a complex production of subjectivities that are entrenched in class, caste, gender, and religion, and that these are simultaneously cultural and economic. Therefore, capitalist exploitation and oppression is always a patriarchal act, but it is also almost always a religious, caste-based, and race-based patriarchal act.

Shaping Globalization

The globalization that we see etched on the city in the form of immigrant landscapes, exotic foods, fusion music, outsourced jobs, and immigrant labour is the constituted materiality of existence. The city synthesizes the constituted materiality of globalization. However, this materiality is not stamped on the cityscape by some super-organic, larger-than-life global machine. Global governing institutions like the World Bank and IMF are often critically analysed as trans-national machines that shape the geography of globalization, and rightly so. However, my attempt here is not just to look at the anthill from the bird's-eye view, but rather, to slice it open and look at the intricate tunnels and paths that comprise that hill. In other words, here I am interested in understanding how exactly the materiality of globalization is shaped. In doing so, I am particularly interested in querying the subject of globalization that constitutes the materiality of globalization and is (re)constituted in the process. Following phenomenologists, I argue that the subject, or subjectivity, is not some nebulous mental faculty separated from the body. In doing away with Cartesian dualism, phenomenologists claimed that the tangible and intangible, the mind and the body, and our position in the world and our point of view of the world are not separate entities, but rather simultaneously exist in the 'body-subject' as an embodied position and can never be synthetically severed. It is that version of the subject or subjectivity that I wish to explore in my attempt to understand the subjectivity of globalization.

However, I argue that phenomenological understanding does not quite go beyond the individual, and we therefore need to take recourse in Marx in order to understand embodied subjectivity in the group context. For Marx consciousness is inescapably bound to the material act of labouring and existing, but this consciousness is never insular; it is always a group consciousness, because existence is a social and collective act of labouring in a group or class. Therefore, class-consciousness is defined by the body-subject's situation in the context of labouring and accumulation. If situated as accumulators of value, the class-consciousness is dialectically constituted with the materiality of accumulation; if situated in the context of extraction, the class is imbricated with the materiality of exploitation. The constituted materiality of all reality, including globalizing realities, must therefore be a class act. The city that synthesizes this materiality of globalization must therefore also be a classed reality. Following post-structural and socialist feminists, I argue that class is always imbued with gender. There can be no genderless class, or classless gender, and hence, the constituted materiality of globalization is informed by a gendered-classed subject that co-constitutes a gendered-classed city. There is another dualism that must be addressed here: the dualism between culture and economy. In other words, is the classed-gendered subject an economic force, or is it a cultural force? There are many within the class perspective that argue for one or the other, or both, but E. P. Thompson, in my opinion, said it best when he argued that class eventuates itself in specific historical-geographical circumstances in diverse economic and cultural ways. Similarly, feminists have understood gendering and gender exploitation in the context of globalization in various ways, some purely as cultural subjectivities, others purely as discursive postionalities, and yet others still as cultural and economic. Eisenstein, in my opinion, did an excellent job of explicating how the economy and culture are inflected in the process of gendering. She argued that the realm of reproduction at home structures the realm of production outside the home, and familial patriarchy, therefore, feeds capitalist patriarchy, and vice versa. If the family is the seat of cultural value systems, and the workplace is the seat of economic norms, then these are always already fused, and reproduction and production structure each other in contextualizing the materiality of women's class oppression. At home, the daughter, wife, and sister are as much a working class as the women worker in the factory is a cultural 'other'. Therefore, gender is always a class position, and class is always gendered.

In this chapter, I attempt to bring these ideas into conversation by querying how the spectacular landscape of cities—like the Akshardham temple complexes in Houston, Atlanta, and Dallas—represent the constituted materiality of a globalization that is shaped by gendered subjects who embody a particular class-consciousness. I look at religious patriarchy and understand its evolution from a more fundamental, textual position to a more contemporary, porous reading of the scriptures, as well as a more porous practice of religion that now improvizes to include the globalizing women who are an important part of its clientele. It is my argument that, through an increased porosity or softening of religious patriarchy, capitalist patriarchy is enabled, or at least left preserved. The women subjects who shape the new global religion, the new immigrant-consciousness, and the new globalizing city emphasize that their economic emancipation is attained through carefully balancing their reproductive and productive roles. In other words, questioning familial patriarchy and calling for its overhaul does not inform the subjectivity of this globalizing subject. The softened religious patriarchy consents to women's participation in production only *after* she has immaculately performed 'her roles' within the household. Being able to do both is the new subjectivity of the globalizing woman. In doing both, the woman subject engages in a class act, the act of accumulation. She directly and indirectly aids accumulation: directly by becoming the modern entrepreneur who is at work, and indirectly by legitimizing the sexual division of labour at home so that her man can participate in production free of any caregiving responsibilities. A globalizing religious patriarchy celebrates her economic emancipation on the condition that patriarchal, capitalist accumulation is not disrupted in any way. Therefore, not only do capitalism and patriarchy depend on each other, capitalist patriarchy and religious patriarchy depend on each other. The gendered subject is always engaged in a class act, and a class position is a gendered act. In this case, most of my middle-class women interviewees, and their male counterparts, shape accumulation through religious and capitalist patriarchy, and that is the constituted materiality of globalization. 'No women allowed behind this point' represents the constituted materiality of global patriarchal capitalism, which is simultaneously cultural and economic. Such is the dialectics of this materiality that separating the cultural questions from the economic ones will result in a disembodied subject, a partial consciousness, and a fragmented city that does not exist in reality.

Notes

1. Based on my interviews.
2. Most women interviewees in India confirmed that they were housewives and were happy to support their husband's productive roles.

7 Conclusions
Spectacular City as Synthesis

I landed at the Dubai airport on my way to India, and as I made my way into the heart of the terminal, I noticed that I was walking through a coniferous forest replete with life-size pines and firs, pine cones, fern-covered rocks, and gurgling streams (Figure 7.1). The disjuncture caught me off guard; did I land at the wrong airport? What is a coniferous forest doing in this land of sand? I glanced outside and breathed a sigh of relief to see the flat and sandy desert landscape outside. The airport encapsulated a transitional space—globalization's twilight zone—between two worlds where ornately carved silver camels, life-size hookahs, and Moroccan lamps brushed shoulders with coniferous forests, Gucci handbags, and frozen yogurt stores. These transitional spaces represent the globalizing aspirations of the local social psyche: the desire to feel the pine needles between one's fingers and the crunch of snow underfoot even when rooted in the desiccating sand of the Arabian Desert. Tall, neon billboards proclaimed malls that fulfil global shopping experiences and doubled as indoor ice-skating rinks and amusement parks featuring tons of freshly made snow. Arab women and men, adorned from head to toe in billowy gowns, fulfil the global tourists' desire for an ethnic fix of the *Arabian Nights* fairy tales. The glossy bathrooms feature western- and eastern-style toilets, and the tourist is mesmerized by the numerous hygienic possibilities that she can choose from, starting with the toilet paper and continuing to the ornate jug that dispenses water through a finely arched nozzle, or to the more technologically friendly telephone hose that allows for

Figure 7.1 Coniferous forest in Dubai airport
Source: Photograph taken by Waquar Ahmed.

a clean-up without physical contact. Travel does not seal off cultural possibilities, as it is no longer necessary to pack one's favourite candy or favourite shaving cream out of fear that the exotic encounters in foreign lands will not accommodate one's familiarities. The globalizing twilight zones re-realize reality, melding, twisting, and turning it on its head so that the hookah bar and the Starbucks café share common walls. The native is no longer the cultural other and the traveller is no longer the alien *sahib*, because the transitional spaces of globalization blend the local and global together into a kaleidoscope of possibilities, from yogurts to falafels and burgers.

Thomas Friedman (1999) collated similar happy, feel-good stories and spun them into tales of free-market democracy's victory. Most people in the non-academic world, understand globalization through his lens; that is, the proliferation of consumptive possibilities all over the world and the intense circulation of people and goods into happy amalgams of hybrid airports, hotels, and people going global. The gritty details of exploited women in the maquiladoras of Mexico, of the garment factories of Bangladesh, of the jobs outsourced from and lost to the US working class, of the corporate take-over of indigenous labels in India, and of Chinese children working day-and-night to produce toys for their western counterparts. These are also transitional spaces of globalization, because they also re-realize reality, melding and twisting it, but instead of opening up possibilities, they limit them and exploit those who are forced to remain rooted in a globalizing world, who are stuck in transitional zones of pain and exploitation. How can these globalizing realities be written about in a way that is not superficial? How can a globalization that is not just about the explosion of ice-cream flavours or the proliferation of women's accessories be understood? How can globalizing of culture be talked about in a deep way?

This book wants to understand culture as more than malls and consumption goods. It wants to understand how culture exists in relation to the economy in comprising the social totality of globalization. Globalization is not a thing or place; it is a way of life, and such a profound one that it permeates all context of reality today. Therefore, social totality is just a conceptual way of referring to the entirety of globalizing reality in its full complexity: the superficial and the deep, the glossy and the gritty, the cultural and the economic. It is this context of complexity that this book hopes to explore, it attempts to communicate an understanding of globalization that is complex without making any attempt to simplify it.

Reality is not simple, and globalization is not simple either. Therefore, this book attempted to find a language that did not reduce reality to a simple caricature of itself, but instead approached it in a way that revealed its complex machinations. I attempted to do that through a dialectical approach. In philosophy, the dialectical approach is distinct from the analytical approach. In approaching something analytically, one dissects reality into sub-sets, sub-components, and sub-parts that can then be individually studied and later combined to explain the process. For example, in analysing the market for shirts, the economist analyses the demand for shirts, the supply of shirts, the income level of consumers, the disposable income of consumers demanding the shirts, and so on and so forth. It is possible to separately analyse each of these variables and then put them together to arrive at a total picture of the reality of the market for shirts. However, in a dialectical approach, concrete components exist in relation to each other, and it is in this relationality that the components together make the whole. Dissecting the components as individual systems that will be later combined decomposes the whole in such a way that it will never to be put back together again. Essence of reality disappears if there is a mechanistic attempt to disintegrate it. This may seem rather abstract—vaguely making sense but not fully graspable—largely because modernity and the post-enlightenment scientific inquiry, from which very few places are immune, teaches analytical thinking and not dialectical thinking. Therefore, dialectics has become counter-intuitive to the ubiquitous common sense of analysis. Think, for example, of a family: the children are the relational extension of their parents, but they are still individuals, and their individuality is in the process of formulation through their interconnectedness with their parents. What gender roles are established, how those gender roles are played, how one identifies one-self, and how one identifies the other is enmeshed in the context of relationality. The daughter relates to the father in a certain way that is different from how she relates to the mother, the son relates to his parents in a different way than his sister, and the son and daughter each relate to the other in a different manner than to their parents. Whether the father will be the role model, or the mother, and how, would all be decided in the contingent and relational context of gendering and role-playing. If each family members were to be discreetly separated, and the relations among brother, sister, father, and mother understood as separate from each other, we would lose the very essence of the family that we are trying to understand. Family, then, becomes a demographic entity rather than a social totality. We live our lives dialectically, and hence produce a reality that is inherently dialectical; yet, when it comes to academic enquiry, because of our grounding in post-enlightenment scientific traditions, we kill dialectics as we academically conceptualize the real world. This book hopes to preserve the dialectical nature of globalizing reality.

By this, I mean that I am interested in understanding how the economic, cultural, political, and social aspects of globalization unfold relationally. In other words, I have consciously decided to not attempt an economic analysis of globalization, or a cultural analysis of globalization, or a political analysis of globalization. I have decided to understand the dialectics of globalization by revealing how culture, economy, society, and politics, but specifically culture and economy, are interconnected in forming the totality of globalization. The argument is that, when we live in the world, it is not as if the economic processes unfold separately from cultural and political processes. There are no sealed-off spatial containers inside which culture is happening, no walled spaces behind which the economy is unfolding, and no sequence in which they unfold. Therefore, if the economy and culture are inseparably inflected, there must be a way to understand and explain this inflection. Much work has been invested in understanding economic globalization: the academic left has looked at globalization in its neoliberal formulations and post-Fordist manifestation as late-capitalism, as new imperialism, and neo-colonization, while the academic right has understood it as free-market democracy. Similarly, a look at cultural globalization understands it as the corporatization of culture, a process of homogenization through which the McDonalds, Barbies, and Coca Colas are erasing local tastes and preferences, local ways of dressing, eating, and relating. It is a loss of authenticity in favour of commodified culture. Others argue that globalization is not all homogenization, because locally unique cultural forces interact with global cultural processes in unique ways to create new versions of globalization. McDonalds sells noodles in China but does not sell beef in India, and Barbie sometimes wears the kimono in Japan and the saree in India. The 'exotic other' does not stand as a mute recipient of globalization, but is incorporated as an ingredient, and the landscape of globalization is therefore more than just banal cultural standardization.

In this book, I search for an approach that can explore culture as intertwined with the economy. Some conceptual paths have already been provided, like the base and superstructure approach to culture economy present in some versions of Marxism. Other approaches include Weberian idealism, which understands culture as the solvent that formulates economic rationality; in other words, culture—or more specifically—religious worldviews, inform, and mediate the kind of economic regimes that will manifest in places. In geography, 'cultural-economic spatial dialectic' and 'socio-spatial dialectic' are the other conceptual moments that have been suggested as ways of understanding the interrelations between culture, economy, and space/place. I discuss why the base–superstructure approach often becomes an economic determinism that severs culture from the economic determinant—production—and then treats it as produced (after the fact) as a superstructural manifestation. By changing the nature of production, culture can be changed. Culture does not, in any instance, produce the economy, but is instead, always and in every instance, produced by it. This, I argue becomes a causal analysis, a partial eye that chooses to segregate production (economy) from its relational context and conceptually imprison it as something that comes first and causes everything else to come after itself. Causal analysis sequences reality in a way that reality does not actually exist. There exist many Marxist critiques of this crude, determinist vision, and I discuss Raymond Williams's brilliant effort to transcend this base–superstructure dualism by introducing the concept of 'mediation' and 'constituted materiality'. Base and superstructure are in a continuous process of mediation, and together they constitute the materiality of existence.

I also look at the spatially explicit stance towards the dialectical approach introduced in geography. The argument here is that space, place, territory, region, and nation inflect in unique ways with cultural, economic, and political processes. However, the social sciences often forget space, and treat processes as if they occur in an aspatial vacuum. They lose the nuanced contributions that cities, places, regions, and nations make to these processes. Hence, there must be a way to include space in a dialectical analysis of society. Soja's 'socio-spatial dialectic' (discussed in Chapter 2) was an effort in that direction. The idea that society produces its own space and space in turn, informs society acquired great momentum and circulation. In other words, cities have a certain kind of landscape, and these landscapes influence social processes. For instance, slums and ghettos determine social processes like redlining, in which certain addresses are outlined in red by bankers to indicate that they are high-risk areas for loan repayment. I argue that the problem with *including* space with society (as in 'socio-spatial') is the problematic assumption that it was, at some moment, removed from the social totality. In reality, however, space and processes (economic, cultural, and otherwise) are always already welded together, because they happen together and manifest together. Therefore, to conceptual append space to society is to assume that society does not already consist of space. Many geographic and non-geographic works that are oblivious to the built environment, the landscape, and the inequalities etched by space certainly exist, but rectifying such omissions cannot involve synthetic additions and semantic changes. It must involve a complete re-orientation of how we approach reality; that is, an emphatic abandonment of the analytical approach in exchange for a dialectical stance. In moving away from an analytical stance, I move away from how the world has normally been approached by analytical traditions: identify a process and problem—for example, neoliberalism, McDonaldization, or imperialism—then study how and where they operate, and, in explaining their operations, critique them, and possibly suggest solutions. Instead, I begin with the city as an exemplar of social totality, or reality. It is not as if the rural world is unreal; rather, the urban world is my reality, and hence I prefer to stick to it. The city is social totality, not a sub-set or a smaller segment of that totality. It is not a closed system or a unique site, but a concept. As a concept, it is not just a geographic site, and therefore it cannot be added together with information from other cities in order to explain a process or problem, or treated as a system with its own inner logic that is distinct from larger–scale entities like the nation or globe. The city, in my approach, is a material–conceptual totality in the same way that the ocean is to a fish. I approach the city as constituting the materiality of globalization, or as revealing the DNA of globalization. The city synthesizes culture and economic processes in a dialectical whole. This dialectical whole is globalization and it can be understood by approaching the city-as-synthesis. Therefore, the purpose is not to identify a process, see how it operates at a geographic site, and then connect it to globalization with an arrow. The purpose is to approach the city in its culture economic complexity in order to understand globalization; this constitutes the dialectical approach. In remaining true to this dialectical approach, I have consciously blurred the boundaries between capitalism and religion demonstrating how they bleed into one another in accumulating and alienating. Therefore, an alternative globalization would require 'acting out' (Marin 1984: 241), or as Jameson (1984: 89) argued, a new 'cognitive mapping' that can remove stupefaction through a process of disalienation.

I dialectically approach the US cities of Atlanta, Houston, and Irving-Dallas, and the Indian cities of Gandhinagar and Delhi. I approach them through the temple complexes of the BAPS Swaminarayan sect, a reformist movement within Hinduism that started in Gujarat but has swiftly become highly global, with thousands of temple complexes all over the world, a dense network of transnational followers, a vociferous cyber presence, and, most importantly, a spectacular physical presence in the form of gigantic and superfluous temple complexes that are made of intricately carved marble. In the US context, these marbles are flown from Italy to India for carving, and then brought back to temple sites in the US to be put together. Construction workers are brought from India to build the temple according to Hindu scriptures, with plenty of help from the local immigrant population. The temple becomes an immigrant narrative of reviving the home, community, nostalgia, cultural icon, and legacy that ties one's offspring to India, grounding them to Indian culture as it is envisioned by their first-generation immigrant parents. The complexes double as museums, recreation centres, clubs, hub of religious and secular activities, and retail centres for spiritual and other goods. They globalize India, ground patriotism, reformulate racial imaginaries, formulate American multiculturalism, and transact business. They are a perfect example of globalization as it is co-constituted by the inflection of culture and economy. The temple complexes in India, on the other hand, are unique spectacles, a fantastic representation of postmodern spirituality manifested through the concept of a theme park. According to an ascetic connected to the Delhi temple, spirituality is too abstract, and so one needs spectacles and concrete ways of formulating those spectacles so that people actually internalize the abstractness of spirituality. Monks were sent on world tours to study theme-park entertainment complexes and laser-and-water shows all over Europe and the US, and then to bring glo-balization to Gandhinagar and Delhi in the form of Vedic boat rides, fibre-optic displays, and fire-and-water laser shows that tell the tales of the Upanishads. The spiritual experiences are packaged in separate landscapes within the temple and can be experienced by purchasing tickets at each entry point. This spectacular city-as-synthesis reveals globalization in its complex economic and cultural entirety. This book uses examples from the Swaminarayan narratives to reveal the cultural economic materiality of globalization. I also argue that this cultural economic synthesis is not an inert process of goods, cash, ideas, and spirituality transnationally floating through networks and flows as if on autopilot. Rather, globalization is actually shaped by people and their subjectivities. I combine phenomenological notions of the subject with Marx's ideas of class-consciousness to indicate that the subject of global-ization is a body-subject, a material-subjective totality who synthesizes both the tangible and intangible qualities of being and becoming, thus disrupting the Cartesian object–subject dichotomy. This body subject is also a class subject and a gendered subject. Therefore, the subject of globalization is embedded in class and gender relations, hence, the Swaminarayan narratives of globalization are simultaneously classed and gendered. Marxists have shown how capitalism exploits class through wage relations in the context of labouring, and social feminists have revealed how capitalism, in the production sphere, both draws from and depends on the sex-division of labour at home; in other words, how patriarchy and capitalism work together. In the chapter on 'subjecting-globalization', I indicate how capitalist patriarchy depends on religious patriarch to constitute the class-based and gendered nature of globalization.

Spectacular Cities synthesize the dialectics of globalization by consti-tuting their culture economic materiality in unison. In that sense they hope to reveal the complexity of globalization through a conceptual stance that can approach reality in totality. Understanding globalizing reality as totality has been intended as an alternative to network, or flow, or global versus local, or economic, or cultural approaches, which often tend to segment reality.

Bibliography

Ahmadiyya Muslim Community. 2014. Available at: http://www.ahmadiyya.us/about-ahmadiyya-muslim-community (accessed on 26 June 2014).

Ahmed, W. 2008. 'Indigenous Communities and Their Marginalized Space in India'. In *Studies in Indian Economy*, ed. K. R. Gupta, 188–218. New Delhi: Atlantic Publishers and Distributors (P) Ltd.

Ahmed, W. and I. Chatterjee. 2013. 'Contradictory Policies of Neoliberalizing India'. *Human Geography* 6(2): 85–97.

Albritton, R. 1999. *Dialectics and the Deconstruction in Political Economy*. London: Macmillan Press Ltd.

Amin, Samir. 1974. *Accumulation on a World Scale*. 2 vols. New York: Monthly Review Press.

Appadurai, A. 1990. 'Disjuncture and Difference in the Global Cultural Economy'. *Theory, Culture, Society* 7: 295–310.

———. 1996. *Modernity at Large: Cultural Dimensions of Globalization*. Minneapolis, London: University of Minnesota Press.

Bahai.org. 2014. Available at: http://www.bahai.org (accessed on 25 June 2014).

———. 2014. 'About BAPS: Who We Are'. Available at: http://www.baps.org/About-BAPS/WhoWeAre.aspx (accessed on 7 July 2014).

Balgopal, K. 2002. 'Reflections on "Gujarat Pradesh of Hindu Rashtra"'. *Economic and Political Weekly*, 1 June. Available at: http://www.epw.org.in/showarticles.php (accessed in April 2005).

BAPS Swaminarayan Sanstha, Dallas. 2014. Seventh Annual BAPS Women's Conference. Available at: http://www.baps.org/News/2014/BAPS-Womens-Conference-6054.aspx (accessed on 21 September 2014).

Barber, B. R. 2000. 'Jihad vs. Mcworld'. In *Globalization and the Challenges of a New Century*, ed. P. O'Meara, H. D. Mehlinger, and M. Krain, 23–33. Bloomington: Indiana University.

Baudrillard, J. 1981. *For a Critique of the Political Economy of the Sign*. St Louis: Teleos.

———. 1993. *Symbolic Exchange and Death*. London: Sage.

———. 1994. *Simulacra and Simulation*. Ann Arbor: University of Michigan Press.

Baviskar, A. 2003. 'Between Violence and Desire: Space, Power, and Identity in the Making of Metropolitan Delhi'. *International Social Science Journal* 55: 89–98.

Berger, P. and S. Pullberg. 1965. 'Reification and the Sociological Critique of Consciousness'. *History and Theory* 4(3): 196–211.

Berry, B. J. L. 1989. 'Geography of the Global Economy: Cultures, Corporations, and the Nation-state'. *Economic Geography* 65(1): 1–18.

Bourne, L. S. 1976. 'Urban Structure and Land Use Decisions'. *Annals of the Association of American Geographers* 66: 531–47.

Brenner, N. and N. Theodore. 2002. 'Cities and the Geographies of "Actually Existing Neoliberalism"'. *Antipode* 34: 349–79.

Brown, C. 2001. 'The Idea of World Community'. In *The Global Transformations Reader*, ed. D. Held and A. McGrew, 453–61. Cambridge: Polity Press.

Bryman, A.1999. 'The Disneyization of Society'. *The Sociological Review* 47(1): 25–47.

Bunnel, T., P. A. Barter, and S. Morshidi. 2002. 'City Profile Kuala Lumpur Metropolitan Area: A Globalizing City Region'. *Cities* 19(5): 357–70.

Burgess, E. W. 1925. 'The Growth of the City: An Introduction to a Research Project'. In *The City: Suggestions of Investigation of Human Behavior in the Urban Environment*, ed. R. Park, E.W. Burgess, and R.D. McKenzie, 47–62. Chicago: Chicago University Press.

Carroll, W. and R. S. Ratner. 1994. 'Between Leninism and Radical Pluralism: Gramscian Reflections on Counter-hegemony and New Social Movements'. *Critical Sociology* 20(3): 3–26.

Castells, M. 2000a. 'Materials for an Exploratory Theory of Network Society'. *British Journal of Sociology* 51(1): 5–24.

———. 2000b. 'The Network Society'. In *Globalization and the Challenges of a New Century*, ed. P. O'Meara, H. D. Mehlinger, and M. Krain, 76–81. Cambridge: Polity Press.

Chakravarti, U. 1962. 'Conceptualizing Brahmanical Patriarchy in Early India: Gender, Caste, Class, and State'. In *Caste, Class, and Gender*, ed. M. Mohanty, 271–95. New Delhi: Sage.

———. 1993. 'Conceptualizing Brahmanical Patriarchy in Early India: Gender, Caste, Class, and State'. *Economic and Political Weekly* 28(14): 579–85.

Chatterjee, P. 2004. *The Politics of the Governed: Reflections on Popular Politics in Most of the World*. New York: Columbia University Press.

Chatterjee, I. 2009. 'Deconstructing Vegas: A Class Project?' *Human Geography* 2 (2): 83–5.

———. 2011. 'Governance as "Performed", Governance as "Inscribed": New Urban Politics in Ahmedabad'. *Urban Studies* 48(12 September): 2571–90.

———. 2012. 'Feminism, the False Consciousness of Neoliberal Capitalism?' *Gender, Place and Culture* 19(6 December): 790–809.

———. 2014. *Displacement, Revolution, and the New Urban Condition*. Delhi, London: New York: Sage.

Chossudovsky, Michel. 2003. *The Globalisation of Poverty and the New World Order.*
2nd ed. Shanty Bay, Ontario, Canada: Global Outlook.

Cohen, G. A. 1978. *Karl Marx's Theory of History: A Defense*. Oxford: Clarendon Press.

Cosgrove, D. and S. Daniels. 1988. *The Iconography of Landscape*. Cambridge: Cambridge University Press.

Crossly, N. 1995. 'Merleau-Ponty, the Elusive Body and Carnal Sociology'. *Body & Society* 1(43): 43–63.

Das, V. 1976. 'Indian Women: Work, Power and Status'. In *Indian Women from Purdah to Modernity*, ed. B. R. Nanda, 129–45. New Delhi: Vikas.

Davis, M. 2004. 'The Urbanization of the Empire: Megacities and the Laws of Chaos'. *Social Text* 81, 22(4 Winter): 9–15.

Dawat-e-Islami. 2014. Available at: http://www.dawateislami.net/donation/qurbani_intro.do (accessed on 26 June 2014).

Descartes, R. 1969. *Discourse on Method and the Mediation*. Harmondsworth: Penguin.

Disneyland website. Disneyland Resorts. Available at: https://disneyland.disney.go.com (accessed on 7 August 2014).

Duncan, J.S. 1980. 'The Superorganic in American Cultural Geography'. *Annals of the Association of American Geographers* 70:181–98.

Eisenstein Z. 1999. 'Constructing a Theory of Capitalist Patriarchy and Socialist Feminism'. *Critical Sociology* 25(196): 196–217.

ELCA.org. 2014. Available at: http://search.elca.org/Pages/WorldMap.aspx (accessed on 26 June 2014).

Fernandez-Kelly, M. P. 1983. *For We Are Sold, I and My People: Women in Industry in Mexico's Frontier*. Albany: SUNY Press.

First United Methodist Church of Hurst. 2014. Available at: http://www.fum-churst.org/africa/ (accessed on 25 June 2014).

Florida, R. and A. Jonas. 1991. 'U.S. Urban Policy: The Post-War State and Capitalist Regulation'. *Antipode* 23(4): 349–84.

Fraser, N. 2009. 'Feminism, Capitalism, and the Cunning of History'. *New Left Review* 56: 97–117.

Friedman, T. L. 1999. *The Lexus and the Olive Tree*. New York: Farrar, Straus and Giroux.

Ganesh, K. 1985. 'Women's Seclusion and the Structure of Caste'. Paper presented at the Asian Regional Conference on Women and the Household, New Delhi.

Gimenez, E. M. 2004. 'Connecting Marx and Feminism in the Era of Globalization: A Preliminary Investigation'. Socialism and Democracy. Available at: http://sdonline.org/35/connecting-marx-and-feminism-in-the-era-of-globalization-a-preliminary-investigation/ (accessed on 3 October 2011).

Gold, J. and G. Revill. 2000. 'Landscape, Defense and the Study of Conflict'. In *Landscapes of Defense*, ed. J. Gold and G. Revill, 1–20. London: Prentice Hall.

Gottdiener, M. 1997. *The Theming of America: Dreams, Visions, and Commercial Space*. Boulder, Co: Westview Press.

Gregory, D. 2004. 'Palestine and the "War on Terror"'. *Comparative Studies of South Asia, Africa and the Middle East* 24: 183–95.

Guha-Banerjee, S. 2011. 'New Urbanism, Neoliberalism, and Urban Restructuring'. In *India's New Economic Policy: A Critical Analysis*, ed. W. Ahmed, A. Kundu, and R. Peet, 76–96. New York: Routledge.

Hannigan, J. 2002. 'Fantasy City: Pleasure and Profit in the Postmodern Metropolis'. In *Readings in Urban Theory*, ed. S. Fainstein and S. Cambell, 305–24. Oxford: Blackwell Publishers.

Hardt, M. and A. Negri. 2000. *Empire*. Harvard University Press.

Harvey, David. 1975. 'The Geography of Capitalist Accumulation: A Reconstruction of the Marxian Theory'. *Antipode* 7(2): 9–21.

———. 1978. 'The Urban Process under Capitalism'. *International Journal of Urban and Regional Research* 2(1–4): 101–31.

———. 1989a. *The Condition of Postmodernity*. Cambridge, Massachusetts: Blackwell.

———. 1989b. 'From Managerialism to Entrepreneurialism: The Transformation of Urban Governance in Late Capitalism'. *Geografiska Annaler* 71(B): 3–17.

———. 1996. *Justice, Nature and the Geography of Difference*. Malden, MA: Blackwell.

———. 2000. *Spaces of Hope*. Berkeley: University of California Press.

———. 2001. 'Time–space Compression and the Postmodern Condition'. In *Globalization and the Challenges of a New Century*, ed. P. O'Meara, H.D. Mehlinger, and M. Krain, 82–91. Cambridge: Polity Press.

———. 2003. *The New Imperialism*. Oxford, New York: Oxford University Press.

———. 2005. *A Brief History of Neoliberalism*. Oxford: Oxford University.

Hegel, G.W.F. 2010. *Phenomenology of Spirit*. New York: Digireds.com

Hetne, B. 2001. 'Global Market versus Regionalism'. In *Globalization and the Challenges of a New Century*, ed. P. O'Meara, H. D. Mehlinger and M. Krain, 68–75. Cambridge: Polity Press.

Hirst, P. and G. Thompson. 2001. 'Globalization and the History of the International Economy'. In *Globalization and the Challenges of a New Century*, ed. P. O'Meara, H. D. Mehlinger, and M. Krain, 274–86. Cambridge: Polity Press.

Hobsbawm, E. 1998. 'The Nation and Globalization'. *Constellations* 5(1): 1–9.

Jameson, F. 1984. 'Postmodernism, or the Cultural Logic of Late Capitalism'. *New Left Review* 146: 53–92.

Jordan, M. 2014. 'Growing Number of Hispanics in U.S. Leave Catholic Church'. *The World Street Journal*, 7 May. Available at: http://online.wsj.com/news/articles/SB10001424052702303417104579546130945494804 (accessed on 27 June 2014).

Kamat, S. and B. Mathew. 2003. 'Mapping Political Violence in a Globalized World: A Case of Hindu Nationalism'. *Social Justice* 30(3):4–16.

Kaushik, H. 2011. 'Cell Towers Killing Sparrows, Bees, Says MoEF Study'. *The Times of India*, 25 October. Available at: http://timesofindia.indiatimes.com/city/ahmedabad/Cell-towers-killing-sparrows-bees-says-MoEF-study/articleshow/10481535.cms (accessed on 27 June 2014).

Kirby, A. 2002. 'Everything Is Solid, After All'. *Cities* 19: 1–2.

Lee, J. 2007. 'BAPS as a NRI Network and Its Presence in India'. *International Area Studies Review* 10(2): 151–62.

Lenin, V. 1999. *Imperialism: The Highest Stage of Capitalism*. Australia: Resistance Books.

Levitt, P. 2006. 'God Needs No Passport'. *Harvard Divinity Bulletin* 3(3 Autumn). Available at http://www.hds.harvard.edu/news-events/harvard-divinity-bulletin/articles/god-needs-no-passport (accessed on 24 June 2014).

Mahadevia, D. 2002. 'Communal Space over Life Space'. *Economic and Political Weekly* 30 November. Available online at http://www.epw.org.in/showarticles.php (Downloaded on 6 April 2005).

Mahadevia, D. and H. Narayanan. 2006. 'Shanghaing Mumbai: Politics of Evictions and Resistance in Slum Settlements'. Paper presented at the conference on Tackling Exclusion: Shelter, Basic Services and Citizen's Rights in Globalizing Megacities of Asia, New Delhi, June.

Mann, M. 2001. 'Has Globalization Ended the Rise and the Rise of the Nation-state?' In *Globalization and the Challenges of a New Century*, ed. P. O'Meara, H. D. Mehlinger, and M. Krain, 136–47. Cambridge: Polity Press.

Marcuse, P. 2009. 'From Critical Urban Theory to the Right to the City'. *City* 13(2–3 June–September): 185–97.

Marin, L. 1984. *Utopics: Spatial Play*. New Jersey: Humanities Press.

Marinelli, M. 2009. 'Negotiating Beijing's Identity at the Turn of the Twentieth Century'. In *Dissent and Cultural Resistance in Asia's Cities*, ed. M. Butcher and S. Velayutham, 33–52. London and New York: Routledge.

Marston, S. 2000. 'The Social Construction of Scale'. *Progress in Human Geography* 24: 219–42.

Marston, S., J. Jones, and K. Woodward. 2005. 'Human Geography without Scale'. *Transactions of the Institute of British Geographers* 30: 416–32.

Marx K., 1970. Preface to *A Contribution to a Critique of Political Economy*. Moscow: Progress Publishers.

Marx, K. and F. Engels. 1975. *Collected Works*. Vol. 4. Moscow: Progress.

———. 2002. *The Communist Manifesto*. London: Penguin Books.

Merleau-Ponty, M. 1962. *The Phenomenology of Perception*. London: RKP.

Mitchell, D. 2003. 'Cultural Landscapes: Just Landscapes or Landscapes of Justice?' *Progress in Human Geography* 27: 787–96.

Murray, G. 2006. 'France: The Riots and the Republic'. *Institute of Race Relations* 47 (4): 26–45.

National Association of Evangelicals. Available at: http://www.nae.net/membership (accessed on 26 June 2014).

Nehru, J. 1985. *The Discovery of India*. Oxford: Oxford University Press.

Nieto, G. and A. Franze.1997. 'The Projection of Social Conflict through Urban Space: The Plaza de la Corona Boreal'. *Current Anthropology* 38: 461–6.

Ohmae, K. 2000. 'The Rise of the Region State'. In *Globalization and the Challenges of a New Century*, ed. P. O'Meara, H.D. Mehlinger, and M. Krain, 93–100. Cambridge: Polity Press.

Olwig, K. 1996. 'Recovering the Substantive Nature of Landscape'. *Annals of the Association of American Geographers* 86: 630–53.

Ong, A. 2000. 'Gender and Labor Politics of Postmodernity'. In *Globalization and the Challenges of a New Century*, ed. P. O'Meara, H. D. Mehlinger, and M. Krain, 253–81. Bloomington: Indiana University Press.

Peck, J. and A. Tickell. 2002. 'Neoliberalizing Space'. *Antipode* 34(3): 380–404.

Peet, R. 1978. 'Materialism, Social Formation, and Socio-spatial Relations: An Essay in Marxist Geography'. *Cashiers De Geographie Du Quebec* 22(56): 147–57.

———. 1997. 'The Cultural Production of Economic Forms'. In *Geographies of Economies*, ed. R. Lee and J. Wills, 37–46. London: Arnold.

———. 2000. 'Culture, Imaginary and Rationality in Regional Economic Systems'. *Environment and Planning A* 32: 1215–34.

———. 2007. *Geography of Power: Making Global Economic Policy*. London: Zed books.

Peet, R., B. Born, M. Davis, K. Fehrer, S. Feldman, S.R. Khan, M. Labban, K. McArdle, C. Marcano, L. Meierotto, D. Niles, T. Ponniah, M.C. Schmidt, G.

Schwarz, J. Shagwert, M.P. Staton, and S. Stratton. 2003. *Unholy Trinity: The IMF, World Bank and WTO*. London: Zed Books.

Peet, R. and E. Hartwick. 2009. *Theories of Development*. New York: The Guilford Press.

Pratt, G. 2004. *Working Feminism*. Philadelphia, PA: Temple University Press.

Promo Spanish American Church. 2014. Available at: http://www.youtube.com/watch?v=dexe1jQtkYk (accessed on 25 June 2014).

Raval, S. 2012. *Renunciation, Reform and Women in Swaminarayan Hinduism*. Ahmedabad, India: Swaminarayan Aksharpith.

Richert, S.P. 2014. 'Why Can't Women Be Priests in the Catholic Church? The Reasons for the All-Male Priesthood'. Available at: http://catholicism.about.com/od/beliefsteachings/f/Women_Priests.htm (accessed on 17 September 2014).

Ritzer, G. and E. Malone. 2000. 'Globalization Theory: Lessons from the Exportation of McDonaldization and the New Means of Consumption'. *American Studies* 41 (2/3, Summer–Fall): 97–118.

Rowntree, L. 1996. 'The Cultural Landscape Concept in Human Geography'. In *Concepts in Human Geography*, ed. E. Earle, K. Mathewson, and M. S. Kenzer, 127–59. Latham, MD: Rowman and Littlefield.

Roy, A. 2005. 'Urban Informality: Towards an Epistemology of Planning'. *Journal of American Planning Association* 71(2): 147–58.

———. 2009. 'Civic Governmentality: The Politics of Inclusion in Beirut and Mumbai'. *Antipode* 41(1): 159–79.

Said, E. 1978. *Orientalism*. London: Penguin Books.

Sassen, S. 1991. *The Global City: New York, London, Tokyo*. United Kingdom: Princeton University Press.

———. 2002. 'Locating Cities on the Global Circuits'. *Environment and Urbanization* 14: 13–30.

Sauer, C. 1925. 'The Morphology of Landscape'. In *University of California Publications in Geography* 2: 19–54. Reprinted in J. Leighly (ed.), *Land and Life: A Selection of Writings of Carl Ortwin Sauer* (Berkeley, CA: University of California Press), 315–50.

Sayers, S. 1990. 'Marxism and the Dialectical Method: A Critique of G.A. Cohen'. In *Socialism, Feminism and Philosophy: A Radical Philosophy Reader*, ed. S. Sayers and P. Osborne, 140–69. London, New York: Routledge.

Shah, G. 2002. 'Caste, Hindutva and Hideousness'. *Economic and Political Weekly*. 13 April. Available at: http://www.epw.org.in/showarticles.php (accessed on April 2005).

Slaughter, A. M. 2000. 'The Real New World Order'. In *Globalization and the Challenges of a New Century*, ed. P. O'Meara, H. D. Mehlinger, and M. Krain, 112–22. Bloomington: Indiana University Press.

Smith, N. 1979. 'Geography, Science, and the Post-positivist Mode of Explanation'. *Progress in Human Geography* (3): 356–83.

———. 1996. *The New Urban Frontier: Gentrification and the Revanchist City*. New York: Routledge.

———. 2000. 'Scale'. In *The Dictionary of Human Geography*, 4th edition, ed. R.J. Johnston, D. Gregory, G. Pratt, and M. Watts, 724–7. Oxford: Blackwell.

———. 2005. 'The Endgame of Globalization'. *Political Geography* 25: 1–14.

Soja, E. 1980. 'The Socio-spatial Dialectic'. *Annals of the Association of American Geographers* 70(2): 207–25.

———. 2010. *Seeking Spatial Justice*. Minneapolis: University of Minnesota Press.

Sorkin, M. 2002. 'See You in Disneyland'. In *Readings in Urban Theory*, ed. S. Fainstein and S. Cambell, 335–53. Oxford: Blackwell Publishers.

Srinivas, M. N. 1962. 'Caste in Modern India'. In *Caste, Class, and Gender*, ed. M. Mohanty, 154–82. New Delhi: Sage.

Stewart, Jon. 2000. *The Unity of Hegel's Phenomenology of Spirit: A Systematic Interpretation*. Evanston: Northwestern University Press.

Stiglitz, J. 2002. *Globalization and Its Discontent*. New York: WW Norton & Company Inc.

Strange, S. 2001. 'The Declining Authority of the States'. In *Globalization and the Challenges of a New Century*, ed. P. O'Meara, H. D. Mehlinger, and M. Krain, 148–55. Cambridge: Polity Press.

Swyngedow, E. 1997. 'Neither Global nor Local: Glocalization and the Politics of Scale'. In *Spaces of Globalization: Reasserting the Power of the Local*, ed. K. Cox, 137–66. New York: Guilford.

Taylor, P. J. 1995. 'Beyond Containers: Internationality, Interstateness, Interterritoriality'. *Progress in Human Geography* 19(1): 1–15.

Thompson, E. P. 1978. 'Eighteenth-Century English Society: Class Struggle without Class?' *Social History* 3(2 May): 133–65.

Vasquez, M. A. and M. F. Marquardt. 2003. *Globalizing the Sacred: Religion across the Americas*. New Jersey and London: Rutgers University Press.

Weber, M. 1992. *The Protestant Ethic and the Spirit of Capitalism*. London, New York: Routledge.

Weinstein, R. 1992. 'Disneyland and Coney Island: Reflections on the Evolution of the Modern Amusement Park'. *Journal of Popular Culture* 26(1 Summer): 131–64.

Williams, R. 1980. *Problems in Materialism and Culture*. Verso: London.

———. 1981. *The Sociology of Culture*. New York: Schocken Books.

———. 2009. *Marxism and Literature*. Oxford, New York: Oxford University Press.

Yeoh, B. and T. C. Chang. 2001. 'Globalizing Singapore: Debating Transnational Flows in the City'. *Urban Studies* 38(7): 1025–44.

Index

abstraction, 23, 27, 30, 33, 125–6
accumulation, 13–15, 28–30,
    32, 51, 57, 114–19, 131, 133,
    137–8, 141–2, 151, 154–5, 161–2,
    169–72, 174
aestheticization, 56, 111, 113
alienation, 12–13, 82, 114, 116–17,
    124–6, 133, 135, 137–42, 156
Archimedean point, 131, 138
analysis, 6–7, 13, 15–19, 20–4,
    27–30, 33, 37, 45, 52, 64, 120–5,
    135, 140, 141, 149, 151, 153–4,
    157–9, 169, 171, 178–80

base, 2, 6–7, 10, 15, 20, 22–4, 30, 34,
    35, 38–9, 53, 56, 93, 119, 135,
    122–3, 135, 136, 157, 180

class, 14–15, 20, 27–32, 43–4,
    48–9, 67, 74, 93, 111, 115, 118,
    120, 122, 125, 135, 136, 141–2,
    146–64, 172–4, 183
class consciousness, 14–15, 155, 159,
    169, 171–3, 183
cognitive map, 12, 124–6, 132,
    138–9, 141, 142, 182

constituted materiality, 7–9, 14–15,
    23–4, 34–5, 86, 145–6, 158,
    171–4, 180
contradiction, 11, 13, 51, 32, 54,
    84–5, 107, 114–17, 119–21,
    137–8, 141–2
critical distance, 123–4, 131, 134,
    138–9, 142, 143
cultural consumption, 134
cultural logic, 10, 41, 52–3, 56, 66,
    113, 122–4, 137, 141
cultural production, 13, 53, 118,
    120–3, 126, 128, 131, 137, 140,
    142
cultural stupefaction, 126, 132, 141–2

degenerate utopia, 119–20, 143
deterritorialization, 54, 64, 133
dialectics, 3–7, 9–12, 15, 24, 32–3,
    35, 66, 81, 109, 133, 135, 138–9,
    144, 155, 158, 163, 165, 169,
    171, 174, 178, 179, 183
disalienation, 12–13, 124–6, 133,
    138, 139–40, 142, 182
discourse, 21, 37, 41, 83, 119, 121,
    141, 147, 148–9, 153, 160, 165–6

disjuncture, 40, 85, 103, 105–6,
    108–9, 128, 113, 116–17, 119–20
Disneyland, 12, 110–11, 126–7, 134,
    139, 141–3
Disneyization, 2, 42, 44, 111, 133

economic determinism, 6, 18, 180
embeddedness, 155

fantasy, 12–13, 110, 112–13, 116–18,
    127, 129, 131–6, 138–42
Fordist, 9, 46, 48–9, 51, 53, 55–56,
    58, 65–6, 85, 112, 179
free market, 16, 38, 51, 114

gender, 14–15, 30, 44, 55, 79, 126,
    141, 144, 146, 147–83
gendered subject, 14, 147, 153, 169,
    173–4, 183
globalization, 1–16, 34–67, 80–109,
    132–83

homogenization, 16, 40, 42, 51, 64,
    88, 133, 179

landscape, 1, 4, 8–12, 14–15, 18,
    30–1, 34, 40–4, 49–50, 55–8,
    64–9, 77, 79–83, 86, 90, 92–3,
    103, 105–11, 114–15, 127, 131,
    138, 140, 142, 159, 165, 171,
    173, 175, 180–1, 183
late capitalism 10, 52–3, 56, 66, 68,
    113, 117, 118, 120–1, 123–4, 143
liberalization, 8–9, 45, 49–50, 52–3,
    56, 58, 65–6, 85, 94, 106, 154

MacWorld, 51
materialism, 6, 10–12, 18, 21, 27,
    80, 83–5, 88, 92–3, 102, 105–9,
    145
mediation, 6–7, 20, 23, 34, 60, 137,
    180

McDonaldization, 2, 42–4, 106, 133,
    181
modernity, 5, 10, 36–7, 50, 54, 56,
    64, 66, 80, 111–12, 178
multiculturalism, 12, 54, 100, 102,
    106–8, 133, 150, 182

idealism, 6, 11, 18, 84, 107, 180
indigenization, 43, 64, 86, 135
informalization, 8–9, 49–50, 149,
    154–5
intersubjectivity, 146

nation, 4, 7–8, 11–13, 16, 22, 29, 31,
    36–42, 46–9, 53–60, 62, 68–70,
    77–8, 81–2, 84–5, 93–5, 98,
    100–3, 106–8, 126, 129, 130–43,
    154, 156, 180, 181–3
neoliberalism, 2, 16, 38, 39, 65,
    150–4

patriarchy, 14–15, 147, 150, 156–64,
    166–74, 183
phenomenology, 147, 159
post-Fordist, 9, 48–9, 53, 55–6, 58,
    65, 66, 85, 112, 179
post-liberalization, 9, 45, 49–50,
    52–3, 56, 58, 65, 66, 85
postmodern, 3, 10, 12–13, 52–3,
    56–7, 64–9, 80, 112–13, 117–18,
    121–4, 126, 131–2, 134–5, 137,
    140–3, 182
positionality, 155

reality in totality, 183
reterritorialization, 54, 64, 133

semiotic, 43, 112–13, 117–18, 120,
    123
signification, 6, 10, 15, 23–4, 35, 53,
    111–12, 123, 144–5
situatedness, 155

socio-spatial dialectic, 7, 27–33, 180
spatial, 2, 4, 6–7, 9–10, 18, 22, 24,
    27–34, 54, 64, 69, 82, 85, 110,
    113–14, 144, 146, 156, 163,
    179–81
spectacle, 12, 52, 56, 69, 86, 102,
    110, 112, 125–7, 129, 132, 134,
    138–43, 182
spectacular, 12, 13, 15, 16, 56, 80,
    87, 103, 116, 118, 121, 124, 126,
    127, 132, 134, 138, 139, 140–2,
    173, 182–3
subject, 12–15, 19–20, 28, 83,
    86–7, 94, 124–5, 131, 138, 141–2,
    144–60, 163–74, 183

subjectivity, 13–14, 20, 145–52, 159,
    164, 166, 172–74
superstructure, 6–7, 10, 15, 20, 22–4,
    30, 34–5, 56, 106, 119, 121, 123,
    136, 180
structural adjustment, 9, 16, 38, 47,
    49, 65

time–space compression, 8
transcendental idealism, 11, 84, 107
transnationalism, 68, 100, 102
transcendental materialism, 10–11,
    83–5, 88, 107

utopia, 110, 112–25, 132, 139–43

About the Author

Ipsita Chatterjee is Assistant Professor, Department of Geography, University of North Texas, USA. She has previously taught at the University of Texas at Austin and Pennsylvania State University. She has a Ph.D. in geography from Clark University, Massachusetts, USA, and is the author of *Displacement, Revolution, and the New Urban Condition: Theories and Case Studies* (2014). Her research interests focus on globalization and urban transformation particularly relating to class, racial, gender, and ethnophobic exploitations in cities. Chatterjee uses Marxist and feminist theories to critique these contemporary urban conditions. She is the mother of a delightful four-year-old girl, Nadia.